ESSAYS ON THE PRINCIPLES
OF MORALITY AND NATURAL RELIGION

From
J.P.Smith

You would home my Leibniz
too if I didn't bin
that nonsense.

NATURAL LAW AND
ENLIGHTENMENT CLASSICS

Knud Haakonssen
General Editor

Henry Home, Lord Kames

NATURAL LAW AND
ENLIGHTENMENT CLASSICS

Essays on the Principles of Morality and Natural Religion

Corrected and Improved, in a Third Edition. Several Essays Added Concerning the Proof of a Deity

Henry Home, Lord Kames

Edited and with an Introduction by
Mary Catherine Moran

Major Works of Henry Home, Lord Kames

LIBERTY FUND

Indianapolis

Introduction, annotations © 2005 Liberty Fund, Inc.

09 08 07 06 05 C 5 4 3 2 1
09 08 07 06 05 P 5 4 3 2 1

Library of Congress Cataloging-in-Publication Data
Kames, Henry Home, Lord, 1696–1782.
Essays on the principles of morality and natural religion:
several essays added concerning the proof of a deity /
Henry Home, Lord Kames;
edited and with an introduction by Mary Catherine Moran.
3rd ed., corrected and improved.
p.   cm.
(Natural law and enlightenment classics)
Includes bibliographical references and index.
ISBN 0-86597-448-9 (alk. paper)—ISBN 0-86597-449-7 (pbk: alk. paper)
1. Ethics.   I. Moran, Mary Catherine.   II. Title.   III. Series.
BJ1005.K2   2005
170—dc22   2004061555

LIBERTY FUND, INC.
8335 Allison Pointe Trail, Suite 300
Indianapolis, Indiana 46250-1684

CONTENTS

INTRODUCTION

Lord Kames's *Essays on the Principles of Morality and Natural Religion* is at once a typical example of and an original contribution to the Scottish Enlightenment's distinctive attempt to construct a moral science based on the principles of natural law. From Gershom Carmichael in the 1690s to Thomas Reid and Adam Ferguson in the 1780s, the teaching and writing of moral philosophy in eighteenth-century Scotland drew upon a tradition of natural jurisprudence derived from Grotius, Pufendorf, and Locke.[1] If its contractarian account of the bases of government provided a suitably whiggish explanation for the emergence of civil society, natural law also offered insights into what Hutcheson called "mankind as a system," which was governed by the fundamental "law of sociality"[2] that entailed various

1. Francis Hutcheson, *A System of Moral Philosophy,* 2 vols. (London, 1755), vol. 2, bk. II, chap. 16, "Concerning the general Rights of Human Society, or Mankind as a System"; Adam Ferguson, *Principles of Moral and Political Science,* 2 vols. (Edinburgh, 1792; reprint, New York: AMS Press, 1973). Hutcheson's *System* was based on the written lectures that he developed as professor of moral philosophy at the University of Glasgow, while Ferguson's *Principles* is based on the moral philosophy lectures that he delivered at the University of Edinburgh. Carmichael's writings are now available in *Natural Rights on the Threshold of the Scottish Enlightenment, The Writings of Gershom Carmichael,* ed. James Moore and Michael Silverthorne (Indianapolis: Liberty Fund, 2002). On the significance of natural jurisprudence for Scottish Enlightenment theory, see Knud Haakonssen, *Natural Law and Moral Philosophy: From Grotius to the Scottish Enlightenment* (Cambridge, 1996); Istvan Hont, "The language of sociability and commerce: Samuel Pufendorf and the theoretical foundations of the 'four-stages theory'," in *The Languages of Political Theory in Early Modern Europe,* ed. Anthony Pagden (Cambridge, 1987), pp. 253–76; and James Moore and Michael Silverthorne, "Gershom Carmichael and the natural jurisprudence tradition in eighteenth-century Scotland," in *Virtue and Commerce,* pp. 73–87.

2. Samuel Pufendorf, *On the Duty of Man and Citizen,* ed. James Tully, trans. Michael Silverthorne (Cambridge: Cambridge University Press, 1991), p. 35.

rights and duties to God, to self, and to others. To this natural law frame-work of rights and duties ordained by providence but knowable through reason, the Scottish thinkers typically applied a new moral psychology which emphasized the role of the passions and sentiments. The attempt to synthesize an objectively grounded law with a subjectivist account of moral and social exchange had an enormous influence on the Enlightenment's science of man and society.

While his *Elements of Criticism* (1762) is a classic in the history of aes-thetics and his *Sketches of the History of Man* (1774) part of the canon of Enlightenment historical sociology, Kames's *Essays* has received compara-tively little attention.[3] Yet it deserves to be read alongside Kames's better-known works as an important contribution to the Enlightenment's science of human nature. First published anonymously in 1751 and significantly revised in 1758 and 1779, the *Essays* represents an important contribution to eighteenth-century debate over the foundations of justice and morality and the challenges posed by the skepticism of David Hume. More broadly, in its concern to vindicate the veracity of our common moral intuitions and sense perceptions that are rooted in our very nature, the *Essays* helped found the Scottish Common Sense school. The *Essays* is Kames's most important philosophical work and sheds valuable light on his lifelong preoccupations. At the same time, the book raises issues of continuing importance—the foundations of morality, free will versus determinism, the nature of self and identity.

Kames's Life and Writings

Born at Eccles in the eastern borders borough of Berwickshire in 1696, Henry Home was the son of minor landed gentry with dual political (Whig and Jacobite) and religious (Presbyterian and Episcopalian) loyalties on both the maternal and paternal sides of the family. Because of the family's

---

3. Some thirty years ago, two Kames scholars asserted the significance of the *Essays:* see Arthur E. McGuiness, *Henry Home, Lord Kames* (New York: Twayne Publishers, 1970), esp. chap. 2; and Ian Simpson Ross, *Lord Kames and the Scotland of His Day* (Oxford: Clarendon Press, 1972), esp. chap. 6.

relative poverty, he was educated at home, where he studied Latin, Greek, mathematics, and physics under the tutelage of two nonjuring (and possibly Jacobite) Episcopalian clergymen.[4] In 1712 Kames apprenticed himself to a "writer" (the Scottish term for solicitor) in Edinburgh, but within a few years changed course to prepare for a career as a barrister. He was admitted to the Faculty of Advocates in 1723. At some point during the 1730s, Kames abandoned his Jacobite sympathies to embrace the Whig principles that would help secure him the patronage first of the powerful third Duke of Argyll and then of the duke's nephew John Stuart, Earl of Bute. In 1741 he inherited the Kames estate and married Agatha Drummond, who would inherit her family's estate at Blair Drummond in Stirlingshire in 1766. He became "Lord Kames" when he was appointed to the Court of Sessions (Scotland's highest civil court) in 1752; in 1763 he joined the High Court of the Justiciary (Scotland's highest criminal court), a position he held until days before his death in December 1782.

Kames's judicial career and writings on Scottish law have earned him a place in the annals of eighteenth-century legal history;[5] the rest of his work has secured his position as the quintessential Enlightenment figure in Scotland, a practical man of affairs with significant achievements as a man of letters. In addition to a busy legal career, Kames sat on the boards of two governmental agencies, belonged to a number of the important clubs and societies, and served as patron to the generation of literati who are the high point of the Enlightenment in Scotland. Among those who benefited from his patronage were Adam Smith, whose public lectures at Edinburgh in 1748–1751 were sponsored by Kames,[6] and Smith's student John Millar, who lived at the Kames household for two years while qualifying as an advocate and who owed his chair in civil law at the University of Glasgow to Kames

4. A nonjuror was one who refused to swear an oath of loyalty to William and Mary or their successors.

5. One of his most far-reaching decisions was on literary property, in which he argued against the common law principle of perpetual copyright on the basis of public utility and benefit to society. See Trevor Ross, "Copyright and the Invention of Tradition," *Eighteenth-Century Studies* 26 (Autumn 1992): 1–27.

6. See Adam Smith, *Lectures on Rhetoric and Belles Lettres,* ed. J. C. Bryce (Indianapolis: Liberty Fund, 1985).

and Smith. An avid reader with broad tastes, Kames relied on his Edinburgh publishers to keep him supplied with new material: "Can Lord Kames find no books either of Instruction or amusement to entertain him in the country?" he wrote to the bookseller William Creech in a typical appeal for more books; "Must he recurr to a Second reading of his own books?"[7] This would certainly have kept him occupied, for he had already published widely in law, philosophy, history, aesthetics, and agriculture.

While Kames addressed a remarkably wide variety of topics, from flax-husbandry to education (including female education),[8] his publications are characterized by several recurrent themes. Not surprisingly, many are juridical in nature and are concerned with systematizing the principles and tracing the origins and development of law. In a series of legal digests beginning with *Remarkable Decisions of the Court of Session from 1716 to 1728* (1728),[9] Kames devised a system of classification according to the application of specific rules of law, while *Historical Law-Tracts* (1758) was organized around the basic principle of philosophical history: taking law as part of the history of man, Kames accounted for its progress "from its first rudiments among savages, . . . to its highest improvements in civilized society."[10] "Improvement" was both a practical goal for law, education, agriculture, and other institutions, and a theoretical principle explaining the progress of man and society. Most notably, improvement was the organizing theme of *Sketches of the History of Man* (1774), which aimed at nothing less than a history of the human species, that is, of the gradual unfolding and improvement of the human faculties that he had accounted for in his *Essays*. Indeed, though there are significant differences between the historicism of *Sketches* and the natural law of *Essays*, Kames viewed both within the broader framework of a unified account of human nature based on the gen-

---

7. Kames to William Creech, 5 April 1775, Letters of Henry Home, Lord Kames, 1772–1776, "William Creech Letter Books," Dalguise Muniments, Microfilm RH4/26/1, Scottish Record Office.

8. *Progress of Flax-Husbandry in Scotland* (1766); *Loose Hints on Education* (1781).

9. Followed by *The Decisions of the Court of Sessions from Its First Institution to the Present Time: Abridged and Digested under Proper Heads, in the Form of a Dictionary* (1741), *Remarkable Decisions of the Court of Sessions from the Year 1730 to 1752* (1766), and *Select Decisions of the Court of Sessions from the Year 1752 to the Year 1758* (1780).

10. Preface to *Historical Law-Tracts,* 2 vols. (Edinburgh, 1758), I:v.

eral laws and underlying principles governing the human no less than the natural world.

"The subject of these Essays is man," Kames declared (p. 229), which subject involved a vindication of those principles that were at once the laws of our own nature and the laws of a universal system to which human nature belonged. To this end, the *Essays* is an attack on skepticism in both morality and epistemology. Part I concerns the principles and foundations of morality and justice, while Part II centers on questions of metaphysics and epistemology. No narrow specialist, Kames critically engaged theological rationalists, Lockean epistemology, Humean skepticism, and moral-sense theory and drew upon fields as diverse as medicine, theology, philosophy, aesthetics, and epistemology. In so doing, he addressed a number of interrelated themes, including moral sense, justice, selfhood and identity, the veracity of the senses, and the existence of the Deity. The result is to answer skepticism with a deistic defense of commonsense notions of morality and epistemology.

Morality and Justice

By far the lengthiest essay concerns "The Principles and Foundations of Morality" that are rooted in our very nature. In seeking to "restore morality to its original simplicity and authority" (p. 24), Kames criticizes both sides of the selfish versus social debate. Against the "selfish system"—the egoistic moral psychology associated with Hobbes and Mandeville—Kames supports Shaftesbury's and Hutcheson's argument that man is inherently social with a natural inclination toward benevolence. But while accepting a natural, perceptual moral faculty, he believed that something more than an instinctive orientation toward the good was required to make morality lawlike. Using Butler's notion that reflective conscience adjudicates between self-interest and benevolence, Kames argues that Hutcheson leaves too much to benevolence without adequate foundation for the duties necessary to justice. As Adam Smith put it, citing Kames as "an author of very great and original genius," the *Essays* insist on "that remarkable distinction between justice and all other social virtues."[11]

11. Adam Smith, *The Theory of Moral Sentiments* (Indianapolis: Liberty Fund, 1982), p. 80.

As a central concept in natural law, justice figures prominently in the *Essays*. Justice is "that moral virtue which guards the persons, the property, and the reputation of individuals, and gives authority to promises and covenants" (p. 46). Not only is justice a primary virtue, the sense of justice (and of injustice) is one of the strongest inclinations in human nature. For Kames, one of the most troubling aspects of Humean skepticism is its denial of justice as a natural principle. In the *Treatise of Human Nature* (1739), Hume had undermined a basic premise of natural law by arguing that justice is an artificial, not a natural, virtue.[12] Hume did not mean that justice is unnatural or incompatible with human nature but rather that the sense of justice is not instinctive; justice arises from conventions that are themselves the products of complex social and historical relations. To Kames, this made justice too historically contingent to serve as an objective and authoritative arbiter of human conduct. Kames insisted that Hume's conventionalist account of the origins of justice had got it backward: it is not society which gives rise to justice, but justice which gives rise to society. In the important Scottish divide between historicist and objectivist ideas of justice, this was forceful advocacy for the latter.

Liberty and Necessity

In December 1778, Kames wrote to his printer William Smellie to press for a new edition of the *Essays:*

> I am informed from several hands that no subject at present employs more the thoughts and pens of the learned than that of Liberty and Necessity, which Dr. Priestley has revived and makes a great flourish about. Is not this then the proper time for the Essays on Morality and Natural Religion, in which Liberty and Necessity is handled with great precision? You have been calling for it for two years past; and I intimated to you some time

---

12. David Hume, *A Treatise of Human Nature* (1739; reprint, ed. David Fate Norton and Mary Beth Norton, Oxford: Oxford University Press, 2000), 3.2.1, pp. 307–11.

ago that I was ready, having laboured upon it all the last vacation. If you delay this opportunity, you may happen not to find another so proper.[13]

As Kames knew very well, not all contemporaries agreed that he had handled liberty and necessity "with great precision." With the first edition of *Essays,* he entered the eighteenth-century version of a debate going back to the ancient Stoics: if the universe is governed by necessary laws, to what extent are human actions free? And Kames's treatment of liberty and necessity was as singular in Scottish moral theory as that of justice and morality was mainstream. His attempt to reconcile moral agency with universal laws was so controversial that he narrowly escaped heresy charges before the Scottish presbytery; he "was scarcely warm in his judge's seat when he became subject to attacks from the zealots in the Church of Scotland."[14]

The essay on liberty and necessity views man as a necessary agent. Kames was committed to the doctrine that every part of the universe (both physical and moral) must be governed by the Deity in accordance with causal laws that are "fixed and immutable" (p. 120), but admitted that this involved "a labyrinth of doubts and difficulties" (p. 99). In the material world there is no contingency, all is governed by an omniscient and omnipotent Deity. In the human world, however, this lack of contingency "does not appear so clearly," for "man is the actor here" and man is "endued with will, and he acts from choice" (p. 100). But if every action is directed by immutable laws and final causes, how can man act out of choice? In seeking to resolve the dilemma between determinism and free will, Kames hit upon a radical solution: the Deity had implanted a "deceitful feeling of liberty."

However, if the feeling of liberty was delusive, how could a person be held accountable for actions that were not in fact free? Kames distinguished between the philosophical truth of final causes and the everyday truth (ultimately based on deception) that there is a distinction between "things

13. Kames to William Smellie, 4 December 1778. Fraser-Tytler of Aldourie Papers, NRAS 1073, Highland Council Archive. I am indebted to Richard Sher for sharing his transcription of this letter. William Creech was the Edinburgh partner of the Scottish-born, London-based bookseller (i.e., publisher) William Strahan. Dr. Priestley was Joseph Priestley (1733–1804).

14. Ian Simpson Ross, *Lord Kames and the Scotland of His Day* (Oxford: Clarendon Press, 1972), p. 152.

necessary and things contingent." He offered this analogy: "the precise time and manner of each man's death" is "determined by a train of preceding causes" but we do not act upon this principle; rather we behave as though the time of death were contingent, subject to actions such as "caution against accidents, due use of exercise, medicine, &c."[15] Likewise, though our actions are ultimately governed by final causes, we do and must behave as though they were subject to choice and contingency.

For many contemporaries it was a dangerous line of argument. Not surprisingly, some Scottish clergy reacted vehemently against depicting the Deity as a deceiver and claiming that denial of free will conformed to orthodox Calvinist predestinarianism. Kames's unorthodox views inspired the opprobrium of George Anderson, an evangelical minister of the Church of Scotland who launched a campaign, not only against Kames but also against Hume. Writing to his friend Allan Ramsay in 1752, Hume informed him that "Anderson, the godly, spiteful, pious, splenetic, charitable, unrelenting, meek, persecuting, Christian, inhuman, peace-making, furious Anderson, is at present very hot in pursuit of Lord Kames."[16] In *An Estimate of the Profit and Loss of Religion, Personally and publicly stated: Illustrated with reference to Essays on Morality and Natural Religion* (1753), Anderson urged the Church of Scotland to excommunicate public teachers of atheism and infidelity, such as Kames and Hume. Another minister, John Bonar, entered the fray with a pamphlet addressed to the General Assembly of the Church of Scotland, in which he accused Kames of arguing that "since man is thus necessarily determined in all his actions, and can have nothing more than a deceitful feeling of liberty, [there] can be no sin or moral evil in the world."[17]

Kames responded with a pamphlet (possibly coauthored by the mod-

---

15. *Essays,* 1st ed. (1751), pp. 184–85.

16. David Hume to Allan Ramsay, n.d., *The Letters of David Hume,* 2 vols., ed. J. Y. T. Greig (Oxford: Clarendon Press, 1932), I:224.

17. John Bonar, *An Analysis of the Moral and Religious Sentiments contained in the Writings of Sopho, and David Hume, Esq.: Addressed to the considerations of the Reverend and Honourable Members of the General Assembly of the Church of Scotland* (1755); quoted in Ian Simpson Ross, *Lord Kames and the Scotland of His Day* (Oxford: Clarendon Press, 1972), p. 154.

erate minister Hugh Blair) which he appended to the second and third editions of *Essays*. He managed to emerge relatively unscathed, the Moderate wing of the Church of Scotland voting against excommunication. Still, in the 1758 edition, Kames felt compelled to tone down his statements concerning the deceptive feeling of liberty. In the final edition of 1779, he removed the language of deceit altogether, though without abandoning the argument concerning necessary agency.

Since one of the issues at the heart of the controversy was that of moral agency, it should be noted that Kames also revised another essay that took up this theme. For the third edition, he not only expanded the essay on personal identity but also moved it to Part I, because of "its intimate connection with the moral system." Kames was now concerned to argue—against Hume's notion of a fluid and potentially discontinuous sense of self—that moral agency requires a sense of continuous selfhood: "The knowledge I have of my personal identity is what constitutes me a moral agent, accountable to God and to man for every action of my life. Were I kept ignorant of my personal identity, it would not be in my power to connect any of my past actions with myself. . . . It would answer no good purpose, to reward me for a benevolent act, or to punish me for a crime" (p. 128). Again, the underlying concern is to establish the prerequisites for justice and natural law.

Sense Perception as Common Sense

"Lord Kames's mind," wrote William Smellie with respect to the *Essays*, "was very much inclined to metaphysical disquisitions."[18] This metaphysical inclination found expression in Part II of *Essays*, where Kames examines a number of topics surrounding belief and perception in order to counter skepticism in epistemology and theology. The eight essays in this part have three main concerns: the basis of belief, the evidence of the senses, and the knowledge of the Deity. This part of the book is of particular interest as an

18. William Smellie, "The Life of Henry Home, Lord Kames," in *Literary and Characteristical Lives* (1800; reprint, ed. Stephen Brown, Bristol: Thoemmes Press, 1997), p. 129.

early example of and contribution to the Common Sense philosophy that was developed more fully by Thomas Reid. On this understanding of human nature, there are certain self-evident principles that are universally held because we find them undeniable. These include the principle of causation (every effect must have a cause) and the tenet that qualities perceived by the senses must really exist outside the perceiving mind. Thus Kames, a determined determinist, takes aim at Hume's argument against causation. He also seeks to refute "the inveterate scepticism" of Berkeley, whose denial of "the reality of external objects, strikes at the root of the veracity of the senses" (p. 158). Though the evidence of the senses is sometimes deceptive in particular instances, the senses are basically trustworthy. Indeed, they could not be otherwise, for they have been designed by the Deity to suit the active purposes of man.

The *Essays* concludes with a lengthy essay on the existence of the Deity in which Kames pulls together the different strands of his argument to defend natural theology. He offers several proofs for the existence of the Deity, including arguments from causation and from design. Though skepticism is one of his targets, Kames also takes aim at rationalism. As a young man, he had initiated a correspondence with the rationalist theologian Samuel Clarke to query some of the arguments made in Clarke's *Discourse on the Being and Attributes of God*. Several decades later, Kames published his dissatisfaction with Clarke's rationalism in the final chapter of *Essays*. Kames objected to an approach in which evidence for the existence of the Deity depended on rational proofs intelligible only to the learned: "Is then our Maker known to none but to persons of great study and deep thinking?" (p. 317). Evidence of the Deity must be readily accessible to all people, not only philosophers and theologians, and Kames assured his readers that this was so for knowledge of the Deity depended on feeling and perception, more specifically, on the perception of causation. There was an undeniably egalitarian strain in the notion that the intuitive beliefs of the common man are more valid than the thought experiments of the skeptical philosopher.

In the third edition of his *Essays*, Kames makes several references to his other major contribution to the science of man, *Sketches of the History of Man* (1774). As a typical "conjectural history," *Sketches* accounts for the gradual improvement and refinement of the mind as man progresses through the various stages from savage to civil society. At first glance, the two works might seem incompatible: where *Sketches* emphasizes a gradual improvement over time, *Essays* views human nature as static and unitary. Yet even in *Sketches,* Kames stopped short of a historicism which would view also justice and property as products of history rather than nature. Moreover, *Essays* does hint at a progressive view of human nature with the suggestion that the moral sense refines and improves over time (p. 64).[19] For Kames, the natural history of the species was a gradual, providentially designed unfolding of faculties and inclinations implanted by nature. To understand the role and position of human beings within this larger and divinely ordered system was the goal of a science of human nature.

Note on the Text

The present edition is based on the third edition of 1779. However, all substantial variant readings in the first and second editions are added in the Appendix (pp. 237–64 below). Superscript roman numerals in the text refer to these variant readings.

---

19. For an argument which emphasizes the historicism of the *Essays,* see Ario Helo, "The historicity of morality: Necessity and necessary agents in the ethics of Lord Kames," *History of European Ideas,* 27 (2001): 239–55.

ESSAYS

ON THE

PRINCIPLES

OF

MORALITY

AND

NATURAL RELIGION:

CORRECTED AND APPROVED,

IN A

THIRD EDITION.

SEVERAL ESSAYS ADDED CONCERNING
THE PROOF OF A DEITY

EDINBURGH:
Printed for John Bell; and John Murray, London.

M,DCC,LXXIX.

PREFACE TO
THE FORMER EDITIONS

It is proper to acquaint the reader, that the following Essays are not thrown together without connection. The first, by the investigation of a particular fact, is designed to illustrate the nature of man, as a social being. The next considers him as the subject of morality. And as morality supposes freedom of action, this introduces the disquisition on Liberty and Necessity. These make the first part of the work. The rest of the Essays, ushered in by that on Belief, hang upon each other. A plan is prosecuted, in support of the authority of our senses, external and internal; where it is occasionally shown, that our reasonings on some of the most important subjects, rest ultimately upon sense and feeling. This is illustrated in a variety of instances; and from these, the author would gladly hope, that he has thrown new light upon the principles of human knowledge:—All to prepare the way for a proof of the existence and perfections of the Deity, which is the chief aim in this undertaking. The author's manner of thinking, may, in some points, be esteemed bold, and new. But freedom of thought will not displease those who are led, in their inquiries, by the love of truth. To such only he writes: and with such, he will have the merit of a good aim, of having searched for truth, and endeavoured to promote the cause of virtue and religion.

PREFACE TO
THE PRESENT EDITION

I must acknowledge it to have been once my opinion, that there is in man a sense of being able to act against motives, or against our inclination and choice, commonly termed *liberty of indifference.* I was carried along in the current of popular opinion; and could not dream but that this sense really existed, when I found it vouched by so many grave writers. I had at the same time the clearest conviction that man is a necessary agent; and therefore justly concluded that this sense must be delusive. I yielded to another popular opinion, that not only praise and blame, merit and demerit, as attributed to human actions, but also contrition and remorse, are inconsistent with necessity; and must be founded on the same delusive sense of liberty of indifference. From these premises, I was led though reluctantly to admit, that some of our moral feelings and emotions must be founded on a delusion. I was sensible of the odium of a doctrine that rests virtue in any measure upon such a foundation; but so firm is my reliance on divine wisdom in the formation of man, that I was not apprehensive of harm in adhering to truth, however unpalatable it might be in some instances. Before a second edition was called for, I discovered fortunately that the feelings and emotions of the moral sense are perfectly consistent with moral necessity; and I gladly laid hold of that opportunity to acknowledge my error. Having so far rescued the moral system from this pretended delusive sense, I was strongly inclined to think, that we had no notion of being able to act against motives; and in the second edition I ventured to say so. But upon reviewing the subject for the present edition, I clearly saw that we really have a notion of being able to act against motives; which renewed my perplexity, till it occurred to me, that that notion is suggested by the irregular influence of passion, and that we never have it in our cool moments; consequently, that it is not a delusion of nature, but of passion only. Candour I shall always esteem essential in addressing the public, no less than in private dealings; and now I am happy in thinking that morality rests on a foundation that has no delusion in it.

In the second edition however, there is another error that I was not able to disintangle myself from. In the Essay of Liberty and Necessity, our notions of *chance* and *contingency* are held to be delusive; and consequently, that so far we are led by our nature to deviate from truth. It is a harsh doctrine that we should be so led astray in any instance. As that doctrine never sat easy upon me, I discovered it to be also erroneous; and the error is corrected in the present edition, where I hope it is made clearly out, that the notion we have of chance and contingency, is intirely conformable to the necessary chain of causes and effects. And now, rejoice with me my good reader, in being at last relieved from so many distressing errors.

In correcting the Essay on Personal Identity, having discovered its intimate connection with the moral system, I transferred it from the second Part to the first. And in its place are put several new Essays contributing in some degree to the demonstration given of the Deity.

HENRY HOME.

1779.

CONTENTS

Part I.

7

Part II.

ESSAYS

ON THE

PRINCIPLES

OF

MORALITY

AND

NATURAL RELIGION

PART I

❧ ESSAY I ❧

Our Attachment to Objects of Distress

A noted French critic,* treating of poetry and painting, undertakes a subject attempted by others unsuccessfully, which is, to account for the strong attachment we have to objects of distress, imaginary as well as real.

> It is not easy (says he) to account for the pleasure we take in poetry and painting, which has often a strong resemblance to affliction, and of which the symptoms are sometimes the same with those of the most lively sorrow. The arts of poetry and painting are never more applauded than when they succeed in giving pain. A secret charm attaches us to representations of this nature, at the very time our heart, full of anguish, rises up against its proper pleasure. I dare undertake this paradox, (continues our author), and to explain the foundation of this sort of pleasure which we have in poetry and painting; an undertaking that may appear bold, if not rash, seeing it promises to account to every man for what passes in his own breast, and for the secret springs of his approbation and dislike.

Let us attend him in this difficult undertaking. The following proposition is laid down by him as fundamental:

> That man by nature is designed an active being: that inaction, whether of body or mind, draws on languor and disgust: and that this is a cogent motive to fly to any sort of occupation for relief. Thus (adds he) we fly by instinct to every object that can excite our passions, and keep us in agitation, notwithstanding the pain such objects often gives, which causes

---

* l'Abbé du Bos.

11

vexatious days and sleepless nights: but man suffers more by being without passions, than by the agitation they occasion.[1]

This is the sum of his first section. In the second he goes on to particular instances. The first he gives is compassion; which makes us dwell upon the miseries and distresses of others, though thereby we are made to partake of their sufferings; an impulse that he observes is entirely owing to the foregoing principle, which makes us chuse occupation, however painful, rather than be without action. Another is public executions.

> We go in crouds (says he) to a spectacle the most horrid that man can behold, to see a poor wretch broken upon the wheel, burnt alive, or his intrails torn out. The more dreadful the scene, the more numerous the spectators. Yet one might foresee, even without experience, that the cruel circumstances of the execution, the deep groans and anguish of a fellow-creature, must make an impression, the pain of which is not effaced but in a long course of time. But the attraction of agitation prevails more than the joint powers of reflection and experience.

He goes on to mention the strange delight the Roman people had in the entertainments of the amphitheatre; criminals exposed to be torn to pieces by wild beasts, and gladiators in troops hired to butcher one another. He takes this occasion to make the following observation upon the English nation.

> So tender-hearted are that people, that they observe humanity towards their greatest criminals. They allow not of torture; alledging it better to leave a crime unpunished, than to expose an innocent person to those torments authorised in other Christian countries to extort a confession from the guilty. Yet this people, so respectful of their kind, have an infinite pleasure in prize-fighting, bull-baiting, and such other savage spectacles.

He concludes with showing, that it is this very horror of inaction, which makes men every day precipitate themselves into play, and deliver themselves over to cards and dice.

---

1. Jean-Baptiste Dubos (1679–1742), *Réflexions critiques sur la poésie et sur la peinture* (Paris, 1719), Introduction, p. 1; pt. 1, sec. 1, pp. 5–7.

None but fools and sharpers (says he) are moved to play by hope of gain. The generality are directed by another motive. They neglect those diversions where skill and address are required, chusing rather to risk their fortunes at games of mere chance, which keep their minds in continual motion, and where every throw is decisive.[2]

Here is our author's account, fairly stated. It has, I acknowledge, an air of truth; but the following considerations made me doubt. In the first place, if the pain of inaction be the motive which carries us to the spectacles above mentioned, we must expect to find them frequented by none but those who are oppressed with idleness. But this does not hold. All sorts of persons flock to them. Pictures of danger, or of distress, have a secret charm which attracts men from the most serious occupations, and operate equally upon the active and the indolent. In the next place, were there nothing in these spectacles to attract the mind, abstracting from the pain of inaction, there would be no such thing as a preference of one object to another, upon any other ground than that of agitation; and the more the mind was agitated, the greater would be the attraction of the object. But this is contrary to experience. There are many objects of horror and distaste that agitate the mind exceedingly, which even the idlest fly from. And a more apt instance need not be given, than what our author himself cites from Livy;* who, speaking of Antiochus Epiphanes, has the following words. *Gladiatorum munus Romanae consuetudinis, primo majore cum terrore hominum insuetorum ad tale spectaculum, quam voluptate dedit. Deinde saepius dando, et familiare oculis gratumque id spectaculum fecit, et armorum studium plerisque juvenum accendit.* This spectacle we see was at first so far from being attractive to the Greeks, that it was their aversion, till custom rendering it familiar, and less agitating, it came at last to be relished. Upon the same account, the bear-garden, which is one of the chief entertainments of the

2. Ibid., pt. 1, sec. 2, pp. 12–13, 19, 22.
* Lib. 41 ["Gladiatorial contest exhibited in Roman fashion frightened the spectators, who were unused to such sights, more than it pleased them. By frequently giving these exhibitions, he familiarised the eyes of his people to them so that they learned to enjoy them and he created amongst most of the younger men a passion for arms." Livy, *History of Rome* (New York: E. P. Dutton, 1912), vol. 4, 41.20.]

English, is held in abhorrence by the French, and other polite nations. It is too savage an entertainment, to be relished by those of a refined taste.

Were man a being whose only view, in all his actions, is either to attain pleasure, or to avoid pain; which our author lays down as a preliminary, borrowed from Mr Locke (chap. *Of Power,* sect. 37 and 43.);[3] it would, upon that supposition, be hard if not impossible, to give any satisfactory account why we should incline, with our eyes open, to frequent entertainments that must necessarily give us pain. But when we more attentively examine human nature, we discover many and various impulses to action, independent of pleasure and pain. Let us prosecute this thought, because it may probably lead to a solution of the problem.

When we attend to the emotions raised in us by external objects, or to any of our emotions, we find them greatly diversified. They are strong or weak, distinct or confused, *&c.* There is no division of emotions more comprehensive than into agreeable or disagreeable. It is unnecessary, and would perhaps be in vain, to search for the cause of these differences. More we cannot say, but that such is the constitution of our nature, so contrived by the Author of all things, in order to answer wise and good purposes.

There is another circumstance to be attended to in these emotions; that *affection* enters into some of them, *aversion* into others. To some objects we have an affection, and we desire to possess and enjoy them: other objects raise our aversion, and move us to avoid them. No object can move our affection but what is agreeable, nor our aversion but what is disagreeable. Whether it be the effect of every agreeable object to raise affection, we have no occasion at present to inquire. But it is of importance to observe, that many objects are disagreeable, perhaps painful, that raise not aversion in any degree. Objects of horror and terror, loathsome objects, and many others raise aversion. But there are many emotions or passions, some of them of the most painful sort, that raise no aversion. Grief is a most painful passion, and yet is not accompanied with any degree of aversion. On the contrary, it is attractive, no less so than many of our pleasant emotions: we

3. John Locke, *An Essay Concerning Human Understanding* (London, 1690; reprint, ed. Peter H. Nidditch, Oxford: Clarendon Press, 1975), II.xxi.37, pp. 254–5; II.xxi.43, pp. 259–60.

cling to the object that raises our grief, and love to dwell upon it. Compassion is an instance of the like nature. Objects of distress raise no aversion in us, though they give us pain. On the contrary, they draw us to them, and inspire us with a desire to afford relief.

During infancy, appetite and desire are our sole impulses to action. But in the progress of life, when we learn to distinguish the objects around us as productive of pleasure or pain, we acquire by degrees impulses to action of a different sort. Self-love is a strong motive to search about for every thing that may contribute to happiness. Self-love operates by means of reflection and experience; and every object, as soon as discovered to contribute to our happiness, raises in us of course a desire of possessing. Hence it is, that pleasure and pain are the only motives to action, as far as self-love is concerned. But our appetites and passions are not all of them of this kind. They frequently operate by direct impulse, without the intervention of reason, in the same manner as instinct does in brute creatures. As they are not influenced by any sort of reasoning, the view of shunning misery or acquiring happiness, makes no part of the impulsive motive. It is true, that the gratification of our passions and appetites, is agreeable; and it is also true, that, in giving way to a particular appetite, the view of pleasure may, by a reflex act, become an additional motive to the action. But these things must not be confounded with the direct impulse arising from the appetite or passion; which, as I have said, operates blindly, and in the way of instinct, without any view to consequences.

To ascertain the distinction betwixt actions directed by self-love and actions directed by particular appetites and passions, it must be further remarked, that the aim of self-love is always to make us happy, but that other appetites and passions have frequently a very different tendency. This will be plain from induction. Revenge gratified against the man we hate, is agreeable. It is a very different case, where we have taken offence at a man we love. Friendship will not allow me, however offended, to hurt my friend. "I cannot find in my heart to do him mischief; but I would have him made sensible of the wrong he has done me." Revenge thus denied a vent, recoils, and preys upon the vitals of the person offended. It displays itself in peevishness and bad humour; which must work and ferment, till time or acknowledgment of the wrong, carry it off. This sort of revenge is turned against the man himself who is offended; and examples there are of persons in this pettish humour, working great mischief to themselves, in order to make the offenders sensible of the wrong. Thus, no example is more common, than that of a young woman disappointed in love, who prone to augment her distress, throws herself away upon any worthless man that will ask her the question. My next example will be still more satisfactory. Every one must have observed, that when the passion of grief is at its height, the very nature of it is to shun and fly from every thing that tends to give ease or comfort. In the height of grief, a man rushes on to misery, by a sort of sympathy with the person for whom he is grieved. Why should I be happy when my friend is no more, is the language of this passion. In these circumstances, the man is truly a self-tormentor. And here we have a singular phaenomenon in human nature; an appetite after pain, an inclination to render one's self miserable. This goes farther than even self-murder; a crime that is never perpetrated but in order to put an end to misery, when it rises to such an height as to be insupportable.

We now see how imperfect the description is of human nature, given by Mr Locke, and by our French author. They acknowledge no motive to action, but what arises from self-love; measures laid down to attain pleasure, or to shun pain. Many appetites and passions, with the affection and aversion involved in them, are left entirely out of the system. And yet we may say, with some degree of probability, that we are more frequently influenced by these than by self-love. So various is human nature, and so complicated its acting powers, that it is not readily to be taken in at one view.

We return to our subject, after having unfolded those principles of action with which it is connected. It may be gathered from what is above laid down, that nature, which designed us for society, has linked us together in an intimate manner, by the sympathetic principle, which communicates the joy and sorrow of one to many. We partake the afflictions of our fellows: we grieve with them and for them; and, in many instances, their misfortunes affect us equally with our own. Let it not therefore appear surprising, that, instead of shunning objects of misery, we chuse to dwell upon them; for this is truly as natural as indulging grief for our own misfortunes. And it must be observed at the same time, that this is wisely ordered by providence: were the social affections mixed with any degree of aversion, even when we suffer under them, we should be inclined, upon the first notice of an object in distress, to drive it from our sight and mind, instead of affording relief.

Nor must we judge of this principle as any way vitious or faulty: for besides that it is the great cement of human society, we ought to consider, that, as no state is exempt from misfortunes, mutual sympathy must greatly promote the security and happiness of mankind. That the prosperity and preservation of each individual should be the care of many, tends more to happiness in general, than that each man, as the single inhabitant of a desert island, should be left to stand or fall by himself, without prospect of regard or assistance from others. Nor is this all. When we consider our own character and actions in a reflex view, we cannot help approving this tenderness and sympathy in our nature. We are pleased with ourselves for being so constituted: we are conscious of inward merit; and this is a continual source of satisfaction.

To open this subject a little more, it must be observed, that naturally we have a strong desire to be acquainted with the history of others. We judge of their actions, approve or disapprove, condemn or acquit; and in this the busy mind has a wonderful delight. Nay, we go farther. We enter deep into their concerns, take a side; we partake of joys and distresses with those we favour, and show a dislike to others. This turn of mind makes history, novels, and plays, the most universal and favourite entertainments. It is natural to man as a sociable creature; and we venture to affirm, that the most sociable have the greatest share of this sort of curiosity, and the strongest attachment to such entertainments.

Tragedy is an imitation or representation of human characters and actions. It is a feigned history, which commonly makes a stronger impression than what is real; because, if it be a work of genius, incidents will be chosen to make the deepest impressions; and will be so conducted as to keep the mind in continual suspense and agitation, beyond what commonly happens in real life. By a good tragedy, all the social passions are excited. We take a sudden affection to some of the personages represented: we come to be attached to them as to our bosom-friends; and we hope and fear for them, as if the whole were a true history.

To a dry philosopher, unacquainted with theatrical entertainments, it may appear surprising, that imitation should have such an effect upon the mind, and that the want of truth and reality should not prevent the operation of our passions. But whatever may be the physical cause, one thing is evident, that this aptitude of the mind of man to receive impressions from feigned as well as from real objects, contributes to the noblest purposes of life. Nothing contributes so much to improve the mind and confirm it in virtue, as being continually employed in surveying the actions of others, entering into the concerns of the virtuous, approving their conduct, condemning vice, and showing an abhorrence at it; for the mind acquires strength by exercise, as well as the body. But were this sort of discipline confined to scenes in real life, the generality of men would be little the better for it, because such scenes rarely occur. They are not frequent even in history. But in compositions where liberty is allowed of fiction, it must be want of genius, if the mind be not sufficiently exercised, till it acquire the greatest sensibility, and the most confirmed habits of virtue.

Thus, tragedy engages our passions, no less than true history. Friendship, concern for the virtuous, abhorrence of the vitious, compassion, hope, fear, and the whole train of the social passions, are roused and exercised by both of them equally.

This may appear to be a fair account of the attachment we have to theatrical entertainments: but when the subject is more narrowly examined, some difficulties occur, to which the principles above laid down will scarce afford a satisfactory answer. It is not wonderful that young people flock to such entertainments. The love of novelty, desire of occupation, beauty of action, are strong attractions: and if one be once engaged, of whatever age, by entering into the interests of the personages represented, the attraction becomes strong; and the foresight of running into grief and affliction will not disengage us. But we generally become wise by experience; and it may appear surprising, when distress is the never-failing effect of such entertainments, that persons of riper judgment do not shun them altogether. Doth self-love lie asleep in this case, which is for ordinary so active a principle? One should naturally think, that as repeated experience must make us sufficiently wise to keep out of harm's way; deep tragedies would be little frequented by persons of reflection. Yet the contrary is true in fact; the deepest tragedies being the most frequented by persons of all ages, by those especially of delicate feelings upon whom the strongest impressions are made. A man of that character, who is scarce relieved from the deep distress he was thrown into the night before by a well-acted tragedy, does, in his closet, coolly and deliberately resolve to go to the next entertainment of the kind, without feeling the smallest obstruction from self-love.

This leads to a speculation, perhaps one of the most curious that belongs to human nature. Contrary to what is generally understood, the foregoing speculation affords a palpable proof, that even self-love does not always operate to avoid pain and distress. In examining how this is brought about, there will be discovered an admirable contrivance in human nature, to give free scope to the social affections. Keeping in view what is above laid down, that of the painful passions some are accompanied with aversion, some with affection; we find, upon the strictest examination, that those painful passions, which, in the direct feeling, are free from any degree of aversion, have as little of it in the reflex act. Or, to express the thing more familiarly, when we reflect upon the pain we have suffered by our concern for others, there is no degree of aversion mixed with the reflection, more than with the pain itself which was raised by a sight of the object. For illustration's sake, let us compare the pain which arises from compassion with any bodily pain. Cutting one's flesh is not only accompanied with strong aversion in the direct feeling, but with an aversion equally strong in reflecting upon the action afterward. We feel no such aversion in reflecting upon the mental pains above described. On the contrary, when we reflect upon the pain which the misfortune of a friend gave us, the reflection is accompanied with an eminent degree of satisfaction. We approve ourselves for suffering with our friend, value ourselves the more for that suffering, and are ready to undergo chearfully the like distress upon the like occasion. Self-love gives no opposition.

When we examine those particular passions, which, though painful, are yet accompanied with no aversion; we find they are all of the social kind, arising from that eminent principle of sympathy, which is the cement of human society. The social passions are accompanied with appetite for in-dulgence when they give us pain, no less than when they give us pleasure. We submit willingly to such painful passions, and reckon it no hardship to suffer under them. In being thus constituted, we have the consciousness of regularity and order, and that it is *right* and *meet* we should suffer after this manner. Thus the moral affections, even such of them as produce pain, are none of them attended with any degree of aversion, not even in reflecting upon the distress they often bring us under. Sympathy in particular attaches us to an object in distress so powerfully as even to overbalance self-love, which would make us fly from it. Sympathy accordingly, though a painful passion, is attractive; and in affording relief, the gratification of the passion is not a little pleasant. And this observation tends to set the moral affections in a very distinguished point of view, in opposition to those that are either malevolent, or selfish.

Many and various are the springs of action in human nature, and not one more admirable than what is now unfolded. Sympathy is an illustrious principle, which connects persons in society by ties stronger than those of blood. Yet compassion, the child of sympathy, is a painful emotion; and were it accompanied with any degree of aversion, even in reflecting upon the distress it occasioned, that aversion would by degrees blunt the passion, and at length cure us of what we would be apt to reckon a weakness or disease. But the Author of our nature hath not left his work imperfect. He has given us this noble principle entire, without a counterbalance, so as to have a vigorous and universal operation. Far from having any aversion to pain occasioned by the social principle, we reflect upon such pain with satisfaction, and are willing to submit to it upon all occasions with chearfulness and heart-liking, just as much as if it were a real pleasure. And, thus, tragedy is allowed to seize the mind with all the different charms which arise from the exercise of the social passions, without the least obstacle from self-love.

Had the principle of sympathy occurred to our author, he would have found it sufficient to explain our voluntarily partaking with others in their distress, without having need of so imperfect a cause as aversion to inaction. Without entering deep into philosophy, he might have had hints in abundance from common life to explain it. In every corner, persons are to be met with of such a sympathising temper, as to chuse to spend their lives with the diseased and distressed. They partake with them in their afflictions, enter heartily into their concerns, and sigh and groan with them. These pass their lives in sadness and despondency, without having any other satisfaction than what arises upon the reflection of having done their duty.

And if this account of the matter be just, we may be assured, that those who are the most compassionate in their temper, will be the fondest of tragedy, which affords them a large field for indulging the passion. Admirable indeed are the effects brought about by this means: for passions, as they gather strength by indulgence, so they decay by want of exercise. Persons in prosperity, unacquainted with distress and misery, are apt to grow hard-hearted. Tragedy is an admirable resource in such a case. It serves to humanize the temper, by supplying feigned objects of pity, which have nearly the same effect to exercise the passion that real objects have. And thus, we are carried by a natural impulse to deal deep in affliction, occasioned by representations of feigned misfortunes; and the passion of pity alone would throng such representations, were there nothing else to attract the mind, or to afford satisfaction.

It is owing to curiosity, that public executions are so much frequented. Sensible people endeavour to correct an appetite, the indulging of which produces pain; and upon reflection is attended with no degree of self-approbation. Hence it is, that such spectacles are the entertainment of the vulgar chiefly, who allow themselves blindly to be led by curiosity with little attention whether it will contribute to their good or not.

With respect to prize-fighting and gladiatorian shews, nothing animates and inspires us more than examples of courage and bravery. We catch the spirit of the actor, and turn bold and intrepid as he appears to be. On the other hand, we enter into the distresses of the vanquished, and have a sympathy for them in proportion to the gallantry of their behaviour. No wonder then that such shews are frequented by persons of the best taste. We are led by the same principle that makes us fond of perusing the lives of heroes and of conquerors. And it may be observed by the bye, that such spectacles have an admirable good effect in training up the youth to boldness and resolution. In this therefore I see not that foreigners have reason to condemn the English taste. Spectacles of this sort deserve encouragement from the state, and to be made an object of public police.

As for gaming, I cannot bring myself to think that there is any pleasure in having the mind kept in suspense, and as it were upon the rack, which must be the case of those who venture their money at games of hazard. Inaction and idleness are not by far so hard to bear. I am satisfied that the love of money is at the bottom. Nor is it a solid objection, That people will neglect games of skill and address, to venture their money at hazard; for this may be owing to indolence, diffidence, or impatience. There is indeed a curious speculation with regard to this article of gaming, that pleasure and pain attend good and bad success at play, independent of the money lost or win. It is plain, that good luck raises the spirits, as bad luck depresses them, without regard to consequences: and to that is owing our concern at game, when we play for trifles. To what principle in our nature that concern is owing, I leave to be investigated by others, as it is not necessarily connected with the subject of the present Essay.

I lay hold of the present edition to investigate the point left open in the former. This earth produces little for the use of man but what requires the preparation both of art and industry; and man, by nature artful and industrious, is well fitted for his situation. Were every thing furnished to his hand without thought or labour, he would sink below the lowest of the brute creation. I say, *below,* because the lowest creature perfect in its kind, is superior to a creature of whatever kind that is corrupted. Self-love moves us to labour for ourselves; benevolence to labour for others. And emulation is added to enforce these principles. Emulation is visible even in children, striving for victory without knowing what moves them. In striving for fame, power, riches, emulation makes a splendid figure: it operates vigorously in works of skill, nor does it lye dormant in competitions that depend mostly or intirely on chance, such as playing with cards or dice. It is true, that the pleasure of victory without a view to gain, is extremely faint; and it pains me to observe that the desperate risks voluntarily submitted to in games of chance, are mostly, if not intirely instigated by avarice.

Foundation and Principles of Morality[i]

INTRODUCTION

Superficial knowledge produces the boldest adventurers, because it gives no check to the imagination when fired by a new thought. Shallow writers lay down plans, contrive models, and are hurried on to execution by the pleasure of novelty, without considering whether, after all, there be any solid foundation to support the spacious edifice. It redounds not a little to the honour of some late inquirers after truth, that, subduing this bent of nature, they have submitted to the slow and more painful method of experiment; a method that has been applied to natural philosophy with great success. The accurate Locke, in the science of logics, has pursued the same method, and has been followed by several ingenious writers. The mistress-science alone is neglected; and it seems hard that less deference should be paid to her than to her hand-maids. Every author gives a system of morals, as if it were his privilege to adjust it to his own taste and fancy. Regulations for human conduct are daily framed, without the least consideration, whether they arise out of human nature, or can be accommodated to it. And hence many airy systems, that relate not to man nor to any other being. Authors of a warm imagination and benevolent temper, exalt man to the angelic nature, and compose laws for his conduct, so refined as to be far above the reach of humanity. Others of a contrary disposition, forcing down all men to a level with the very lowest of their kind, assign them laws more suitable to brutes than to rational beings. In abstract science, writers may more innocently indulge their fancies. The worst that can happen is, to mislead us in matters where error has little influence on practice. But they who deal in moral philosophy ought to be cautious; for their errors seldom fail to

23

ɥave a bad tendency. The exalting of nature above its standard, is apt to disgust the mind, conscious of its weakness, and of its inability to attain such an uncommon degree of perfection. The debasing of nature tends to break the balance of the affections, by adding weight to the selfish and irregular appetites. Beside these bad effects, clashing opinions about morality are apt to tempt men who have any hollowness of heart, to shake off all principles, and to give way to every appetite: and then adieu to a just tenor of life, and consistency of conduct.

These considerations give the author of this essay a just concern to proceed with the utmost circumspection in his inquiries, and to try his conclusions by their true touchstone, that of facts and experiments. Had this method been strictly followed, the world would not have been perplexed with that variety of inconsistent systems, which unhappily have rendered morality a difficult and intricate science. An attempt to restore it to its original simplicity and authority, must be approved, however short one falls in the execution. Writers differ about the origin of the laws of nature, and they differ about the laws themselves. As the author is not fond of controversy, he will attempt a plan of the laws of nature, drawn from their proper source, laying aside what has been written on this subject.

CHAPTER I

Foundation of Morality

In searching for the foundation of the laws of our nature, the following reflections occur. In the first place, two things cannot be more intimately connected than a being and its actions: for the connection is that of cause and effect. Such as the being is, such must its actions be. In the next place, the several classes into which nature has distributed living creatures, are not more distinguishable by an external form, than by an internal constitution, which manifests itself in an uniformity of conduct, peculiar to each species. In the third place, any action conformable to the common nature of the species, is considered by us as regular and proper. It is according to order, and according to nature. But if there exist a being of a constitution different from that of its kind, the actions of this being, though conformable to its own peculiar constitution, will, to us, appear whimsical and disorderly. We shall have a feeling of disgust, as if we saw a man with two heads or four hands. These reflections lead us to the foundation of the laws of our nature. They are to be derived from the common nature of man, of which every person partakes who is not a monster.

As the foregoing observations make the groundwork of all morality, it may not be improper to enlarge a little upon them. Looking around, we find creatures of very different kinds, both as to external and internal constitution. Each species having a peculiar nature, ought to have a peculiar rule of action resulting from its nature. We find this to hold in fact; and it is extremely agreeable to observe, how accurately the laws of each species are adjusted to the frame of the individuals which compose it, so as to procure the conveniencies of life in the best manner, and to produce regularity and consistency of conduct. To give but one instance: the laws which govern sociable creatures, differ widely from those which govern the savage and solitary. Among solitary creatures, who have no mutual connection, there is nothing more natural nor more orderly, than to make food one of another. But for creatures in society to live after that manner, must be the effect of jarring and inconsistent principles. No such disorderly appearance is discovered upon the face of this globe. There is, as above observed, a harmony betwixt the internal and external constitution of the several classes of animals; and this harmony affords a delightful prospect of deep design, effectively carried into execution. The common nature of every class of beings is perceived by us as perfect; and if, in any instance, a particular being swerve from the common nature of its kind, the action produces a sense of disorder and wrong. In a word, it is according to order, that the different sorts of living creatures should be governed by laws adapted to their peculiar nature. We consider it as fit and proper that it should be so; and it is beautiful to find creatures acting according to their nature.

The force of these observations cannot be resisted by those who admit of final causes. We make no difficulty to pronounce, that a species of beings who have such or such a nature, are made for such or such an end. A lion has claws, because nature made him an animal of prey. A man has fingers, because he is a social animal made to procure food by art not by force. It is thus we discover for what end we were designed by nature, or the Author of nature. And the same chain of reasoning points out to us the laws by which we ought to regulate our actions: for acting according to nature, is acting so as to answer the end of our creation.

CHAPTER II

Moral Sense

Having made out that the nature of man is the foundation of the laws that ought to govern his actions, it will be necessary to trace out human nature, so far as regards the present subject. If we can happily accomplish this part of our undertaking, it will be easy, in the synthetical method, to deduce the laws that ought to regulate our conduct. And we begin with examining in what manner we are related to beings and things around us; a speculation that will lead to the point in view.

As we are placed in a great world, surrounded with beings and things, some beneficial, some hurtful; we are so constituted, that scarce any object is indifferent to us: it either gives pleasure or pain; witness sounds, tastes, and smells. This is the most remarkable in objects of sight, which affect us in a more lively manner than objects of any other external sense. Thus, a spreading oak, a verdant plain, a large river, are objects that afford delight. A rotten carcase, a distorted figure, create aversion; which, in some instances, goes the length of horror.

With regard to objects of sight, whatever gives pleasure is said to be *beautiful:* whatever gives pain, is said to be *ugly.* The terms *beauty* and *ugliness,* in their proper signification, are confined to objects of sight. And indeed such objects, being more highly agreeable or disagreeable than others, deserve well to be distinguished by a proper name. But, as it happens with words that convey a more lively idea than ordinary, the terms are applied in a figurative sense to almost every thing that gives a high relish or disgust. Thus, we talk of a beautiful theorem, a beautiful thought, and a beautiful passage in music. And this way of speaking has become so familiar, that it is scarce reckoned a figurative expression.

Objects considered simply as existing, without relation to any end or any designing agent, are in the lowest rank or order with respect to beauty and ugliness; a smooth globe for example, or a vivid colour. But when external objects, such as works of art, are considered with relation to some end, we feel a higher degree of pleasure or pain. Thus, a building regular in all its parts, pleases the eye upon the very first view: but considered as a house for dwelling in, which is the end purposed, it pleases still more, supposing it to be well fitted to its end. A similar sensation arises in observing the operations of a well-ordered state, where the parts are nicely adjusted to the ends of security and happiness.

This perception of beauty in works of art or design, which is produced not barely by a sight of the object, but by viewing the object as fitted to some use, and as related to some end, includes in it what is termed *approbation:* for approbation, when applied to works of art, means our being pleased with them or conceiving them beautiful, in the view of being fitted to their end. *Approbation* and *disapprobation* are not applicable to the lowest class of beautiful and ugly objects. To say, that we approve a sweet taste, or a flowing river, is really saying no more but that we are pleased with such objects. But the term is justly applied to works of art, because it means more than being pleased with such an object merely as existing. It imports a peculiar beauty, which is perceived, upon considering the object as fitted to the use intended.

It must be further observed to avoid obscurity, that the beauty which arises from the relation of an object to its end, is independent of the end itself, whether good or bad, whether beneficial or hurtful: it arises from considering its fitness to the end purposed, whatever that end be.

When we take the end itself under consideration, there is discovered a beauty or ugliness of a higher kind than the two former. A beneficial end strikes us with a peculiar pleasure; and approbation belongs also to this feeling. Thus, the mechanism of a ship is beautiful, in the view of means well fitted to an end. But the end itself, of carrying on commerce and procuring so many conveniencies to mankind, exalts the object, and heightens our approbation and pleasure. By an end, I mean what it serves to procure and bring about, whether it be an ultimate end, or subordinate to something farther. Considered with respect to its end, the degree of its beauty depends on the degree of its usefulness. Let it be only kept in view, that as the end or use of a thing is an object of greater dignity and importance than the means, the approbation bestowed on the former rises higher than that bestowed on the latter.

These three orders of beauty may be blended together in many different ways, to have very different effects. If an object in itself beautiful be ill fitted to its end, it will, upon the whole, be disagreeable. This may be exemplified in a house regular in its architecture and beautiful to the eye, but incommodious for dwelling. If there be in an object an aptitude to a bad end, it will, upon the whole, be disagreeable, though it have the second modification of beauty in perfection. A constitution of government formed with the most perfect art for enslaving the people, may be an instance of this. If the end be good but the object not well fitted to the end, it will be beautiful, or ugly, as the goodness of the end, or unfitness of the means, is prevalent. Of this instances will occur at first view, without being suggested.

The foregoing modifications of beauty and deformity, apply to all objects, animate and inanimate. A voluntary agent produceth a peculiar species of beauty and deformity, which may be distinguished from all others. The actions of living creatures are more interesting than the actions of matter. The instincts and principles of action of the former, give us more delight than the blind powers of the latter; or, in other words, are more beautiful. No one can doubt of this fact, who is in any degree conversant with the poets. In Homer every thing lives: even darts and arrows are endued with voluntary motion. And we are sensible, that nothing animates a poem more than the frequent use of this figure.

Hence a new circumstance in the beauty and deformity of actions, considered as proceeding from intention, deliberation, and choice. This circumstance, which is of the utmost importance in the science of morals, concerns chiefly human actions: for we discover little of intention, deliberation, and choice, in the actions of inferior creatures. Human actions are not only agreeable or disagreeable, beautiful or deformed, in the different views above mentioned, but are further distinguished in our perception of them, as *fit* and *meet* to be done, or as *unfit* and *unmeet*. These are simple perceptions, capable of no definition. But let any man attentively examine what passeth in his mind, when the object of his thought is an action proceeding from deliberate intention, and he will soon discover the meaning of these words, and the perceptions which they denote. Let him reflect upon a signal act of generosity to a person of merit, relieving him from want or from a cruel enemy: let him reflect on a man of exemplary patriotism bearing patiently rank oppression, rather than break the peace of society. Such conduct will not only be agreeable to him, and appear beautiful, but will be agreeable and beautiful, as *fit* and *meet* to be done. He will approve the action in that quality, and he will approve the actor for his humanity and disinterestedness. This distinguishing circumstance intitles the beauty and deformity of human actions to peculiar names: they are termed *moral beauty* and *moral deformity.* Hence the *morality* and *immorality* of human actions; founded on a faculty termed the *moral sense.*

It gives no clear notion of morality, to rest it upon simple approbation, as some writers do. I approve a well constructed plough or waggon for its usefulness. I approve a fine picture or statue for the justness of its representation; and I approve the maker for his skill. I approve an elegant dress on a fine woman; and I approve her taste. But such approbation is far from being the same with that which is occasioned by human actions deliberately done in order to some end. If the end be beneficial, the action is approved as right and fit to have been done: if hurtful, it is disapproved as wrong and unfit to have been done. None of these qualities are applicable to the instances first given. [ii]

Of all objects whatever, human actions are the most highly delightful or disgustful, and possess the highest degree of beauty or deformity. In these every circumstance concurs: the fitness or unfitness of the means, the goodness or badness of the end, the intention of the actor; which give them the peculiar character of *fit* and *meet,* or *unfit* and *unmeet.*

Thus we find the nature of man so constituted, as to approve certain actions, and to disapprove others; to consider some actions as *fit* and *meet* to be done, and others as *unfit* and *unmeet.* What distinguisheth actions to make them objects of the one or the other perception, will be explained in the following chapter. And with regard to some of our actions, another circumstance will be discovered, different from what have been mentioned, sounding the well known terms of *duty* and *obligation,* directing our conduct, and constituting what in the strictest sense may be termed a law. With regard to other beings, we have no *data* to discover the laws of their nature, other than their frame and constitution. We have the same *data* to discover

the laws of our own nature; and over and above, a peculiar sense of approbation or disapprobation, termed the moral sense. And one thing extremely
remarkable will be explained afterwards, that the laws which are fitted to
the nature of man and to his external circumstances, are the same that we
approve by the moral sense.

CHAPTER III

Duty and Obligation

Though these terms are of the utmost importance in morals, I know not
that any author hath attempted to explain them, by pointing out those
principles or perceptions which they express. This defect I shall endeavour
to supply, by tracing these terms to their proper source, without which the
system of morals cannot be complete; because these terms point out to us
the most precise and essential branch of morality.

Lord Shaftesbury, to whom the world is greatly indebted for his inesti-
mable writings, has clearly and convincingly made out, "that virtue is the
good, and vice the ill of every one."[1] But he has not proved virtue to be our
duty, otherways than by showing it to be our interest; which comes not up
to the idea of duty. For this term plainly implies somewhat indispensable
in our conduct; what we ought to do, what we ought to submit to. Now,
a man may be considered as foolish for acting against his interest; but he
cannot be considered as wicked or vitious. His Lordship indeed, in his essay
upon virtue,* approaches to an explanation of duty and obligation, by asserting the subordinancy of the self-affections to the social. But though he
states this as a proposition to be made out, he drops it in the subsequent
part of his work, and never again brings it into view.

---

1. Anthony Ashley Cooper, Third Earl of Shaftesbury (1671–1713), *Inquiry Concerning
Virtue or Merit*, in *Characteristics of Men, Manners, Opinions, Times* (London, 1711; re-
print, ed. Lawrence E. Klein, Cambridge: Cambridge University Press, 1999), p. 230.
First published in 1699, the *Inquiry* argued that man has a "natural sense of right and
wrong," which Shaftesbury called a "moral" sense (pt. 3, sec. 1, pp. 177–9.)
* Page 98.

Hutcheson, in his essay upon beauty and virtue,* founds the morality of actions on a certain quality of actions, that procures approbation and love to the agent. But this account of morality is also imperfect, as it makes no distinction between duty and simple benevolence. It is scarce applicable to justice; for the man who, confining himself strictly to it, is true to his word and avoids harming others, is a just and moral man, is intitled to some share of esteem; but will never be the object of love or friendship. He must show a disposition to the good of mankind, of his friends at least and neighbours, he must exert acts of humanity and benevolence; before he can hope to procure the affection of others.

But it is chiefly to be observed, that in this account of morality, the terms *obligation, duty, ought* and *should,* have no distinct meaning; which shows, that the entire foundation of morality is not taken in by this author. It is true, that toward the close of his work, he attempts to explain the meaning of the term *obligation;* but without success. He explains it to be, either, "a motive from self-interest, sufficient to determine those who duly consider it to a certain course of action;" which surely is not moral obligation; or "a determination, without regard to our own interest, to approve actions, and to perform them; which determination shall also make us displeased with ourselves, and uneasy upon having acted contrary to it;" in which sense, he says, there is naturally an obligation upon all men to benevolence.[2] But this account falls short of the true idea of obligation; because it makes no destinction betwixt it and that simple approbation of the moral sense which can be applied to heroism, magnanimity, generosity, and other exalted virtues, as well as to justice. Duty however belongs to the latter only; and no

---

* Page 101.

2. Francis Hutcheson's *An Inquiry into the Original of Our Ideas of Beauty and Virtue* (London, 1725) consists of two separate essays bound in one volume. Kames quotes from the second essay (*Inquiry II*), *An Inquiry concerning the Original of our Ideas of Virtue or Moral Good,* pp. 249–51. Francis Hutcheson (1694–1746) was Chair of Moral Philosophy at the University of Glasgow, where he taught his famous successor Adam Smith, and a major influence on the generation of literati associated with the high point of the Enlightenment in Scotland. Hutcheson drew upon Shaftesbury's somewhat looser notion of a natural moral sense to posit an innate moral sense, a distinctive faculty of perception, analogous to the external senses, through which people recognize and distinguish between vice and virtue.

man reckons himself under an obligation to perform any action that belongs to the former.

Neither is the author of the treatise upon human nature more successful, when he endeavours to resolve the moral sense into pure sympathy.* According to that author, there is no more in morality, but approving or disapproving an action, after we discover by reflection that it tends to the good or hurt of society. This would be too faint a principle to control our irregular appetites and passions. It would scarce be sufficient to restrain us from incroaching upon our friends and neighbours; and, with regard to strangers, would be the weakest of all restraints. We shall by and by show, that morality has a more solid foundation. In the mean time, it is of importance to observe, that, upon this author's system, as well as Hutcheson's, the noted terms of *duty, obligation, ought* and *should, &c.* have no meaning.

We shall now proceed to explain these terms, by pointing out the perceptions which they express. And, in performing this task, there will be discovered a wonderful and beautiful contrivance of the Author of our nature, to give authority to morality, by putting the self-affections in a due subordination to the social. The moral sense has in part been explained above; that by it we perceive some actions to be *fit* and *meet* to be done; and others to be *unfit* and *unmeet*. When this observation is applied to particulars, it is an evident fact, that we have a sense of *fitness* in kindly and beneficent actions: we approve ourselves and others for performing actions of this kind; as, on the other hand, we disapprove the unsociable, peevish, and hard-hearted. But in one class of actions, an additional circumstance is regarded by the moral sense. Submission to parents, gratitude to benefactors, and the acting justly to all, are perceived not only as fit and meet, but as our indispensable duty. On the other hand, the injuring others in their persons, in their fame, or in their goods are perceived not only as *unfit* to be done, but as absolutely *wrong* to be done, and what, upon no account, we *ought* to do. What is here asserted, is a matter of fact, which can admit of no other proof than an appeal to every man's own perceptions. Lay prej-

* Vol. 3 Part 3 [David Hume, *A Treatise of Human Nature* (London, 1739; reprint, ed. David Fate Norton and Mary J. Norton, Oxford: Oxford University Press, 2000), 3.3.7–12, pp. 368–70.]

udice aside, and give fair play to what passes in the mind: I ask no other concession. There is no man, however irregular in his life and manners, however poisoned by a wrong education, but must be sensible of these perceptions. And indeed the words which are to be found in all languages, and which are perfectly understood in the communication of sentiments, are an evident demonstration of it. *Duty, obligation, ought* and *should,* would be empty sounds, unless upon supposition of such perceptions. We do not consider actions that come under the notion of duty or obligation, or prohibited by them, as in any degree under our own power. We have the consciousness of necessity, and of being bound and tied to performance, as if under some external compulsion.

It is proper here to be remarked, that benevolent and generous actions are not objects of this peculiar sense. Hence, such actions, though considered as *fit* and *right* to be done, are not however considered to be our *duty,* but as virtuous actions beyond what is strictly our duty. Benevolence and generosity are more beautiful, and more attractive of love and esteem, than justice. Yet, not being so necessary to the support of society, they are left upon the general footing of approbatory pleasure; while justice, faith, truth, without which society cannot subsist, are objects of the foregoing peculiar sense, to take away all shadow of liberty, and to put us under a necessity of performance. The virtues that are exacted from us as duties, may be termed *primary:* the other which are not exacted as duties, may be termed *secondary.*

Dr. Butler, a manly and acute writer, hath gone farther than any other, to assign a just foundation for moral duty. He considers conscience or reflection,*

> as one principle of action, which, compared with the rest as they stand together in the nature of man, plainly bears upon it marks of authority over all the rest, and claims the absolute direction of them all, to allow or forbid their gratification.

* Preface to the later editions of his sermons. [Preface to the 2d ed. (1729) and to subsequent editions of Joseph Butler (1692–1752), *Fifteen Sermons Preached at the Rolls Chapel* (1st ed., London, 1726); in *The Works of Joseph Butler,* 3 vols. (Oxford: Clarendon Press, 1896; reprint, Bristol: Thoemmes Press, 1995), 2:13. Against the psychological egoism of Thomas Hobbes, Butler argued that human nature is a complex system in which the principles of self-love and benevolence are guided by conscience or reflection.]

And his proof of this proposition is, "that a disapprobation or reflection is in itself a principle manifestly superior to a mere propension." Had this admirable writer handled the subject more professedly than he had occasion to do in a preface, it is more than likely he would have put it in a clear light. But he has not said enough to afford that light the subject is capable of. For it may be observed, in the first place, that a disapprobation of reflection is far from being the whole of the matter. Such disapprobation is applied to moroseness, selfishness, and many other partial affections, which are, however, not considered in a strict sense as contrary to our duty. And it may be doubted, whether a disapprobation of reflection be, in every case, a principle superior to a mere propension. We disapprove a man who neglects his private affairs, and gives himself up to love, hunting, or any other amusement: nay, he disapproves himself. Yet from this we cannot fairly conclude, that he is guilty of any breach of duty, or that it is unlawful for him to follow his propension. We may observe, in the next place, what will be afterward explained, that conscience, or the moral sense, is none of our principles of action, but their guide and director. It is still of greater importance to observe, that the authority of conscience does not consist merely in an act of reflection. It arises from a direct perception, which we have upon presenting the object, without the intervention of any sort of reflection. And the authority lies in this circumstance, that we perceive the action to be our duty, and what we are indispensably bound to perform. It is in this manner that the moral sense, with regard to some actions, plainly bears upon it the marks of authority over all our appetites and passions. It is the voice of God within us, which commands our strictest obedience, just as much as when his will is declared by express revelation.

What is here stated will I hope clearly distinguish duty or moral obligation from benevolence: I know of no words in our language to make the distinction more clear. The overlooking this distinction is a capital defect in the writers who acknowledge morality to be founded on an innate sense: it has led them to reduce the whole of virtue to benevolence; and consequently, to hold mankind as bound to perform the highest acts of benevolence, because such acts produce the highest approbation. This doctrine cannot be altogether harmless, because it converts benevolence into indispensable duty, contrary to the system of nature. A young man who enters the world full of such notions soon discovers it to be above his power to conform his conduct to them. Will he not be naturally led to consider morality as a romance or chimera? If he escape that conclusion, he may justly consider himself as remarkably fortunate. [iii]

A very important branch of the moral sense remains still to be unfolded. In the matters above mentioned, performing of promises, gratitude, and abstaining from harming others, we have the peculiar sense of duty and obligation: but in transgressing these duties, we have not only the sense of vice and wickedness, but we have further the sense of merited punishment, and dread of its being inflicted upon us. This dread may be but slight in the more venial transgressions. But, in crimes of a deep dye, it rises to a degree of anguish and despair. Hence remorse of conscience, which, upon the commission of certain crimes, is a dreadful torture. This dread of merited punishment operates for the most part so strongly upon the imagination, that every unusual accident, every extraordinary misfortune, is by the criminal judged to be a punishment purposely inflicted upon him. During prosperity, he makes a shift to blunt the stings of his conscience. But no sooner does he fall into distress or into any depression of mind, than his conscience lays fast hold of him: his crime stares him in the face; and every accidental misfortune is converted into a real punishment. "And they said one to another, We are verily guilty concerning our brother, in that we saw the anguish of his soul, when he besought us; and we would not hear: therefore is this distress come upon us. And Reuben answered them, saying, Spake I not unto you, saying, Do not sin against the child; and ye would not hear? therefore behold also, his blood is required."*

One material circumstance is here to be remarked, which widens the difference still more betwixt the primary and secondary virtues. As justice, and the other primary virtues, are more essential to society, than generosity, benevolence, or any other secondary virtue, they are more indispensable. Friendship, generosity, softness of manners, form peculiar characters, and serve to distinguish one person from another. But the sense of justice and of the other primary virtues, belongs to man as such. Though it exists in very different degrees of strength, there perhaps never was a human creature

* Genesis xlii. 21, 22.

altogether void of it. And it makes a delightful appearance in the human constitution, that even where this sense is weak, as it is in some individuals, it notwithstanding retains its authority as the director of their conduct. If there be a sense of justice, it must distinguish right from wrong, what we *ought* to do from what we *ought not* to do; and, by that very distinguishing faculty, justly claims to be our guide and governor. This consideration may serve to justify human laws, which make no distinction among men, as endued with a stronger or weaker sense of justice.

And here we must pause a moment, to indulge some degree of admiration upon this part of the human system. Man is evidently intended to live in society; and because there can be no society among creatures who prey upon one another, it was necessary, in the first place, to provide against mutual injuries. Further, man is the weakest of all creatures separately, and the very strongest in society; therefore mutual assistance is the chief end of society; and to this end it was necessary, that there should be mutual trust and reliance upon engagements, and that favours received should be thankfully repaid. Now, nothing can be more finely adjusted than the human heart, to answer these purposes. It is not sufficient that we approve every action that is essential to the preservation of society: it is not sufficient, that we disapprove every action that tends to its dissolution. Approbation or disapprobation merely, is not sufficient to subject our conduct to the authority of a law. These sentiments have in this case the peculiar modification of duty, that such actions are what we ought to perform, and what we are indispensably bound to perform. This circumstance converts into a law, what without it can only be considered as a rational measure, and a prudential rule of conduct. Nor is any thing omitted to give it the most complete character of a law. The transgression is attended with apprehension of punishment, nay with actual punishment; as every misfortune which befals the transgressor is considered by him as a punishment. Nor is this the whole of the matter. Sympathy is a principle implanted in the breast of every man; we cannot hurt another without suffering for it, which is an additional punishment. And we are still further punished for our injustice or ingratitude, by incurring the aversion and hatred of all men.

CHAPTER IV

Different Ranks of Moral Virtues

It is a truth universally admitted, that no man thinks so highly of himself or of another, for having done a just, as for having done a generous action: yet every one must be sensible, that justice is to society more essential than generosity; and why we should place the greater merit upon the less essential action, may appear unaccountable. This matter deserves to be examined, because it discloses more and more the science of morals; and to this examination we shall proceed, after making some further observations upon the subject of the preceding chapter.[iv]

The primary virtues, as observed in that chapter, being duties essential to the subsistance of society, are entirely withdrawn from our election and choice. They are perceived as indispensably obligatory upon us; and the transgression of them as laws of our nature, is attended with severe and never-failing punishment. In a word, there is not a characteristic of positive law which is not applicable, in the strictest sense, to these laws of our nature; with this material difference, that the sanctions of these laws are greatly more efficacious than any that have been invented to enforce municipal laws. The secondary virtues, which contribute to the improvement of society, but are not strictly necessary to its subsistance, are left to our own choice. They have not the character of necessity impressed upon them, nor is the forbearance of them attended with a sense of guilt. On the other hand, the actions which belong to this class, are objects of the strongest perceptions of moral beauty; of the highest degree of approbation, both from ourselves and others. Offices of undeserved kindness, requital of good for evil, generous toils and sufferings for the good of our country, come under this class. These are not made our *duty*. There is no motive to the performance, which in any proper sense can be called a law. But there are the strongest motives that can consist with perfect freedom. The performance is rewarded with a consciousness of self-merit, and with the praise and admiration of all the world, which are the highest and most desirable rewards human nature is susceptible of.

There is so much of enthusiasm in this branch of moral beauty, that it is not wonderful to find persons of a free and generous turn of mind captivated with it, who are less attentive to the primary virtues. The magnanimous, who cannot bear restraint, are guided more by generosity than by justice. The sense however of strict duty is, with the bulk of mankind, a more powerful incitement to honesty, than praise and self-approbation are to generosity. And there cannot be a more pregnant instance of wisdom than in this part of the human constitution; it being far more essential to society, that all men be just and honest, than that they be patriots and heroes.

From what is above laid down, the following observation naturally arises, that with respect to the primary virtues, the pain of transgressing our duty is much greater than the pleasure which results from obeying it. The contrary holds in the secondary virtues. The pleasure which arises from performing a generous action is much greater than the pain of neglect. Among the vices opposite to the primary virtues, the most striking appearances of moral deformity are found; among the secondary virtues, the most striking appearances of moral beauty.

We are now prepared to carry on the speculation suggested in the beginning of this chapter. In ranking the moral virtues according to their dignity and merit, one would readily imagine, that the primary virtues should be intitled to the highest class, as being more essential to society than the secondary. But, upon examination, we find that this is not the order of nature. The first rank in point of dignity is assigned to the secondary virtues, which are not the first in point of utility. Generosity, in the sense of mankind, hath more merit than justice; and other secondary virtues, undaunted courage, magnanimity, heroism, rise still higher in our esteem. Is not nature whimsical and irregular, in ranking after this manner the moral virtues? One at first view would think so. But, like other difficulties that meet us in contemplating the works of nature, this arises from partial and obscure views. When the whole is surveyed as well as its several parts, we discover, that nature has here taken her measures with peculiar foresight and wisdom. Let us only recollect what is inculcated in the foregoing part of this essay, that justice is enforced by natural sanctions of the most effectual kind, by which it becomes a law in the strictest sense, a law that never can be transgressed with impunity. To extend this law to generosity and the other secondary virtues, and to make these our duty, would produce an inconsistency in human nature. It would make universal benevolence a strict duty, to which the limited capacity and more limited abilities of man, bear no proportion. Generosity, therefore, heroism, and all the extraordinary exertions of virtue, must be left to our own choice, without annexing any punishment to the forbearance. Day-light now begins to break in upon us. If the secondary virtues must not be enforced by punishment, it becomes necessary that they be encouraged by reward; for without such encouragement, examples would be rare of sacrificing one's own interest to that of others. And after considering the matter with the utmost attention, I cannot imagine any reward more proper than that actually bestowed, which is to place these virtues in the highest rank, to give them a superior dignity, and to make them productive of grand and lofty emotions. To place the primary virtues in the highest rank, would no doubt be a strong support to them. But as this could not be done without displacing the secondary virtues, detruding them into a lower rank, and consequently depriving them of their reward, the alteration would be ruinous to society. It would indeed more effectually prevent injustice and wrong; but would it not as effectually prevent the exercise of benevolence, and of numberless reciprocal benefits in a social state? If it would put an end to our fears, so it would to our hopes. And, to say all in one word, we would, in the midst of society, become solitary beings; worse if possible than being solitary in a desart. Justice at the same time is not left altogether destitute of reward. Though it reaches not the splendor of the more exalted virtues, it gains at least our esteem and approbation; and, which is still of greater importance, it never fails to advance the happiness of those who obey its dictates, by the mental satisfaction it bestows.

CHAPTER V

Principles of Action

In the three chapters immediately foregoing, we have taken pains to inquire into the moral sense, and to analyze it into its different parts. Our present task must be to inquire into those principles in our nature which move us to action. These must be distinguished from the moral sense; which, properly speaking, is not a principle of action. Its province, as shall forthwith be explained, is to instruct us, which of our principles of action we may indulge, and which of them we must restrain. It is the voice of God within us, regulating our appetites and passions, and showing us what are lawful, what unlawful.

Our nature, as far as concerns action, is made up of appetites and passions which move us to act, and of the moral sense by which these appetites and passions are governed. The moral sense is not intended to be the first mover: but it is an excellent second, by the most authoritative of all motives, that of duty. Nature is not so rigid to us her favourite children, as to leave our conduct upon the motive of duty solely. A more masterly and kindly hand is visible in the architecture of man. We are impelled to motion by the very constitution of our nature; and to prevent our being carried too far, or in a wrong direction, conscience is set as at the helm. That such is our nature, may be made evident from induction. Were conscience alone, in any case, to be the sole principle of action, it might be expected to be so in matters of justice, of which we have the strongest sense as our indispensable duty. We find however justice not to be an exception from the general plan. For is not love of justice a principle of action common to all men; and is not affection between parents and children equally so, as well as gratitude, veracity, and every primary virtue? These principles give the first impulse, which is finely seconded by the influence and authority of conscience. It may therefore be safely pronounced, that no action is a duty, to the performance of which we are not prompted by some natural motive or principle. To make such an action our duty, would be to lay down a rule of conduct contrary to our nature; or that has no foundation in our nature.

This is a truth little attended to by those who have given us systems of natural laws. No wonder they have gone astray. Let this truth be kept close in view, and it will put an end to many a controversy about these laws. If, for example, it be laid down as a primary law of nature, That we are strictly bound to advance the good of all, regarding our own interest no farther than as it makes a part of the general happiness; we may safely reject such a law, unless it be made appear, that there is a principle of benevolence in man prompting him to pursue the happiness of all. To found this disinterested scheme wholly upon the moral sense, would be a vain attempt. The moral sense, as above observed, is our guide only, not our mover. Approbation or disapprobation of those actions, to which, by some natural principle, we are antecedently directed, is all that can result from it. If it be laid down on the other hand, That we ought to regard ourselves only in all our actions; and that it is folly, if not vice, to concern ourselves for others; such a law can never be admitted, unless upon the supposition that self-love is our only principle of action.

It is probable, that in the following particular, man differs from the brute creation. Brutes are entirely governed by principles of action, which, in them, obtain the name of instincts. They blindly follow their instincts, and are led by that instinct which is strongest for the time. It is *meet* and *fit* they should act after this manner, because it is acting according to the whole of their nature. But for man to suffer himself to be led implicitly by instinct or by his principles of action, without check or control, is not acting according to the whole of his nature. He is endued with a moral sense or conscience, to check and control his principles of action, and to instruct him which of them he may indulge, and which of them he ought to restrain. This account of the brute creation is undoubtedly true in the main: whether so in every particular, is of no importance to the present subject, being suggested by way of contrast only, to illustrate the peculiar nature of man.

A full account of our principles of action would be an endless theme. But as it is proposed to confine the present short essay to the laws which govern social life, we shall have no occasion to inquire into any principles of action, but what are directed to others; dropping those which have self alone for their object. And in this inquiry, we set out with the following question, In what sense are we to hold a principle of universal benevolence, as belonging to human nature? This question is of importance in the science of morals: for, as observed above, universal benevolence cannot be a duty, if we be not antecedently promp[t]ed to it by a natural principle. When we consider a single man, abstracted from all circumstances and all connections, we are not conscious of any benevolence to him; we feel nothing within us that prompts us to advance his happiness. If one be agreeable at first sight and attract any degree of affection, it is owing to looks, manners, or behaviour. And for evidence of this we are as apt to be disgusted at first sight, as to be pleased. Man is by nature a shy and timorous animal. Every new object gives an impression of fear, till upon better acquaintance it is discovered to be harmless. Thus an infant clings to its nurse, upon the sight of a new face; and this natural dread is not removed but by experience. If every human creature did produce affection in every other at first sight, children, by natural instinct, would be fond of strangers. But no such instinct discovers itself. The fondness of a child is confined to the nurse, the parents, and those who are most about it; till by degrees it opens to a sense of other connections. This argument may be illustrated by a low, but apt instance. Dogs have by nature an affection for the human species; and puppies run to the first man they see, show marks of fondness, and play about his feet. There is no such general fondness of man to man by nature. Certain circumstances are always required to produce and call it forth. Distress indeed never fails to beget sympathy. The misery of the most unknown gives us pain, and we are prompted by nature to afford relief. But when there is nothing to call forth our sympathy; where there are no peculiar circumstances to interest us or beget a connection, we rest in a state of indifference, and are not conscious of wishing either good or ill to the person. Those moralists therefore who require us to lay aside all partial affection and to act upon a principle of equal benevolence to all men, require us to act upon a principle, which has no place in our nature.

In the manner now mentioned, a principle of universal benevolence does certainly not exist in man. Let us next inquire if it exist in any other manner. The happiness of mankind is an object agreeable to the mind in contemplation; and good men have a sensible pleasure in every study or pursuit by which they can promote it. Benevolence, not equally directed to all men, gradually decreaseth according to the distance of the object, till it dwindles away to nothing. But here comes in a happy contrivance of nature, to supply the want of benevolence to distant objects; which is, to give power to an abstract term, such as our religion, our country, our government, or even mankind, to raise benevolence or public spirit. The particular objects under each of these classes, considered singly and apart, may have little or no force to produce affection; but when comprehended under one general view, they become an object that dilates and warms the heart. In this manner, a man is enabled to embrace in his affection all mankind: and in this sense man is endued with a principle of universal benevolence.

Any person who can reflect upon this branch of human nature without some degree of emotion, must be of a very cold temperament. There is perhaps not one scene to be met with in the natural or moral world where more of design and of consummate wisdom are displayed, than in this under consideration. The authors, who, impressed with reverence for human nature, have endeavoured to exalt it the highest, could none of them stretch their imagination beyond a principle of equal benevolence to every individual. And a very fine scheme it is in idea; but, unluckily it is entirely of the Utopian kind, altogether unfit for life and action. It hath escaped the consideration of these authors, that man is by nature of a limited capacity; and that his affection, by multiplication of objects, instead of being increased, is split into parts, and weakened by division. A principle of universal equal benevolence, by dividing the attention and affection, instead of promoting benevolent actions, would be an obstruction to them. The mind would be distracted by the multiplicity of objects that have an equal influence, so as to be eternally at a loss where to begin. But the human system is better adjusted than to admit of such disproportion betwixt ability and affection. The chief objects of a man's love are his friends and relations. He reserves some share to bestow on his neighbours. His affection lessens gradually, in proportion to the distance of the object, till it vanish altogether. But were this the whole of human nature with regard to benevolence, man would be but an abject creature. By a very happy contrivance, objects which, because of their distance, have little or no influence, are gathered together in one general view, and made to have the very strongest effect; exceeding, in many instances, the most lively affection that is bestowed on a particular object. By this happy contrivance, the attention of the mind, and its affections are preserved entire, to be bestowed upon general objects, instead of being dissipated among an endless number of individuals. Nothing more ennobles human nature than this principle of action: nor is there any thing more wonderful, than that a general term which has no precise meaning, should be the foundation of a more intense affection than is bestowed, for the most part, upon particular objects, even the most attractive. When we talk of our country, our religion, our government, the ideas annexed to these general terms, are obscure and indistinct. General terms are extremely useful in language; serving, like mathematical signs, to communicate our thoughts in a summary way. But the use of them is not confined to language: they serve for a much nobler purpose, that of exciting us to generous and benevolent actions of the most exalted kind; not confined to individuals, but grasping whole societies, towns, countries, kingdoms, nay all mankind. By this curious mechanism, the defect of our nature is amply remedied. Distant objects, otherways invisible, are rendered conspicuous: accumulation makes them great; and greatness brings them near the eye: affection is preserved, to be bestowed entire, as upon a single object. And, to say all in one word, this system of benevolence, which is really founded on human nature and not the invention of man, is infinitely better contrived to advance the good and happiness of mankind, than any Utopian system that ever has been produced by the warmest imagination.

Upon the opposite system of absolute selfishness, there is no occasion to lose a moment. It is evidently chimerical, because it has no foundation in human nature. It is not more certain that there exists the creature man, than that he hath principles of action directed entirely upon others; some to do good, and others to do mischief. Who can doubt of this, when friendship, compassion, gratitude, on the one hand; and on the other, malice and resentment, are considered? It hath indeed been observed, that we indulge such passions and affections merely for our own gratification. But no person can relish this observation, who is in any measure acquainted with human nature. The social affections are in fact the source of the deepest afflictions, as well as of the most exalted pleasures, as has been fully laid open in the foregoing essay. In a word, we are evidently formed by nature for society, and for indulging the social as well as the selfish passions; and therefore to contend, that we ought to regard ourselves only and to be influenced by no principles but what are selfish, is directly to fly in the face of nature, and to lay down a rule of conduct inconsistent with it.

These systems being laid aside, as deviating from the nature of man, the way lies open to come at what are his true and genuine principles of action. The first thing that nature consults, is the preservation of her creatures. Hence the love of life is made the strongest of all instincts. Upon the same foundation, pain is in a greater degree the object of aversion, than pleasure is of desire. Pain warns us of what tends to our dissolution: pleasure is often sought after unwarily, and by means dangerous to health and life. Pain comes in as a monitor of our danger; and nature, consulting our preservation in the first place and our gratification in the second only, wisely gives pain more force to draw us back, than it gives pleasure to push us on.

The second principle of action is self-love, or desire of our own happiness and good. This is a stronger principle than benevolence, or love bestowed upon others: wisely so ordered; because every man has more power, knowledge, and opportunity, to promote his own good than that of others. Thus individuals are mostly left to their own care. It is agreeable to the limited nature of such a creature as man, that it should be so; and, consequently, it is wisely ordered, that every man should have the strongest affection for himself.

The foregoing principles having *self* for their object, come not properly under the present undertaking. They are barely mentioned, to illustrate, by opposition, the following principles, which regard others. Of this sort, the most universal is the love of justice, without which there can be no society.[v] Veracity is another principle, no less universal. Fidelity, a third principle, is circumscribed within narrower bounds; for it cannot exist without a peculiar connection betwixt two persons, to found a reliance on the one side, which requires on the other a conduct corresponding to the reliance. Gratitude is a fourth principle, universally acknowledged. And benevolence possesses the last place, diversified by its objects, and exerting itself more vigorously or more faintly, in proportion to the distance of particular objects, and the grandeur of those that are general. This principle of action has one remarkable quality, that it operates with much greater force to relieve those in distress, than to promote positive good. In the case of distress, sympathy comes to its aid; and, in that circumstance, it acquires the name of *compassion.*

These several principles of action are ordered with admirable wisdom, to promote the general good in the best and most effectual manner. When we act on these principles, we act for the general good, even when it is not our immediate aim. The general good is an object too remote, to be the sole impulsive motive to action. It is better ordered, that in most instances individuals should have a limited aim, what they can readily accomplish. To every man is assigned his own task; and if every man do his duty, the general good will be promoted much more effectually, than if it were the aim in every single action.

The above-mentioned principles of action belong to man as such, and constitute what may be called the common nature of man. Many other principles exert themselves upon particular objects in the instinctive manner, without the intervention of any sort of reasoning or reflection; appetite for food, animal love, &c. Other particular appetites, passions, and affections, such as ambition, avarice, envy, &c. constitute the peculiar nature of some individuals; being distributed in different proportions. It belongs to the science of ethics, to treat of these particular principles of action.

CHAPTER VI

Justice and Injustice

Justice is that moral virtue which guards the persons, the property, and the reputation of individuals, and gives authority to promises and covenants. And as it is made out above, that justice is one of those primary virtues which are enforced by the strongest natural laws, it would be unnecessary to say more upon the subject, were it not for a doctrine espoused by the author of a treatise upon human nature, that justice, so far from being one of the primary virtues, is not even a natural virtue, but established in society by a sort of tacit convention, founded upon a notion of public interest.[3] The figure this author deservedly makes in the learned world, will not admit

---

3. "The sense of justice and injustice is not deriv'd from nature, but arises artificially, tho' necessarily from education, and human conventions" (Hume, *Treatise*, 3.2.1.17, p. 311).

of his being passed over in silence. To people beside who live in society, it cannot but be agreeable to learn how solidly founded the principle of justice is, and how finely contrived to protect them from injury.

Our author's doctrine, as far as concerns that branch of justice by which property is secured, comes to this: That, in a state of nature, there can be no such thing as property; and that the idea of property arises, after justice is established by convention, securing every one in their possessions. In opposition to this singular doctrine, there is no difficulty to make out, that property is founded on a natural sense independent altogether of agreement or convention; and that violation of property is attended with remorse, and a perception of breach of duty. In prosecuting this subject, it will appear how admirably the springs of human nature are adapted one to another, and to external circumstances.

The surface of this globe, which scarce yields spontaneously food for the wildest savages, is by labour and industry made so fruitful, as to supply man, not only with necessaries, but even with materials for luxury. Men originally made shift to support themselves, partly by prey, and partly by the natural fruits of the earth. In this state they in some measure resemble beasts of prey, who devour instantly what they seize, and whose care is at an end when the belly is full. But man was not designed by nature to be an animal of prey. A tenor of life where food is so precarious, requires a constitution that can bear long fasting and immoderate eating, as occasion offers. Man is of a different make. He requires regular and frequent supplies of food, which could not be obtained in his original occupations of fishing and hunting. He found it necessary therefore to abandon this manner of life, and to become shepherd. The wild creatures, such of them as are gentle and proper for food, were brought under subjection. Hence herds of cattle, sheep, goats, &c. ready at hand for sustenance. This contrivance was succeeded by another. A bit of land is divided from the common; it is cultivated with the spade or plough; grain is sown, and the product is stored for the use of a family. Reason and reflection prompted these improvements, which are essential to our well-being, and in a good measure necessary even for bare subsistence. But self-preservation, is of too great moment to be left entirely to the conduct of reason. To secure against neglect or indolence, man is provided with a principle that operates instinctively without reflection; and that is the hoarding appetite, common to him with several other animals. No author, I suppose, will be so bold as to deny this disposition to be natural and universal, considering how solicitous every man is for a competency, and how anxious the plurality are to swell that competency beyond bounds. The hoarding appetite, while moderate, is so natural and so common as not to be graced with a proper name. When it exceeds just bounds, it is known by the name of *avarice*.

The compass I have taken is wide, but the shortest road is not always the smoothest or most patent. I come now to the point, by putting a plain question, What sort of creature would man be, endued as he is with a hoarding appetite, but with no sense or notion of property? He hath a constant propensity to hoard for his own use; conscious at the same time that his stores are no less free to others than to himself;—racked thus perpetually betwixt the desire of appropriation, and consciousness of its being in vain. I say more: the hoarding appetite is an instinct obviously contrived for assisting reason, in moving us to provide against want. This instinct, like all others in the human soul, ought to be a cause adequate to the effect intended to be accomplished by it. But this it cannot be, independent of a sense of property. For what effectual provision can be made against want, when the stores of every individual are, without any check from conscience, left free to the depredations of the whole species? Here would be a palpable defect or inconsistency in the nature of man. If I could suppose this to be his case, I should believe him to be a creature made in haste, and left unfinished. I am certain there is no such inconsistency to be found in any other branch of human nature; nor indeed, as far as we can discover, in any other creature that is endued with the hoarding appetite. Every bee inhabits its own cell, and feeds on its own honey. Every crow has its own nest; and punishment is always applied, when a single stick happens to be pilfered. But we find no such inconsistency in man. The cattle tamed by an individual, and the field cultivated by him, were held universally to be his own from the beginning. A relation is formed betwixt every man and the fruits of his own labour, the very thing we call property, which he himself is sensible of, and of which every other is equally sensible. *Yours* and *mine* are terms in all languages, familiar among savages, and understood even by children. This is a fact, which every human creature can testify.

This reasoning might be illustrated by many apt analogies. I shall mention but one. Veracity, and a disposition to believe what is affirmed for truth, are corresponding principles, which make one entire branch of the human nature. Veracity would be of no use were men not disposed to believe; and, abstracting from veracity, a disposition to believe, would be a dangerous quality; for it would lay us open to fraud and deceit. There is precisely the same correspondence betwixt the hoarding appetite and the sense of property. The latter is useless without the former; witness animals of prey, who having no occasion for property, have no notion of it. The former again, without the latter, is altogether insufficient to produce the effect for which it is intended by nature.

Thus it is clear, that the sense of property owes not its existence to society. But in a matter of so great importance in the science of morals, I cannot rest satisfied with a successful defence. I aim at a complete victory, by insisting on a proposition directly opposite to that of my antagonist, namely, That society owes its existence to the sense of property; or at least, that without this sense no society ever could have been formed. In the proof of this proposition, we have already made a considerable progress, by evincing that man by his nature is a hoarding animal and loves to store for his own use. In order to the conclusion, we have but one farther step to make; which is, to consider what originally would have been the state of man, supposing him destitute of the sense of property. The answer is extremely obvious, That it would have been a state of universal war — of men preying upon each other — of robbing and pilfering the necessaries of life where ever found, without regard to industry, or the connection that is formed betwixt an individual and the fruits of his own labour. Courage and bodily strength would have stood in place of right, and nothing left for the weak, but to hide themselves and their goods. And to do Hobbes justice, who, as well as our author, denies the sense of property to be natural, he fairly owns this reasoning to be just, and boldly asserts that the state of nature is a state of war, all against all. In a word, destitute of the sense of property, men would naturally be enemies to each other, no less than they are to wolves and foxes at present. Now, if this must have been the original condition of man, let our author say, by what over-ruling power, by what miracle, individuals so disposed ever came to unite in society. We may pronounce with great assurance, that so signal a revolution in the state of man could never have been compassed by natural means. Nothing can be more evident than that relying upon the sense of property and of justice, a few individuals ventured at first to unite for mutual defence and mutual support; and finding the manifold comforts of such a state, that they afterward gradually united into larger and larger societies.[vi]

It must not be overlooked, that the sense of property is fortified by another principle. Every man has a peculiar affection for what he calls his *own*. He applies his skill and industry with great alacrity to improve his own subject: his affection to it grows with the time of his possession; and he puts a much greater value upon it, than upon any subject of the same kind that belongs to another.[vii]

But this is not all that is involved in the sense of property. We not only suffer pain in having our goods taken from us by force; for that would happen were they destroyed or lost by accident: we have the sense of *wrong* and *injustice*. The person who robs us has the same sense; and every mortal who beholds the action, considers it as vitious, and contrary to *right*.

Holding it not altogether sufficient to have overturned our author's doctrine, we proceed to make some observations upon it, in order to show how ill the parts of it hang together.

And, in the first place, he appears to reason not altogether consistently in making out his system. He founds justice on a general sense of common interest.* And yet, at no greater distance than a few pages, he endeavours to make out,† and does it successfully, that public interest is a motive too remote and too sublime to affect the generality of mankind, and to operate with any force in actions so contrary to private interest, as are frequently those of justice and common honesty.[4]

In the second place, abstracting from the sense of property, it does not appear that a sense of common interest would necessarily lead to such a regulation, as that every man should have the undisturbed enjoyment of what he hath acquired by his industry or good fortune. Supposing no sense

* Vol. 3. p. 59.
† Vol. 3. p. 43.
4. Kames cites from Hume's *Treatise*, 3.2.2.22, pp. 319–20; 3.2.1.11, p. 309.

of property, I do not see it inconsistent with society to have a Lacedemonian constitution, that every man may lawfully take what by address he can make himself master of, without force or violence.[5] The depriving us of that to which we have no right, would be doing little more than drinking in our brook, or breathing in our air. At any rate, a regulation so refined would never be considered of such importance as to be established at the very commencement of society. It must come late, if at all, and be the effect of long experience and great refinement in the art of living. It is very true, that, abstaining from the goods of others, is a regulation, without which society cannot subsist. But the necessity of this regulation ariseth from the sense of property, without which a man would suffer little pain in losing his goods, and would have no notion of wrong or injustice. There appears not any way to evade the force of this reasoning, but to deny the reality of the sense of property. Others may, but our author cannot with a good grace. An appeal may be safely made to his own authority. For what else but that sense has suggested to him the necessity in the institution of every society, to secure individuals in their possessions? He cannot but be sensible, that, abstracting from the affection for property, the necessity would be just nothing at all. But our perceptions operate calmly and silently; and there is nothing more common, than to strain for far-fetched arguments in support of conclusions which are suggested by the simplest and most obvious perceptions.

A third observation is, that since our author resolves all virtue into sympathy, why should he with-hold the same principle from being the foundation of justice? Why should not sympathy give us a painful sensation, in depriving our neighbour of the goods he has acquired by industry, as well as in depriving him of his life or limb? For it is a fact too evident to be denied, that many men are more uneasy at the loss of their goods, than at the loss of a member.

And, in the last place, were justice founded on a general sense of common interest only, it would be the weakest sense in human nature; especially

5. A reference to the Spartan practice of permitting and even encouraging boys to steal food, as described by Xenophon in the "Constitution of the Lacedaemonians" (2.1.6–9) and by Plutarch in *Lycurgus* (17).

where injustice is committed against a stranger, with whom we are not in any manner connected. Now, this is contrary to all experience. The sense of injustice is one of the strongest that belongs to humanity, and is also of a peculiar nature. It involves a sense of duty transgressed, and of punishment merited for the transgression. Had our author but once reflected upon these peculiarities, he never could have been satisfied with the slight foundation he gives to justice; for these peculiarities are altogether unaccountable upon his system.

I shall close this reasoning with a reflection upon the whole. The subject debated is a strong instance how dangerous it is to erect schemes and assert propositions, without regard to facts and experiments—no less dangerous in morals than in natural philosophy. Had our author examined human nature, and patiently submitted to the making a complete collection of facts, before venturing upon general propositions; I am positive he would have been as far as any man from maintaining that justice is an artificial virtue, or that property is the child of society. Discovering this edifice of his to be a mere castle in the air, without the slightest foundation, he would have abandoned it without any reluctance.

If a man's property be guarded by justice against the violence of others, still more his person and reputation.

That branch of justice which regards promises and covenants, hath also a solid foundation in human nature; notwithstanding what is laid down by our author in two distinct propositions,* "That a promise would not be intelligible, before human conventions had established it; and, That, even if it were intelligible, it would not be attended with any moral obligation."[6] As man is framed for society, mutual trust and confidence, without which there can be no useful society, enter into the character of the human species. Corresponding to these, are the principles of veracity and fidelity. Veracity and fidelity would be of no significancy, were men not disposed to have faith, and to rely upon what is said to them, whether in the way of evidence or engagement. Faith and trust, on the other hand, would be very hurtful principles, were mankind void of veracity and fidelity. For upon that sup-

* P. 102.
6. Hume, *Treatise*, 3.2.5.1, p. 331.

position, the world, as observed above, would be over-run with fraud and deceit. If that branch of justice which restrains us from harming each other, be essential to the very existance of society, fidelity and veracity are not less essential to its well-being: for from them spring mostly the advantages that are peculiar to the social life. It is justly observed by our author, that man in a solitary state is the most helpless of beings; and that by society only he is enabled to supply his defects, and to acquire a superiority over his fellow-creatures; that, by conjunction of forces, our power is augmented; by partition of employments, we work to better purpose; and, by mutual succour, we acquire security. But, without mutual fidelity and trust, we could enjoy none of these advantages; without them, we could not have any comfortable intercourse with each other. Hence it is, that treachery is the vilest of crimes, held in utter abhorrence. It is worse than murder, because it forms a character, and is directed against all mankind; whereas murder is but a transitory act, directed against a single person. Infidelity is of the same species with treachery. The essence of both crimes is the same, to wit, breach of trust. Treachery has only this aggravating circumstance, that it turns the confidence reposed in me against the friend who trusts me. Now, breach of promise is a species of infidelity; and therefore our author has but a single choice: he must maintain either that treachery is no crime, or that breach of promise is a crime. And, in fact, that it is so, every man can bear evidence from his own feelings. The performance of a deliberate promise has, in all ages, been considered as a duty. We have that sense of a promise, as what we are strictly bound to perform; and the breach of promise is attended with the same natural stings which attend other crimes, namely remorse, and a sense of merited punishment.

Our author's notion of a promise is extremely imperfect, as he takes under consideration the person only who makes the promise.* In this act two persons are concerned; the person who makes the promise, and the person

---

* Vol. 3. p. 102. [Arguing that the performance of promises is not natural but artificial and conventional, Hume considers the case of a man "unacquainted with society" in order to demonstrate that "*I promise*" makes no sense outside the context of the social conventions which have already created a sense of obligation to keep one's promises. *Treatise*, 3.2.5.2, p. 331.]

to whom the promise is made. Were there by nature no trust nor reliance upon promises, breach of promise would be a matter of indifferency. The reliance upon us, produced by our own act, constitutes the obligation. We feel ourselves bound to perform; we consider it as our duty. And when we violate our engagement, we have a sense of moral turpitude in disappointing the person who relied upon our faith.

We shall close this subject concerning the foundation of justice, with a general reflection. Running over every branch of our duty, what concerns ourselves as well as our neighbours, we find, that nature has been more provident than to trust us entirely to the guidance of cool reason. If man be a social being, and justice essential to society, it is not agreeable to the analogy of nature, that we should be left to investigate this branch of our duty by a chain of reasoning; especially where the reasoning, according to our author, turns upon so remote an object as public good. May we not apply to justice, what is so beautifully reasoned concerning society, in a dialogue upon happiness,* "If society be thus agreeable to our nature, is there nothing within us to excite and lead us to it? no impulse; no preparation of faculties? It would be strange if there should not." If we be fitted by our nature for society; if pity, benevolence, friendship, love, dislike of solitude and desire of company, be natural affections, all of them conducive to society, it would be strange if there should be no natural affection, no preparation of faculties, to direct us to do justice, which is so essential to society. But nature has not failed us here, more than in the other parts of our constitution. We have a sense of property; we have a sense of obligation to perform our engagements; and we have a sense of wrong in incroaching upon property, and in being untrue to our engagements. Society could not subsist without these affections, more than it could subsist without the social affections, properly so called. We have reason, *a priori,* to conclude equally in favour of both; and we find upon examination that our conclusion is just.

---

* Page 155. [Not traced.]

CHAPTER VII

Primary Laws of Nature

We are now arrived at what is chiefly the purpose of the present essay; and that is, to give a slight sketch, or cursory view, of the primary laws of nature, deduced from human nature, their true source. This task I undertake as a specimen merely of that sort of reasoning which belongs to the subject; for a complete treatise is far beyond my reach. Action ought to be the object of all our inquiries; without which, moral as well as metaphysical reasonings are but empty speculation. And as life and manners are more peculiarly the object of the moral science, the weight and importance of the subject, one would imagine, should have brought authors to one way of thinking. But it is lamentable to find the world divided about these primary laws, almost as much as they commonly are about the most airy and abstract points. Some authors acknowledge no principle in man, and consequently no duty, but what is altogether selfish; and it is curious to observe how they wrest and torture every social principle to give it the appearance of selfishness. Others exalt human nature much above its just standard, give no quarter to selfishness, but consider man as bound to direct every action to the good of the whole, and not to prefer his own interest to that of others. The celebrated Lord Shaftesbury goes so far, as not to admit of any thing like partial benevolence; holding, that if it be not entire and directed to the whole species, it is not benevolence at all.[7] It is not difficult to assign a cause for such difference in opinion; though it may appear strange, that authors should differ so widely about the nature of man, which every man ought to be acquainted with. There is nothing more common in philosophy, as well as in action, than to build castles in the air. Impatient of the slow and cold method of induction, every writer takes the liberty of framing systems according to his own taste and fancy. Fond of the fabric which he hath erected, it is far from his thoughts to try whether it will stand the test of

---

7. Shaftesbury argues that "partial affection, or social love in part, without regard to a complete society or whole, is in itself an inconsistency and implies an absolute contradiction" (*Inquiry Concerning Virtue or Merit,* pt. II, sec. i, p. 205).

stubborn facts. Men of narrow minds and contracted principles, naturally fall in with the selfish system. The system of universal benevolence attracts the generous and warm-hearted. In the midst of various and opposite opinions, the purpose of this essay is, by the patient method of induction, to search for truth; and, after what is above laid down, it will not be difficult to find it.

Let us only recapitulate, that the principles of action impel to action, and that the moral sense is given as an instructor to regulate our actions, to enforce one principle, to restrain another, and to prefer one to another when they are in opposition. Hence the laws of nature may be defined to be, *Rules of our conduct founded on natural principles approved by the moral sense, and enforced by natural rewards and punishments.*

In searching for these laws, it must be obvious from what is above said, that, by the moral sense, a difference is clearly established among our principles of action. Some are enforced by the consciousness of duty; some are left in a measure upon our own will. With respect to the former, we have no liberty, but ought to proceed to action; with respect to the latter, we may freely indulge every natural impulse, where the action is not disapproved by the moral sense. From this short sketch may be readily deduced all the laws of nature which govern human actions; though, in the present essay, the duty which a man owes to himself, where others are not concerned, is not comprehended.

Among the principles of action that compel us to do our duty, the principle of justice takes the lead. It consists of two branches, one to abstain from harming others, and one to perform our positive engagements. With respect to both, we have no liberty; but are bound to perform every act of justice as our indispensible duty. Veracity, fidelity, and gratitude, are principles of action which come under the same class. And with respect to the whole, it ought not to be overlooked, that the internal constitution of man is adjusted with admirable wisdom to his external circumstances as a social being. Were we allowed to prey upon one another like savage animals, there could be no society; and were there nothing in our nature that could bind us to instruct, to comfort, to benefit each other, society would be deprived of all its advantages, and man, in the midst of society, would be a solitary being. Benevolence is another principle of action, which, in many circumstances, by means of peculiar connections, becomes also an indispensible duty. Witness the connection of parent and child. We are obliged to provide for our children; it is strict duty, and the neglect of it causes remorse. In the case of other blood-relations, an only brother for example who depends entirely on us, we feel the same obligation, though in a weaker degree; and thus, through other connections, it diminisheth by successive gradations, till at last the sense of duty is lost in simple approbation, without any obligatory feeling. This is universally the course that nature holds. Her transitions are soft and gentle: she makes things approximate so nicely one to another, as to leave no gap or chasm. One other instance of a connection that produceth a sense of obligation, shall suffice. In the general case of procuring positive good to others or advancing happiness, without any connection save merely that of humanity, it is self-approbation and not strict obligation that is felt. But let us put the case of a person in distress. By this single circumstance, though it forms no intimate connection, the moral sense is influenced, and now it becomes a positive duty to exert our benevolence, by affording relief. The neglect of this duty is attended with remorse and self-condemnation; though not so pungent as where we betray our trust, or are the authors of positive mischief to others. Thus charity is by all men considered as a duty to which we are strictly bound. [viii]

With respect to principles of action that are not enforced by consciousness of duty, these we may restrain at pleasure, but may not always indulge at pleasure. For in various circumstances, the moral sense interposes, and forbids the gratification. Self-preservation is the strongest of all our principles of action, and the means are infinite which may be put in motion for that end. Yet here the moral sense frequently interposes, and gives no indulgence to the transgression of any positive duty, even for the preservation of life. Self-preservation, however it may alleviate, will not justify any wrong done to an innocent person: it will not justify treachery, nor infidelity. For once admitting it lawful to deprive a man of a hand or a foot in order to save my life; why not kill another to save my life? Both must be lawful or neither. The doctrine thus laid down in general, may be liable to misconstruction; and therefore it must be further explained. Self-preservation, it is certain, will not justify an immoral action. But then, in the circumstances of imminent danger, several actions become lawful, which are unlawful in ordinary circumstances. For example, to prevent dying of hunger, a man may take food at short-hand without consulting the proprietor. Seizing upon what belongs to another, is in ordinary circumstances an unlawful act: but in a case that can bear no delay, the act is lawful, because the approbation of the proprietor will be presumed. At any rate, it is his duty to relieve the distressed; and what he ought to give, may justly be forced from him when the delay of applying to a judge would be fatal. Another example, is the case of two men in a shipwreck, laying hold at the same instant of a plank which cannot support both. In this case it becomes lawful to struggle for the sole possession, though one must perish in the struggle: for each has an equal title to act for self-preservation; and if both cannot be preserved, mere force is the only method by which the controversy can be determined. If the moral sense have such authority over the principle of self-preservation, its authority must, if possible, be still more complete over the inferior principles that belong to the same class.

These are the outlines of the laws which govern our actions, comprehending what we *may* do, what we *ought* to do, and what we *ought not* to do. The two latter, as matter of duty, are the proper objects of law, natural and municipal. And no more seems requisite but to point out our duty, by informing us of what we ought to do, and what we ought not to do; seeing actions that come not under the character of duty, may be safely left to our own will. With regard then to what may be called our duty, the first and primary law is the law of restraint, by which we are prohibited to hurt others in their persons, goods, or whatever else is dear to them. This is a law which dictates to us what ought not to be done; and so sacred it is, as to yield to none of our principles of action, not even that of self-preservation. The second, which is a law dictating what we ought to do, binds us to the performance of our promises and covenants. Veracity occupies the next place. This law excludes not fable, nor any liberty of speech which tends to amusement. It excludes deceit only, and obliges us to adhere to truth where truth is expected from us. Fidelity is a fourth law, not less vigorous, though more confined, than veracity; for, as observed above, fidelity presupposes a peculiar connection betwixt two persons, to found a reliance on the one side, and on the other an obligation to fulfil what is justly expected. Gratitude comes next, limited, like fidelity, to particular objects, but more arbitrary as to what it requires of us. Gratitude, without doubt, is strictly our duty; but the measure of performance, and the kind, are left pretty much to our own choice. Benevolence occupies the last place; which, considered abstractly, is not a positive duty. But there are many connections of different sorts that make it a duty. I shall slightly mention a few. The connection of parent and child is one of the strongest, for it makes mutual benevolence an indispensible duty. Benevolence among other blood-relations becomes also a duty in particular circumstances, though here we seldom feel ourselves so firmly bound as in the former connection. Many are the connections, some intimate, some more slight, which come under the law of equity, and which bind us to the performance of certain acts of benevolence. I shall add but one connection more, namely, that which subsists betwixt us and a person in distress. Benevolence in that case becomes the duty of every one who can afford relief.

These several laws are admirably adjusted to our nature and circumstances, and tend in the most perfect manner to promote the ends of society. In the first place, as man is limited in power and capacity, the foregoing laws are accommodated to his nature, ordering and forbidding nothing but what falls within his power. In the second place, peace and security in society are amply provided for, by tying up the hands, as it were, of every person from harming others. In the third place, man is prompted in an admirable manner to be useful to others. It is his positive duty, to relieve the distressed and to perform his engagements. Boundless are the good offices that are enforced by veracity, fidelity, and gratitude. We are incited to do all the good we can, by the pleasure of being useful, and by grateful returns from the persons obliged. And, lastly, in competition betwixt a man himself and others, though his principles of action directed to himself, may be stronger than those directed to others; the superior rewards bestowed by the constitution of our nature upon the latter, may be deemed a sufficient counterbalance to give an ascendant to the social affections, even such of them as are left to our own will.

It may seem strange, that the municipal law of all countries is so little regardful of the laws of nature, as to adopt but a very few of them. There never was a general law in any country, to punish ingratitude, if it was not among the ancient Persians.[8] There is no positive law to enforce compassion, and to relieve those in distress, if the maintenance of the poor be excepted; which, in some countries, is provided for by law. No notice is taken of breach of friendship, by statute; nor of the duty we owe our children, further than of supporting them while they are under age. But municipal laws, being of human invention, are of no great extent. They cannot reach the heart nor its intentions, further than as expressed by outward acts. And these are to be judged of cautiously, and with reserve; because they form a language, dark, and at best full of ambiguities. At the same time, the object of human laws is man, considered singly in the quality of a citizen. When society is formed, and government submitted to, every private right inconsistent with society and government is surrendered. But, in every other respect, individuals reserve their independency and their private rights. Whether a man be virtuous, is not the concern of the society, at least not of its laws; but only whether he transgress the regulations that are necessary to the preservation of society. In this view, great attention is given by legislators to enforce the natural law of restraint. The like attention is given to enforce the natural obligation of engagements, and of fidelity, at least as far as relates to commerce; for infidelity in love and friendship are left to the natural law. Ingratitude is not punished by human laws, because it may be guarded against by positive engagements; nor hard-heartedness with regard to objects of distress, because society may subsist without such a law, and mankind are scarce yet arrived at such refinement in manners, as to have an abhorrence of this crime sufficient to make it an object of human punishment.

There is another substantial reason that confines municipal laws within a much narrower compass than the laws of nature. It is essential to municipal laws, that they be clear, plain, and readily applicable to particular cases; without which judges would be arbitrary, and law made a handle for oppression. For this reason, none of our actions can be the object of positive law, but

---

8. Xenophon's *Cyropaedia* (1.2.6–7) reported that Persian boys learned justice at school, where they brought each other to trial for any number of offences, including that of ingratitude.

what are reducible to a precise rule. Ingratitude therefore cannot be the object of municipal laws, because the quality of the crime depends upon a multiplicity of circumstances, which can never be reduced to a precise rule. Duty to our children, friends, and relations, is mostly in the same case. The duty of relieving the distressed, depends upon many circumstances; the nature of the distress, the connection betwixt the parties, the opportunity and ability of affording relief. The abstinence from mutual harm, and the performance of promises, are capable to be brought under a precise rule, and consequently to be objects of municipal law. The chief attention of the legislature in all countries, was at first to explain and enforce the natural law of restraint, without which society cannot have a being. Municipal law was afterward extended to support promises and covenants and to enforce performance, without which society may exist, but cannot flourish. Gradual improvements in the arts of life, have in later times extended municipal law still farther. The duty of benevolence arising from certain peculiar connections among individuals, is susceptible in many cases of a precise rule. So far benevolence is also taken under the authority of the legislature, and enforced by rules passing commonly under the name of the law of equity.

CHAPTER VIII

Law of Nations

If we can trust history, the original inhabitants of this earth were a brutish and savage race. And we have little reason to doubt of the fact, when, even at this day, we find in distant corners the same sort of people. The state of nature is accordingly represented by most writers, as a state of war; nothing but rapine and bloodshed. From this picture of the first men, one would be apt to conclude, that man is a wild and rapacious animal, little better than a beast of prey, till he be moulded by society into a rational creature. If this conclusion be just, we cannot help being in some pain for the principles above laid down. Brutish manners imply brutish principles of action; and, from this view of the original state of mankind, it might seem that moral virtues are not natural, but acquired by means of education and example in a well-regulated society; in a word, that the whole moral part of the human system is artificial, as justice is represented by a late writer.

But to be satisfied of the error of this conclusion, we need only look back to what has already been said upon the moral sense. If the perception of beauty and deformity in external existences be natural to man, the perception of beauty and deformity, and of a *right* and *wrong*, in actions, is equally so. The influence of education may be great upon a docile mind; but it would be miraculously great, could it create but any one sense. That miracle is reserved for our Maker. Education may well cherish and improve the plants of nature's formation; but cannot introduce any new or original plant. We must therefore attribute the foregoing appearances to some other cause than want of a moral sense; and these appearances may easily be explained, from peculiar circumstances, that overbalance the moral sense, and produce in appearance the same effects which would result from a total absence of that sense. Let us point out these circumstances; for the subject is worthy of our strictest attention. In the first place, we must look back to the original state of man, destitute entirely of those arts which produce the conveniencies of life. In this state, man, a most indigent creature, would be incited by self-preservation to supply his wants the best way he could, without much obstruction from the moral sense. Debates and differences would multiply to be determined by the strong-hand; there being no established rules of conduct to appeal to, nor judges to apply rules to particular cases. In this state, barbarity, roughness, and cruelty, formed the character of the human species. For, in the practice and habit of war, the malevolent principles gain strength and vigour, as the benevolent principles do by the arts of peace. And to this consideration may be added, that man is by nature shy and timorous; and consequently cruel to those he masters. The security obtained in a regular society, puts an end in a great measure to our fears. Man becomes a magnanimous and generous being, not easily daunted, and therefore not easily provoked to acts of cruelty.

It may be observed in the next place, that the rude and illiterate are governed by their appetites and passions, more than by general principles. We have our first impressions from external objects. It is by education and practice that we acquire a facility in forming complex ideas and abstract propositions. The ideas of a common interest, of a country, of a people, of a society under government, of public good, are complex, and not soon acquired even by the thinking part of mankind. They are scarce ever acquired by rustics; and consequently can scarce make any impression on them. One's own interest, considered in general, is too complex an object for the bulk of mankind; and therefore it is, that appetites and passions, aiming at particular objects, are stronger motives to action with the ignorant and un-thinking, than the principle of self-love, or even of self-preservation, when it is not excited by some object that threatens danger. And the same must hold more strongly with regard to the affections of benevolence, charity, and such like, when there is no particular object in view, but only, in general, the good of others.

Man is a complex machine, composed of various principles of motion, which may be conceived as so many springs or weights, counteracting or balancing one another. When these are accurately adjusted, the movement of life is beautiful, because regular and uniform. But if some springs or weights be withdrawn, those which remain, acting now without opposition from their antagonists, will disorder the balance, and derange the whole machine. Remove those principles of action, which, being directed to gen-eral and complex objects, are conducted by reflection; the force of the ap-petites and passions, which act by blind impulse, will of course be doubled. This is precisely the condition of those, who, abandoning the authority of reason, surrender themselves to every appetite. They are tyrannized by pas-sion, and have no consistent rule of conduct. It is no cause of wonder, that the moral sense should not have sufficient authority to command obedience in such a case. This is the character of savages. We have no reason then to conclude from the foregoing picture, that even the greatest savages are des-titute of the moral sense. Their defect rather lies in the weakness of their general principles of action, which are directed to objects too complex for savages readily to comprehend. This defect is remedied by education and reflection; and then it is, that the moral sense, in concert with these general principles, acquires its full authority, which is openly recognised, and chear-fully submitted to.

The contemplation is beautiful, when we compare our gradual improve-ment in knowledge and in morality. Beginning with surveying particular objects, we lay in a stock of simple ideas. Our affections keep pace, being all directed to particular objects; and during this period, we are governed chiefly by out passions and appetites. As soon as we begin to form complex and general ideas, these also become the objects of our affections. Then it is, that love to our country begins to unfold itself, benevolence to our neighbours and acquaintance, affection for our relations. We acquire by degrees the taste of public good, and of being useful in life. The pleasures of society are more and more relished, selfish passions are tamed and subdued, and social affections gain the ascendant. We refine upon the pleasures of society, because our happiness consists chiefly in social intercourse. We learn to submit our opinions: we affect to give preference to others, and readily accommodate ourselves to whatever may render society more complete. The malevolent passions above all, are brought under the strictest discipline, if not totally eradicated. Instead of unbounded revenge for the smallest injury, we acquire a degree of self-denial to overlook trifling wrongs, and in greater wrongs to be satisfied with moderate reparation.

The moral sense also, though rooted in the nature of man, admits of great refinements by culture and education. It improves gradually, like our other powers and faculties, till it comes to be productive of the strongest as well as the most delicate feelings. I will endeavour to explain in what manner this happens. Every one must be sensible of the great advantages of education and imitation. The most polished nations differ only from savages in refinement of taste, which is a source of pleasure and pain, more exquisite than savages are susceptible of. Hence it is, that many actions which make little impression upon savages, appear to us elegant and beautiful; as, on the other hand, actions which give them no pain, raise in us aversion and disgust. This may be illustrated by a comparison betwixt the English and French dramatic performances. The English, a rough and hardy people, take delight in representations, which more refined manners render insupportable to the French. The distresses, on the other hand, represented on the French theatre, are too slight for an English audience: their passions are not raised; they feel no concern. In general, horror, which denotes the highest degree of pain and aversion that can be raised by a harsh action, is an emotion seldom felt among fierce and savage nations where humanity is little regarded. But when the tender affections are improved by society, horror is more easily raised, and objects which move horror, become more frequent.

The moral sense not only accompanies our other senses in their gradual refinement, but receives additional strength upon every occasion from these other senses. For example, a savage inured to acts of cruelty, feels little pain or aversion in putting an enemy to death in cold blood; and consequently, will have no remorse at such an action, other than what proceeds from the moral sense acting by its native strength. But let us suppose a person of so delicate feelings, as scarce to endure a common operation of phlebotomy, and who cannot behold without some degree of horror the amputation of a fractured member; such a person will be shocked to the highest degree, if he see an enemy put to death in cold blood. The grating emotion thus raised in him, must communicate itself to the feelings of the moral sense, and render them more acute. And thus, refinement in taste and manners, operating by communication upon the moral sense, occasions a stronger perception of immorality in every vitious action, than what would arise before such refinement. Upon the whole, the operations of the moral sense in a savage, bear no proportion to its operations in a person possessed of all the advantages of which human nature is susceptible by refined education.

I never was satisfied with the description given of the law of nations, commonly so called, That it is a law established among nations by common consent, for regulating their conduct with regard to each other. This foundation of the law of nations I take to be chimerical. For upon what occasion was this covenant made, and by whom? If it be said, that the sense of common good gradually brought this law into force; I answer, that the sense of common good is too complex and too remote an object to be a solid foundation for any positive law, if it have no other foundation. But there is no necessity to recur to so slender a foundation. What is just now observed, will lead us to a more rational account of these laws. They are no other but gradual refinements of the original law of nature, accommodating itself to the improved state of mankind. The law of nature, which is the law of our nature, cannot be stationary: it must vary with the nature of man, and consequently refine gradually as human nature refines. Putting an enemy to death in cold blood, raises at present distaste and horror, and therefore is immoral; though it was not always so in the same degree. It is considered as barbarous and inhuman to fight with poisoned weapons; and therefore is more remarkably disapproved by the moral sense than it was originally. Influenced by general objects, we have enmity against France, our natural enemy. But this enmity is not directed against individuals; conscious, as we are, that it is the duty of subjects to serve their king and country. Therefore we treat the prisoners of war with humanity. And now it is creeping in among civilized nations, that in war a cartel should be established for exchange of prisoners. The function of an ambassador has ever been held sacred. To treat him ill was originally immoral; because it is treating as an enemy the man who comes to us with friendly intentions. But the improved manners of later times have refined upon the privileges of an ambassador, and extended them far beyond what they were originally. It is true, that these refinements of the law of nature gain strength and firmness from constant exercise. Hereby they acquire the additional support of common consent. And as every nation trusts that these laws will be observed, it is upon that account a breach of faith to transgress them. But this is not peculiar to these institutions which pass under the name of the law of nations. There is the same adventitious foundation for all the laws of nature, which every man trusts will be observed, and upon that faith directs his conduct.

CHAPTER IX

Various Opinions concerning the Foundation of Morality

As truth cannot be confirmed more successfully than by setting it in opposition to error, a view of erroneous opinions concerning the foundation of morality must be acceptable to every reader who is anxious about truth.

That morality depends entirely on the will of God, and that his will creates the only obligation we lie under to be virtuous, is the opinion of several writers. This opinion in one sense, is true; but far from being true in their sense who inculcate it. And, true or false, it does not advance us a single step in the knowledge of our duty. For what does it avail to know that morality depends upon the will of God, till we once know what his will is? If it be said, there is an original revelation of it to us in our nature; this can only mean, that our nature itself makes us perceive the distinction betwixt virtue and vice, which is the very doctrine above laid down. But, say they, God, from the purity and rectitude of his nature, cannot but approve good actions, and disapprove such as are otherways. They do not advert, that this argument supposes a distinction betwixt virtue and vice, antecedent to the will of God. For if, abstracting from his will, virtue and vice were indifferent, which is supposed in the proposition, we have no *data* from the purity of God's nature, or from any other principle, to conclude, that virtue is more the object of his choice than vice. But further, the very supposition of the purity and rectitude of the nature of the divine Being, presupposes a sense or knowledge in us of an essential difference betwixt virtue and vice. Therefore it can never be said, in any proper sense, that our only obligation to virtue is the will of God; seeing that an obligation to virtue is wrought into the very frame of our nature.

In one sense indeed it is true, that morality depends upon the will of God, as he made us with a moral sense to distinguish virtue from vice. But this is saying no more, but that it is God's will, or that it is agreeable to him, we should be virtuous. It is another thing to maintain, that man is indifferent to virtue and vice, and that he is under no obligation to the one more than to the other, unless as far as he is determined by the arbitrary will of a superior or sovereign. That a being may be so framed as to answer this description, may be yielded. But, taking man as he is, endued with a moral sense, it is a direct contradiction to hold, that he is under no obligation to virtue, other than the mere will of God. In this sense, morality no more depends upon the will of God, than upon our own will.

We shall next take a view of a doctrine which may be set in opposition to the foregoing; and that is Dr. Clarke's demonstration of the unalterable obligation of moral duty. His proposition is,

> That, from the eternal and necessary differences of things, there naturally and necessarily arise certain moral obligations, which are of themselves incumbent on all rational creatures, antecedent to all positive institution, and to all expectation of reward or punishment.

And this proposition he demonstrates in the following manner.

> That there is a fitness of certain circumstances to certain persons, and an unfitness of others, antecedent to positive laws; and that, from the different relations of different things, there arises a fitness and unfitness of certain behaviour of some persons. For instance, God is superior to man, and therefore it is fit that man should worship him.[9]

9. Samuel Clarke, *A Discourse Concerning the Unalterable Obligations of Natural Religion,* in *A Discourse concerning the Being and Attributes of God, the Obligations of Natural*

If this demonstration, as it is called, be the only or chief foundation of morals, unlucky it is, that a doctrine of such importance should have so long been hid from mankind. And now that the important discovery is made, it is not however likely to do great service; considering how little the bulk of mankind are able to enter into abstruse reasoning, and how little influence such reasoning generally has when apprehended.

But abstruseness is not the only imperfection of this celebrated argument. It appears to me entirely inconclusive. Laying aside the moral sense, upon which the Doctor founds no part of his demonstration, I should be utterly at a loss, from any given relation betwixt persons, to draw a conclusion of the fitness or unfitness of a certain course of behaviour. "God is our superior, and therefore it is fit we should worship him." I put the question, Upon what principle of reason does this conclusion rest? where is the connecting proposition by means of which the inference is drawn? It is clear to me, that the terms *fitness* and *unfitness,* in their present signification, depend entirely upon the moral sense. *Fitness* and *unfitness* with regard to a certain end or purpose, are qualities of actions which may be gathered from experience. But *fitness* or *unfitness* of actions, as importing *right* or *wrong,* as denoting what we *ought* to do, or abstain from, have truly no meaning, unless upon supposition of a moral sense, which this learned divine never once dreams of founding upon. The Doctor's error is a common one, that he endeavours to substitute reason in place of sentiment. The fitness of worshipping our Creator was obvious to him, as it is to every person, because it is founded on our very nature. It is equally obvious with the preference of honesty to dishonesty. His only mistake is, that, overlooking the *law written in his own heart,* he vainly imagines that his meta-

---

Religion, and the Truth and Certainty of Christian Revelation (9th ed., London, 1738), pp. 176–7. First published in 1711, the *Discourse concerning the Being and Attributes of God* consists of the two series of Boyle lectures that Clarke delivered at St Paul's Cathedral in 1704 and 1705, bound together in one volume. The first set of Boyle lectures, *A Demonstration of the Being and Attributes of God,* was first published in 1705, while the second set, *A Discourse Concerning the Unchangeable Obligations of Natural Religion,* was first published in 1706. Samuel Clarke (1675–1729), Anglican clergyman and rationalist theologian, sought to counter both atheism and deism by demonstrating the existence and attributes of God and the moral certainty of Christianity through a series of incontrovertible proofs that no rational person could deny.

physical argument is just, because the consequence he draws from it happens to be true. And to satisfy even his most devoted disciples that this is the case, let us only suppose, that man by nature had no approbatory or disapprobatory sense of actions; it could never be evinced by any abstract argument, that the worship of the Deity is his duty, or, in the moral sense of fitness, that it is more fit for him to be honest than to be dishonest.

We will take the liberty to add, because it is of importance to the subject in general, that, supposing our duty could be made plain to us by an abstract chain of reasoning, yet we have good ground to conclude, that the Author of nature has not left our actions to be directed by so weak a principle as reason: and a weak principle it must be to the bulk of mankind, who have little capacity to enter into abstract reasoning; whatever effect it may have upon the learned and contemplative. Nature has dealt more kindly by us. We are compelled by cogent principles, to perform all the different duties of life. Self-preservation is not left to the conduct of reason, but is guarded by the strongest instinct, which makes us carefully, or rather mechanically, avoid every appearance of danger. The propagation of the species is enforced by the most importunate of all appetites; and the care of our offspring, by a lively and constant affection. Is nature so deficient, as to leave the duty we owe our neighbour, which stands in the first rank of duties, to be directed by cool reasoning? This is not according to the analogy of nature: nor is it fact; witness compassion, friendship, benevolence, and all the tribe of the social affections. Neither is common justice left upon this footing, the most useful, though not the most exalted virtue. We are compelled to it by a principle common to all men; and every transgression of it is attended with a sense of disapprobation, and of merited punishment.

A late author,* whom I shall just mention by the way, gives a whimsical system of morals. He endeavours to reduce all crimes to that of telling a lie; and, because telling a lie is immoral, he concludes, that the several crimes he mentions are immoral.[10] Robbery, for example, is acting or telling

---

* Wollaston.

10. William Wollaston, *The Religion of Nature Delineated* (London, 1724). Wollaston (1660–1724) defined the morality of an act in terms of its compatibility with universal moral truths, and asserted that "no act (whether word or deed) of any being, to whom

a lie; because it is in effect saying, that the goods I seize are mine. Adultery is acting or telling a lie, because it is in effect maintaining, that my neighbour's wife is not his, but mine. But not to insist upon the absurdity of giving all crimes the same character and confounding their nature, it is evident, that in this argument the very thing is taken for granted that is undertaken to be proved. For why is it a virtual lie to rob one of his goods? Is it not by imposing upon mankind, who must presume those goods to be mine which I take as my own? But does not this evidently presuppose a difference betwixt *meum* and *tuum,* and that I ought not to make free with another's property without his consent? For what other reason are the goods presumed to be mine, but that it is unlawful to meddle with what belongs to another? The same observation is applicable to all his other transmutations; for, in acting or telling the lie, it is constantly taken for granted, that the action is wrong in itself. And this very wrong is the circumstance which, by the author's supposition, imposes upon the spectators. The error therefore of this author is of the same nature with Dr. Clarke's. It is an evident begging of the question: the very thing is taken for granted which is undertaken to be proved. With regard to the present subject, we shall only further observe, that when this curious author draws so strong consequences from telling a lie, it was incumbent upon him to set in the clearest light the immorality of that action. But this he does not so much as attempt, leaving it upon the conviction of one's own mind. This indeed he might safely do; but not more safely than to leave upon the same conviction all the other crimes he treats of.[ix]

A system that resolves every moral sensation of sentiment into sympathy, shall next be introduced. Listen to the author himself.

> As we have no immediate experience of what other men feel, we can form no idea of it but by imagining what we ourselves would feel in the like situation. Our senses will never inform us of what a man suffers on the rack. They cannot carry us beyond our own persons; and it is by the imagination only that we can form any perception of what he suffers. Neither can that faculty help us to this, any other way than by representing to us

---

moral good and evil are imputable, that interferes with any true proposition, or denies any thing to be as it is, can be right" (p. 16).

what would be our own sufferings if we were in his place. His agonies when thus brought home to ourselves, begin at last to affect us; and we then tremble and shudder at the thought of what he feels.*

The foundation here assigned for the various sentiments of morality, ought to have been very strictly examined before venturing to erect so weighty a superstructure upon it. Is it certain that this play of imagination will necessarily raise the passion of sympathy? The celebrated Rousseau affirms the contrary. "Pity is sweet, says he, because in putting ourselves in place of the person who suffers, we feel the pleasure of not suffering as he does."† And considering that the rack is a punishment reserved for atrocious criminals, I should be inclined to think with Rousseau, that the sight of an odious wretch on the rack, instead of sympathizing in his pain, would make one feel pleasure in not suffering as he does; precisely as a ship in a storm makes the spectators at land rejoice in their own security.

But however that may be, my respect to the author of this system as a man of genius and learning, cannot make me blind to a difficulty that appears unsurmountable. If the torments of a man on the rack be not obvious to my sight from his violent perturbation, nor to my hearing from dismal screams and groans, what can I learn from imagining myself to be in his place? He may be happy for ought I know. To give that act of imagination any effect, I ought before hand to know that the person on the rack is suffering violently. Then indeed, the bringing his case home to myself, would naturally inflame my sympathy. I have another argument against this system, which, being more simple and popular, will probably be more relished. That a man should conceive himself to be another, is no slight effort of imagination; and to make sympathy depend on that effort, confines it to persons who have given much exercise to a ductile imagination. Dull people and illiterate rustics are intirely excluded; and yet, among such there appears

---

* Theory of Moral Sentiments, p. 2. [Adam Smith, *The Theory of Moral Sentiments* (1759; reprint, ed. D. D. Raphael and A. L. Macfie, Indianapolis: Liberty Classics, 1982), 1.1.1.2, p. 9. By "sympathy" Smith means not only benevolence or compassion but "our fellow-feeling with any passion whatsoever" (1.1.1.5, p. 10).]

† Emile, liv. 4. [Jean-Jacques Rousseau, *Emile, ou de l'éducation* (1762); *Emile, or, On Education,* ed. and trans. Allan Bloom (New York: Basic Books, 1979), bk. 4, p. 221.]

no defect of sympathy to associates and blood-relations. Nay, we find sympathy eminent even in children; and yet, it would be a hard task to make a child imagine itself to be what it is not. This shows clearly, that sympathy must proceed from some natural principle inherent in all human beings, the young as well as the old.

This principle will appear from the following facts, which every thinking person knows to be true. First, every passion stamps on the countenance certain signs appropriated to it by nature. Next, being taught by nature to connect every external sign with the passion that caused it; we can read in every man's countenance his internal emotions. Third, certain emotions, thus made known, raise in beholders the passion of sympathy.* With respect to the last, nothing is more natural than that a social being should be affected with the passions of its fellows. Joy is infectious: so is grief. Fear communicates itself to the beholders; and in an army, the fright of a few spreads the infection till it becomes an universal panic. These facts are clear and certain; and applying them to the subject before us, is it not evident, that the distress we read in a person's countenance, directly moves our sympathy, without needing any aid from imagination? I appeal to any man who has seen a person on the rack, whether his sympathy was not raised by sight merely, without any effort of imagination. Thus, in the sympathetic system under examination, an intricate circuit is made in order to account for a passion that is raised by a single glance. The system indeed is innocent; but did it hold in fact, its consequences would not be so. Sympathy is but one of many principles that constitute us moral beings; and yet is held furth as the foundation of every moral sentiment. Had not morality a more solid foundation in our nature, it would give very little obstruction to vicious desires or unjust actions. It is observed above, that, according to this system, sympathy would be rare among the lower ranks. And I now add, that if moral sentiments had no foundation but the imagining myself to be an-

* See Elements of Criticism, vol. I. page 446. Edit. 5th. [Kames refers to the chapter on "External Signs of Emotions and Passions" in his *Elements of Criticism,* 5th ed., 2 vols. (Edinburgh and London: 1774), vol. 1, chap. 15. First published in 1762, the *Elements of Criticism* ran through six editions (the sixth edition, with Kames's final revisions, was published in 1785; reprint, Peter Jones, ed., 2 vols., Indianapolis: Liberty Fund, 2005), with many reprints in both Britain and America.]

other, the far greater part of mankind would be destitute of any moral sentiment.

So much for the sake of truth: in every other view controversy is my aversion. One observation more, and I conclude. This system is far from comprehending all our moral sentiments. It may pretend to account for my sentiments regarding others; but my sentiments regarding myself are entirely left out. My distress upon losing an only son, or my gratitude for a kindly office, are sentiments that neither need to be explained by imagining myself to be another person, nor do they admit of such explanation.

The selfish system shall be more strictly examined. The sympathetic system is a harmless conceit; but a system that resolves all morality into self-love, cannot but be dangerous among luxurious nations whose bent to selfish pleasures is already too strong.

Man is a being composed of many parts, external and internal. He has passions that move him; some to advance his own interest, some to advance the interest of others; a few that prompt him to harm himself, many that prompt him to harm others. A variety of connections with persons and things, require these different springs of action. Yet there are writers more ambitious of singularity than of truth, who hold that self-love is the only motive to action; and that in every action, even the most disinterested in appearance, our own good is always the prime mover. With shallow thinkers the selfish system naturally prevails. During childhood, our desires terminate mostly on ourselves; which is wisely ordered, as children have little power to give aid or assistance to others. But as soon as we acquire ability to do good, the social principle is felt. One thing is certain, that however much selfishness may prevail in practice, it never meets with any degree of approbation. All agree to condemn actions that are eminently selfish; and no wonder, for if absolute selfishness be the system of nature, man is little superior to the brute: heroism, magnanimity, generosity, are degraded from an exalted station to be no better than self-love in a mask. And what is still more humbling, every moral duty and obligation are torn up by the root, not a single fibre left to spring again.* These horrid consequences notwith-

---

* Observe how far one may be carried in contradiction to moral principles by adopting zealously selfishness as our only rule of conduct. Lord Chesterfield, in a series of letters

standing, the selfish system is adopted without disguise by every French writer. Considering the humanity and benevolence of that nation in general, an attempt to vilify their own people along with the rest of mankind, was little to be expected from French writers. One of their profound philosophers, Helvetius, boldly maintains, that man is superior to a horse in nothing but in having ten fingers.[11] I owe the following thoughts to an ingenious correspondent.*

> From what I learn, the French writers have all become rank Epicureans. One would think that French *politesse* might consort well with disinterested benevolence. But if we believe themselves, it is all grimace: it is flattering in order to be flattered; like a horse who scratches his fellow that he may be scratched. I detest all systems that depreciate human nature. If it be a delusion to think that the constitution of man is worthy of its Author, let me live and die in that delusion, rather than to behold the vileness of my species. Every good man finds his stomach rise against those who disparage his kindred or his country. Why should it not rise against those

---

to his favorite son, takes great pains to initiate him in this poisonous system. The young man is instructed to regard nothing but his own interest; and to boggle at no wickedness that can advance it. Friendship is nothing; blood-relation nothing; dissimulation and treachery are to be no obstacles in the way of his preferment. One lesson I give for a specimen, which is sedulously inculcated, that one sure way of coming at a man's secret, is under the mask of friendship to corrupt his wife. [Chesterfield, Philip Dormer Stanhope, 4th Earl of (1694–1773), *Letters written by the late Right Honourable Philip Dormer Stanhope, Earl of Chesterfield, to his son, Philip Stanhope, Esq.,* 2 vols. (London, 1774). Though Chesterfield's *Letters* were enormously popular and frequently reprinted, many Scottish moralists shared Samuel Johnson's opinion that "they teach the morals of a whore, and the manners of a dancing master." James Boswell, *Life of Johnson* (London, 1791; reprint, ed. R. W. Chapman, New York: Oxford University Press, 1980, p. 188.)]

11. "If, instead of hands with flexible fingers, nature had finished our wrists with hooves like a horse, who can doubt that humans, without useful arts, without dwellings, without defenses against other animals, completely occupied in securing a subsistence and in avoiding ferocious beasts, would still be wandering in the forests?" (Claude-Adrien Helvétius [1715–1771], *De l'esprit* [Paris, 1758], pt. 1, chap. 1, p. 2). Helvétius's materialist account of human nature, combined with his resolutely anti-clerical stance, made him one of the most controversial of the Enlightenment *philosophes*. His *De l'esprit* (translated as *Essays on the Mind* in 1759) was banned by the Sorbonne and publicly burned at Paris, and Helvétius was forced to write three recantations.

* Doctor Reid.

who disparage his species? Were it not that extremes sometimes meet, I should think it strange to see your Atheist and your high-shod divine contending who should give the blackest representation of human nature. The Atheist acts the more consistent part; for surely, such representations tend more to promote Atheism than to promote religion.[12]

As the selfish system consorts the best with the degeneracy of the present times, any plausible attempt to establish it as the true system of nature, must tend to spread the infection, and to make actions the most grossly selfish pass even without a blush. All good men will join in disgracing it; and I shall think myself happy to contribute a mite. I hope to evince, not only that it gives a false representation of human nature, but that the arguments urged in its defence are weak and inconclusive.

To prevent the being imposed on by words substituted for things, I begin with marking out the distinction between social and selfish actions. The end in view denominates the action to be social or selfish. When I have nothing in view but my own interest, the action is purely selfish: when my only view is the interest of another, the action is purely social. Thus, when affection moves me to serve my friend for his sake, without regard to myself, the action is entirely social: if done partly from the prospect of its affording me a pleasant recollection, it is so far selfish. Instinctive actions which proceed without having any end in view, are neither social nor selfish; as where one is impelled by hunger to eat, without even thinking of its being necessary for health. But when we have in view that eating will contribute to health or to pleasure, the action so far is selfish. An action prompted by the principle of duty solely, is neither social nor selfish: if desire of approbation be added, it is so far selfish. If desire of approbation be the sole motive, it is entirely selfish: I pay a debt for my own sake, not for the sake of a rigorous creditor: if gratitude to a benefactor who assisted me with money at a pinch,

---

12. Kames quotes from a letter by Thomas Reid, 27 February 1778, the full text of which can be found in *The Correspondence of Thomas Reid,* ed. Paul Wood (University Park, Pa.: Pennsylvania State University Press, 2002), pp. 96–8. Thomas Reid (1710–1796), who succeeded Adam Smith as Professor of Moral Philosophy at the University of Glasgow (a position he held from 1764 to 1780), is best known as the founder of the Scottish school of Common Sense philosophy.

be in my view, the action so far is social.* In a word, it is not the motive or impulsive cause that determines an action to be social or selfish, but the end which the actor has in view.

In bringing the selfish system to trial, I begin with enquiring how far the advocates for it admit man to be a social being. Rousseau excepted, I know no writer but who acknowledges in man an appetite for society; and I am willing to believe that a morose and solitary disposition influenced him more to form that opinion, than reason or experience.† An inclination to communicate thoughts and sentiments and to express wishes and wants, is inherent in the human race. For that end was the blessing of speech bestowed on man; and hence books without end. An appetite to be esteemed by our fellow-creatures will readily be admitted by my opponents, as being selfish. Is any thing more natural than to wish well to our benefactors, and ill to our enemies? These gentlemen probably will also admit, that to re-

---

* See Elements of Criticism, vol. I. p. 47, Edit. 5th. [Kames, *Elements of Criticism,* vol. 1, chap. 2, pt. 1, sec. i.]

† "It is the weakness of man, says he, that renders him social. If a man had no use for others, he would never think of an union with them. A being truly happy is a solitary being. I have no conception, that the man who needs nothing can love any thing." (Emile liv. 4.) Not a word here of an appetite for society, though it makes a principal branch in the nature of man; and is the chief cause that makes men flock together. Nor in his famous discourse upon the origin of inequality among men, is there the least hint of it. If he had acknowledged this appetite, one of the most urgent that belongs to human nature, he would never have preferred the savage state before that of society. It is indeed strange, that an eloquent writer, who paints so deliciously the passions even in their nicest tints, should betray such ignorance in accounting for them. Pity, like the appetite for society, is an original branch of human nature, which is raised at the very first sight of a person in distress. Yet observe how far this author goes out of the road to account for this the simplest of all passions.

> Pity, says he, is sweet because, in putting ourselves in place of the person who suffers, we feel the pleasure of not suffering as he does. What is it that can move pity, other than the identifying ourselves with the person who suffers, quitting as it were our own being to take up his. It is self-love that makes me interest myself for him, and my reason for wishing him not to suffer, is that I may not suffer.

Again, "Envy is bitter, because the sight of a man who is happy, far from putting us in his place, makes us regret that we are not happy as he is." Again, "The affection we have derived from self-love is the only principle of human justice." I could entertain the reader with a great deal more of this stuff; but it has an air of ingratitude to censure so deeply an author, in whose works, with all his errors, I find much entertainment. [Rousseau, *Emile,* bk. 4, p. 221.]

taliate upon the latter is equally natural. If so, is not a grateful return to a benefactor, also natural? If a man can act with the sole view of doing mischief to his enemy, what is it in nature that bars him from acting with the sole view of doing good to his friend? A late French writer, pinched with this argument, finds it necessary to deny that there is in man any such principle as benevolence. He discards by the lump good will to others, parental affection, and even love between the sexes. He holds the expression improper, *I love my father, my friend, my mistress;* observing that the expression ought to be, *I love myself in my father, in my friend, in my mistress.* This, it must be acknowledged, is arguing consequentially, however absurdly. Yet with great assurance he condemns the English writers as being strangely bewildered about morality.

> Hutcheson, says he, talks of a moral sense, as if he had never read Locke, who banishes innate ideas, and demonstrates, that we can have no ideas, but from external objects.[13]

I readily yield to these gentlemen, that a man may justly prefer his own interest before that of others; which is wisely ordered even for the general good, as it lies more within a man's reach to benefit himself than others. But cases daily occur when I can serve others without prejudice to myself. If self-interest make no opposition, what can obstruct my benevolence from operating?

Writers for the selfish system seem to entertain some obscure notion of benevolence being inconsistent with self-love. On the contrary, so friendly is the social principle to the selfish, that every thing I do for the sake of another, is a pleasure to myself. Is there a sweeter pleasure than what one feels in having relieved a man of merit from oppression, in having comforted a friend in affliction, in having served the public at a critical time?

> Every one perceives intuitively the comfort of food and raiment, of a snug dwelling, of riches; but that the doing good to others will make us happy, is not so evident; feeding the hungry for example, or cloathing the naked.

13. Not traced. Possibly a reference to Helvétius, whose posthumously published *De L'Homme* (1772) took aim at the "absurdity" of the "much vaunted moral sense" of "les schaftesburystes" (sec. 5, chap. 3, pp. 12–13).

This truth is seen but obscurely by the gross of mankind. The superior pleasure that follows the exercise of benevolence, of friendship, and of every social principle, is not clearly understood till it be frequently felt. To perceive the social principle in its triumphant state, a man, like an unconcerned spectator, must direct his thoughts upon the conduct of his fellow creatures: he will feel a secret charm in every passion that tends to the good of others, and a secret aversion against every unfeeling heart that is indifferent to their happiness and distresses.* Here the superiority of social affections is conspicuous; as little or no pleasure of that kind arises from those that are selfish.

The pleasure a man feels in doing acts of benevolence, has misled selfish writers to think that that pleasure is the only motive we have for doing good to others. They maintain, that in serving my father, my friend, or my mistress, my motive is not affection to them, but a prospect of the pleasure or satisfaction that will result to myself. And they obstinately deny, that there is in nature such a thing as serving those we love for their sake, independent of our own. But a simple denial cannot be thought sufficient against numberless instances of serving those we love, without the least appearance of self-interest. Such instances must be decisive, unless these writers be able to prove, that to serve others without regard to ourselves, is inconsistent with the nature of man. If they succeed in that proof, the selfish system will be established upon a sure foundation. But without that proof, hitherto not attempted, they must submit. Let them therefore prove, or abandon their system altogether: there is no medium.

But not satisfied with reducing my opponents to this dilemma, I undertake to prove, tho' not incumbent on me, that benevolence frequently operates independent altogether of self-love. I admit that the prospect of consequent pleasure may be an additional motive for doing a benevolent action; and so far the action is selfish; but that it cannot be the only motive, will appear as follows. That pleasure attends benevolent actions, we learn from experience only. Therefore, such an action done by one who has no experience, must proceed from some motive independent of the consequent pleasure. Children have no experience, nor are they capable of fore-

---

* Elements of Criticism, vol. I. page 195. Edit. 5th.

seeing distant consequences: yet children express good will to others by kindly acts; from what motive other than benevolence?

But even with respect to those who have felt pleasure in doing good, what gloss will my opponents put upon the following facts? If we give credit to history, or if we can rely on our own experience, there are instances without number of persons acting for the sake of those they love, even against their own interest. What motive other than duty and affection can prompt a man to sacrifice himself for others, stepping in for example to intercept a deadly blow aimed at his father or his prince? Here, the certainty of death admits not any prospect of consequent pleasure. In a shipwreck, people on shore venture their lives to save the crew: the case is urgent, and they have not a moment for reflection. Nor would any faint thought of consequent pleasure be sufficient among the low and illiterate, to overbalance their danger. Sympathy with fellow creatures in deep distress, is with such people the only motive; and that motive operates like a charm. Gratitude for a slight favour, is commonly attended with a selfish motive. But a great and unexpected favour, swells my heart, and inflames my gratitude to my worthy benefactor: I burn to repay his generosity, without a single thought of gratification to myself. The power of stifling selfish motives, is equally remarkable in dissocial passions. Resentment for a slight injury is often accompanied with a prospect of gratification; and so far is selfish. But revenge instigated by an atrocious injury, admits not a thought but against the offender, whom it devotes to destruction; and in that state the action is neither social nor selfish. There is not a man of a benevolent disposition but who can inform you, that he has often acted for the sake of his friend, without any view to himself. These are subborn facts not easily subdued. Will my opponents have the assurance to affirm, that this is all a deceit; and that their assertion ought to be adopted against the testimony of all others?

But now, even in the case of experience I am ready to demonstrate, that the prospect of gratification can never be the sole motive for acting. To prepare the reader for that demonstration, I premise the following *data*, First, that the accomplishment of desire produces a pleasant feeling, termed gratification of the passion.* Next, that where there is no desire, there is no

* Elements of Criticism, vol. I. page 46. Edit. 5th.

gratification. I have no desire to pay a certain debt, but am compelled by a decree: the payment far from producing any gratification, is not a little unpleasant. I make a rash promise, which I have no desire to perform: the performance affords me no gratification. The more vigorous my desire is to do a benevolent deed, the more exquisite is my gratification: the more faint my desire is, the more faint is my gratification. Therefore, where there is no desire, there can be no gratification.

And now to the demonstration. Those who hold self-love to be the only motive to action, maintain that the prospect of gratification is the only motive one can have for voluntary deeds of benevolence. I ask these gentlemen a plain question, When I have it in view to do a benevolent deed, whence arises the prospect of gratification? They must admit that it arises from my desire of performing the benevolent deed; for if I have no desire to perform, the performance will not gratify me, nor consequently will it afford me an antecedent prospect of gratification. It clearly follows, that as the desire to do a benevolent deed must always precede the prospect of gratification, the latter never can be the sole motive. The prospect of gratification may be an additional motive to act, but never can stand single. Let a man attend to what passes in his mind when he acts for the good of one he loves: he will find, that desire to accomplish his purpose is his primary motive; and that the prospect of gratification, is only a consequent view. I am sensible how difficult it is to convince one of an error that has long been disguised under the mask of truth. And yet I entertain some hope, that this demonstration, for it is truly such, will oblige my opponents to abandon their favourite system, and rest satisfied with self-love, as one only of many principles that govern the actions of men.

They who acknowledge no motive to action but self-love, know little of human nature. How will they account for instinctive actions, which have no end in view, social or selfish? how will they account for revenge, which often impels a man to act more against his own interest than against that of the offender? how will they account for my killing my friend in a sudden fit of passion; and wishing the moment after to have rather put an end to my own life? Can actions instigated by envy or peevishness be owing to self-love? Gratification, attending such actions, may be a motive; but is the impulse of the passion no motive? In stormy and impetuous passions, there is seldom a thought of gratification; and the slight and momentary grati-fication that follows, is immediately suffocated by remorse and repentance. Can a prospect of these consequences be a motive for any action? On the contrary, the prospect is powerfully dissuasive, though overbalanced by the violence of the passion. The nature of man is wonderfully various. Avarice, far from consulting my interest, is a bitter enemy to self-love: it locks up my stores, and deprives me of every comfort that wealth can afford. Can self-love account for those singular passions which prompt people to hurt themselves? A man in deep distress is prone to afflict himself, rejecting all consolation. The vexation of a man for having treated his son harshly, is painted in the genuine colours of nature by Terence in the Heauton-timorumenos.

> Decrevi tantisper me minus injuriae,
> Chreme, meo gnato facere, dum fiam miser:
> Nec fas esse ulla me voluptate hic frui;
> Nisi ubi ille huc salvos redierit meus particeps.[14]

Nature goes still farther in this tract. Instances are not extremely rare of persons, stung with remorse for secret crimes, delivering themselves up to justice, in order to suffer condign punishment. Nor shall my opponents escape here under their favourite pretext of gratification; malevolent pas-sions directed against self, being in every stage of their progress unpleasant. Such passions, inveterate foes to self-love, admit not of any selfish motive. This suggests a reflection that must have influence. Seeing there are passions so contrary to self-love as to excite a man to afflict and even to destroy himself; why should we doubt of passions, perfectly concordant with self-love, exciting a man to serve those he loves for their sake?

To conclude, far from admitting self-love to be the sole mover in human

---

14. "I have come to this conclusion, Chremes, that I do my son a less injury, while I am unhappy; and that it is not right for me to enjoy any pleasure here, until such time as he returns home safe to share it with me." The speaker here, Menedemus, has exiled himself to the country to lead a life of self-imposed hardship and privation out of remorse for having driven his son from home (Terence, *Heautontimorumenos: The Self-Tormentor*, 1.1.147–9, in *The Comedies of Terence*, ed. Henry Thomas Riley, New York: Harper and Brothers, 1874).

actions; it is my firm opinion, that it is rather too sparingly distributed among men, the instances being extremely rare of its prevailing over any impetuous passion. I should willingly give my vote for a larger portion, were it not the hazard of making it overbalance the social principle. To envigorate that principle in proportion, would indeed remove the objection; but it would be at the cost of the impetuous passions. And why not, it will be said, for would it not be a great improvement to bridle such passions? It appears so.—And yet, an attempt to mend the works of the Almighty, is to tread on forbidden ground. What might be the consequences cannot readily be forseen; only, that it would leave without exercise many exalted virtues. But this interesting subject does not necessarily enter into the present speculation; and is handled at large in *Sketches of the History of Man.**

The only author I know who holds up utility as the chief foundation of morality, is David Hume Esq.; first in *A Treatise of Human Nature,* and more fully in a following work entitled *An Enquiry concerning the Principles of Morals.* The latter shows uncommon genius exerted in a pleasing stile. The author has given great scope to invention, but has been little attentive to facts and principles. Love of simplicity has betrayed him into the same error with the authors above-mentioned; that of founding morality upon a single principle, overlooking the complex nature of man, composed of many principles. Utility indeed is not made the sole foundation of morality; for it is admitted that benevolence is founded on a moral sense. The author so far is more cautious than the French writers, who reject every principle but self-love. But he denies that we have any original sense of justice, affirming it to be an artificial virtue, of which public good is the only foundation. It must appear to every one, even upon the most superficial view, that if this doctrine hold true, human nature must be an irregular and disjointed machine. Benevolence indeed is an amiable virtue, tending greatly to make society comfortable. Justice however is a virtue of much higher importance, as without it there can be no society among men; more than among lions and tigers. Here then is a system that distinguishes the less

---

* Vol. II. p. 204. Edit. 2d. [A reference to the chapter (or "sketch") on "Appetite for Society—Origin of National Societies" in Kames, Henry Home, Lord, *Sketches of the History of Man,* 2nd ed. (Edinburgh, 1778), vol. 2, bk. 2, sketch 1.]

useful virtue by marks of pre-eminence, that ingrafts it upon our nature, and inforces it by a moral sense; while the more useful virtue is left to the fluctuating notions of men; and extremely fluctuating these notions must be where public good is the object. Is it not surprising, that so acute a philosopher who acknowledges benevolence to be founded upon an innate sense, should refuse that privilege to a virtue much more essential? Does not this look as if he thought that man was made by chance? Yet, a very slight survey of human nature and of our principles of action, must have discovered to him, that justice is founded upon an innate sense as well as benevolence. He must have seen, that notions of right and wrong make an appearance even among children, who cannot have any conception of public good. Had our perceptions of right and wrong no foundation but utility, there never could have prevailed any uniformity of opinion concerning them. Our notions of utility from partiality and prejudice, would be so various, as to leave no shadow of uniformity.

But impartiality will not suffer us to stop our ears against our author's arguments in behalf of his system. His proposition is, "That public utility is the *sole origin* of justice, and that reflections on the beneficial consequences of this virtue, are the *sole foundation* of its merit."[15] Before entering into particulars, it must be observed, that here two very different propositions are jumbled together, as if they were necessary members of a single proposition. It is granted, that the end of justice is public utility, and that its *merit* consists in contributing to that end. But it cannot be granted that public utility is the *sole origin* of justice; because it would be to grant, that there is no such thing in man as a moral sense, or a natural faculty to distinguish right from wrong, just from unjust. If our author can make out this negative proposition, it must be yielded to him, that public utility is not only the sole end of justice but its sole origin. These things premised, it belongs to the reader to judge, whether our author's following arguments tend to evince that negative proposition.

He supposes a golden age where even luxuries are in superfluity, and where friendship and generosity universally prevail. "It would follow, says

15. David Hume, *An Enquiry Concerning the Principles of Morals* (1751; reprint, ed. Tom L. Beauchamp, Oxford: Oxford University Press, 1998), 3.1, p. 83.

he, that men could not have the least idea of justice, nor of separate property."* Whence he concludes that justice derives its existence from its use in our present state. This conclusion does not follow. It only follows, that there may be circumstances in which there would be no occasion to enforce justice by courts of law, nor for separate property. With respect to the former, did friendship and generosity universally prevail, were all men upright and honest, there would indeed be little occasion for courts of law. But does it follow, that therefore man has no sense of right and wrong? The direct contrary follows; for the goodness and rectitude supposed must be founded on a more vivid sense of right and wrong than is common among men. Society would be an uncomfortable state, were the stern authority of a magistrate always necessary to compel men to do their duty. The people of Switzerland, we are told, are so fair in their dealings, as to make a law-suit seldom necessary. Will this infer that these good people have no sense of justice? Is it not a lively sense of justice that makes them so fair in their dealings? With respect to separate property, I have no difficulty to yield, that in a country superabounding with every necessary of life ready for use, there would be no necessity for separate property more than in the air we breathe. But because in one state of things separate property is unnecessary, is it a good inference, that it is necessary in no state. This has not even a plausible appearance. A philosopher ought to be ashamed of such an argument. Would it not be a gross imperfection in man, to be fitted, not for the state he is placed in, but for an imaginary state, that never existed, nor probably ever will exist?

> Reverse, says our author, in any considerable circumstance the condition of man; produce extreme abundance or extreme necessity; implant in the human breast moderation and equity, or perfect rapaciousness or malice: by rendering justice totally useless, you totally destroy its essence and suspend its obligation on mankind.†

* Page 34, 35. [Hume, *An Enquiry Concerning the Principles of Morals*, 3.2–3, p. 83. Kames does not quote verbatim but paraphrases Hume's statement that, "in such a happy state, every other social virtue would flourish . . . but the cautious, jealous virtue of justice would never once have been dreamed of. For what purpose make a partition of goods, when every one has already more than enough? Why give rise to property, where there cannot possibly be any injury?"]

† Page 41. [Ibid., 3.8, p. 85.]

To have the exercise of justice suspended in certain circumstances, and to have its essence totally destroyed, are widely different. It is admitted above, that universal moderation and equity would render courts of law very little useful; and I also admit, that perfect rapaciousness and malice would make men ungovernable. But does it follow from either of these admissions, that man is destitute of a moral sense? Benevolence is admitted by our author to be inherent in the nature of man. A state may be supposed so flourishing as to afford no objects for compassion, a branch of benevolence: its exercise would be suspended; but would its essence be totally destroyed? Let proper objects appear, and it will not lie dormant. Why not the same in justice? I add in general, that more solid evidence is necessary than bare suppositions to prove or disprove controverted facts.

"But, says he, in some cases that actually happen, such as that of famine or a city besieged, the distinctions of property are overthrown, and the obligation to justice ceases." It is far from being clear, that either property or justice ceases even in these cases of extremity.[16] But supposing them to cease, does the argument prove more than that in such cases the great law of self-preservation prevails over that of property?

These, to the best of my understanding, are all the arguments adduced by Mr. Hume to prove that public good is the sole origin of justice; and consequently that there is not in the nature of man a moral sense: whether they are conclusive, every reader must judge for himself. Much labour is bestowed upon proving a proposition that no mortal controverts, namely, that public good is the sole end of justice; which is perfectly consistent with what is all along inculcated in the present Essay, that the moral sense is bestowed on man to fit him for society. Nothing can be more simple than to distinguish between the means and the end, or between the cause and the effect: yet the subject is handled as if the origin and end of justice were the same; and that to prove either is to prove both. He accordingly bends his whole force to prove that public utility is the end of justice; taking for granted, as it would appear, that the same proof would serve to make it also the origin of justice.

---

16. Kames's paraphrase is not entirely accurate. Hume argues that in cases of famine, shipwreck, and other emergencies, "the strict laws of justice are suspended " in favor of "the stronger motives of necessity and self-preservation" (Ibid.).

Justice, I acknowledge, goes for the most part hand in hand with utility: there are however cases where they differ widely. Take the following example. A large sum is deposited privately in my hand by an intimate friend. He dies suddenly, leaving an overgrown fortune to his heir, who is ignorant of the deposit. Every argument from utility would justify me in retaining this sum, as the only fund I have for educating and providing a numerous family of children. But if even in this trying case I stand bound in conscience to restore, of which no honest man can doubt, it follows necessarily, that justice must have a foundation independent of utility. The only answer that can be given is, that justice is founded upon public utility, what concerns the whole society, without regarding the interest of one or other individual. With respect to this case I cannot enter into the distinction. Robbery, it is true, or murder may benefit me; and yet upon the whole may be detrimental to the public. But in the example given, as no person is hurt, the public suffers no prejudice. But letting it pass that my retaining this sum is hurtful to the public, I am greatly mistaken if our author's theory can stand upon that foundation. To complete that theory, it was incumbent on him to show, that there can exist a public, a regular government, independent of an original sense of justice. This however he has not made out, nor attempted to make out. To me it is evident, that without an original sense of justice, there never could have existed any public, any society under government; far less a government with authority sufficient to subdue the rapacity of man, his love of power, and his other selfish and unruly passions. Were there no law antecedent to society but *major vis,* every man would shun those of his own kind, as he would a savage tiger: war would be perpetual of all against all, as happily expressed by Mr. Hobbes.[17] There is in man, it is true, an appetite for society; but that appetite would be blasted in the bud by selfish and dissocial passions. Our author here has been guilty of a palpable error: he founds justice upon public utility; instead of making justice the foundation of every republic that exists or has existed among

17. "Hereby it is manifest, that during the time men live without a common Power to keep them all in awe, they are in that condition that is called Warre; and such a warre, as is of every man, against every man" (Thomas Hobbes, *Leviathan or the Matter, Forme and Power of a Commonwealth Ecclesiastical and Civill* [1651; reprint, ed. Richard Tuck, Cambridge: Cambridge University Press, 1996], pt. 1, ch. 13, pp. 88–9).

men. The cause is mistaken for the effect: nor is this the single instance of the kind that occurs in the enquiry.

It is agreed on all hands, that justice is established among men for making them good citizens, or, in our author's words, for public utility; consequently that public utility is the sole end of justice. It ought however carefully to be attended to, that in no case is it made our duty to act for the public good: we are left at liberty by the moral sense to act for the public good if we incline; but the moral sense lays us under no obligation. The good of mankind, or even of our own country, resulting from an endless variety of combined circumstances, is an object too complex and intricate to be taken under consideration by a creature so limited in capacity as man. And were it made our duty to take public good under consideration, a wide door would be opened to partiality and passion: the opinions of men would be as various as their faces, which would disqualify them entirely for society. Behold the art that is displayed in this branch of our nature! It is more wisely ordered, even for the general good, that we are strictly bound to perform or to forbear certain plain and simple acts, incapable of a mistake; leaving the consequences to providence. We must be obedient to our parents and to magistrates. We must be grateful to our benefactors, kindly to our relations, and faithful to our engagements. We are forbidden to rob, to lie, or in any other way to injure others. These precepts, simple and perspicuous, are made our duty; and we are not left at liberty to act by any other rule.

Mr. Hume holds "public good to be the foundation of justice, and justice to be the foundation of property."[18] The first proposition being discussed above, it occurs upon the other, that at any rate it is too extensive; for surely, it is not meant that duty to parents, performance of promises, or other obligations of that kind, are the foundation of property; but only that justice as relative to subjects of property is its foundation. Now, with respect to the proposition thus limited, I beg leave to refer the reader for a proof of the contrary, to the sixth chapter of the present essay, where the following

---

18. Not a direct quote, but Kames's paraphrase of Hume's position that the interest of society is "the sole foundation of justice and property" (*An Enquiry concerning the Principles of Morals*, 3.34, n. 12, p. 93).

see p. 32-3 (duty & obligations)

propositions are clearly demonstrated, First, that property is founded on an innate sense; and that every violation of property is a moral wrong, attended with remorse, a severe punishment. Next, that property as well as justice are essential to society; and that no society can exist without them. The cause here is mistaken for the effect, precisely as in the other proposition affirming public utility to be the foundation of justice.

A stronger objection cannot lie against any moral system, than that it discords with human nature. Were utility the only foundation of morals, justice would be intitled to a higher degree of approbation, than patriotism, generosity, or any other secondary virtue; because justice undoubtedly is more essential to the public than any of these. The contrary however holds in truth. The transgression of justice meets indeed with severe punishment, remorse in the transgressor and disapprobation from others; while the neglect of any secondary virtue passes with impunity. But the exercise of justice meets with little approbation compared with what is bestowed upon the exercise of any secondary virtue. The reason of the difference is obvious. Generosity and other secondary virtues being voluntary, the man thinks himself highly obliged who profits by them. No man thinks himself obliged by an act of justice, because every one is bound to be just.

I conclude this branch of the system with a few reflections. That man is a social animal, is evident from his appetite for society, and from various principles directing his conduct in it. Were he not endued with a sense of property and with a sense of right and wrong, he would in society resemble lions and leopards that have no appetite for society. Even in so simple a thing as the taking nourishment, he is not left to reason as his sole guide; but is provided with an appetite for food, a faithful monitor, directing both the time and the quantity. But your great philosophers take no pleasure to dissect the human heart; though that anatomy be necessary for unfolding the true system of nature. They love to surprise the world with some pompuous system, entirely their own. A complete system of morals is erected upon self-love, or upon benevolence, or upon utility, or upon a play of imagination. Such bold structures may charm by their novelty; but cannot long stand the test of cool investigation. The late Lord Bolinbroke, the vainest of writers, exceeds all in affectation of singularity. He gravely maintains, that compassion has not for its foundation any instinct or innate principle.[19] Yet for this strange doctrine he can find no better reason, than that savages and men-eaters seem to have as strong an instinct for cruelty as for compassion. Could that profound philosopher be ignorant of what every school-boy knows, that man is composed of different principles and passions, prevailing, sometimes one, sometimes another, according to circumstances? But whatever may be imagined by writers ambitious of singularity, men of plain sense will tell them, that both justice and compassion are natural principles; to prove which there is no need of reasoning; because every man who has not a system to defend will acknowledge, that these principles are engraved on his own heart.

Not satisfied with deriving justice and even property from utility as its genuine offspring, the same taste for simplicity has prompted our author to derive also from utility every virtue, so as to rank in the same class with the primary virtues almost every thing that is useful. His notion is, that whatever in character or conduct we approve as useful, is virtue, intitled to moral approbation. He accordingly includes in the class of virtues, every intellectual ability, penetration for example, secrecy, courage, industry. These qualities are indeed useful to the possessor; but to call every thing virtue that is useful, is strangely to pervert the meaning of words. But he does not stop there: moral approbation is applied to qualities still inferior, such as cheerfulness, politeness, wit, and even cleanliness. Nay, he employs a whole section to make out, that bodily strength, beauty, riches, enter into the same class with the primary virtues. He even admits into the same class that quality in a male which characterizes him a *good woman's-man,* "a like principle, says he, operating more extensively is the general source of moral affection and approbation."* What more effectual service to vice could any person do, than in this manner to depretiate virtue?

---

19. In his *Reflections Concerning Innate Moral Principles* (published in 1752, though written in 1724 while he was in exile in France), Henry St. John, Viscount Bolingbroke (1678–1751) argued that self-love was innate while benevolence had to be cultivated by education and experience.

* Page 135. ["'Tis a general remark, that those we call good *women's men,* who have either signaliz'd themselves by their amorous exploits, or whose make of body promises

But virtue will maintain its dignity in spite of all the engines that can be levelled against it. The sense of right and wrong in voluntary actions, is what eminently distinguishes virtue from the many trifling qualities confounded with it by this author. He jumbles all of them into one mass by the test of approbation; and yet has not attempted to give any precise meaning to that term. We approve every thing that is either agreeable or useful; but such approbation is far inferior to what is bestowed on virtuous actions. Is the approbation of a pleasant prospect, of a fine picture, of a commodious habitation, sufficient to denominate such objects virtuous? Our author admits, that it is not sufficient.

> For, says he, though a species of approbation attends inanimate objects when beneficial, it is so weak and so different from the approbation bestowed on beneficial magistrates or statesmen, that they ought not to be ranked under the same class or appellation.*

This is a most unwary concession; for it overturns at one stroke his darling system of utility. A strong approbation is now to be held the criterion of virtue, not utility. A criterion more vague and arbitrary, never certainly entered into the mind of any thinking person: to one of a lively imagination an object would be virtuous, not to one who has but a small share of that faculty: nay, to the same person it would be virtuous or not, as the spirits are high or low. If it be this author's plan to exclude from the moral system inanimate objects, it cannot be from defect of utility; for as many objects of that kind afford both food and raiment, they are highly useful.

I do not recollect that our author has delivered an opinion, whether any of the brute creation ought to be included in his moral system. If utility be made the criterion, all of them cannot be excluded; as many are highly useful by their labour and by affording food and raiment. Upon his rectified system some of them must be included, such as merit high approbation for

---

any extraordinary vigour of that kind, are well receiv'd by the fair sex, and naturally engage the affections even of those, whose virtue prevents any design of ever giving employment to those talents." Hume, *Treatise,* 3.3.5.2.]

* Page 75. [Hume, *An Enquiry Concerning the Principles of Morals,* 5.1, fn. 17, pp. 104–5.]

their many admirable properties; witness the faithfulness of a dog to his master, zeal to serve him, and care of his property. Reflect only upon the gratitude of a lion to Androcles, and many instances of the same kind.[20] This is a pregnant instance how far a man's fancy can mislead him, when he once deviates from the path of nature and truth. As the moral sense is the true criterion of virtue, virtue undoubtedly is confined to the human species, and cannot in any just sense be attributed to any inferior being.

When a system is not founded on nature and truth, it requires much attention to avoid contradictions. Our author here has fallen into a palpable contradiction. He refuses moral approbation to the inanimate objects above mentioned; and yet more than once bestows moral approbation upon riches. They are indeed useful; but is not a fine garden or a commodious habitation also useful? Here I have an opportunity to retort our author's argument.

> Though a species of approbation attends riches, it is so weak and so different from the approbation bestowed on beneficial magistrates or statesmen, that they ought not to be ranked under the same class or appellation.

To soften this contradiction, he admits that the approbation given to riches, to bodily strength, and to other particulars mentioned above, is inferior in degree to what is given to justice and humanity; but still insists, that in both the approbation is of the same kind. If they be of the same kind, disapprobation of their contraries must be also of the same kind. One man betrays his trust, is inhuman to his parents, or ingrateful to his benefactor: another is a sloven, means well but frequently blunders, or is aukward in his address, or blunt in his manners. I appeal to any person, whether the disapprobation be of the same kind in these two examples; whether we feel the least of that indignation against the sloven, which we feel against the

---

20. "Gratitude is the sign of noble souls" is the moral of Aesop's tale of Androcles, in which the escaped slave nursed a wounded lion back to health and the two lived together until both man and lion were captured. When Androcles was thrown to the lion as punishment, he faced not a bloodthirsty adversary but his old and grateful friend. Aesop, *Fables,* retold by Joseph Jacobs, vol. 17, *The Harvard Classics* (New York: Collier & Son, 1909–14).

betrayer. To this strange conclusion our author is led by making approbation depend entirely on utility. Was he ignorant, that approbation, as far
as concerns virtue, is founded on the moral sense? By that sense certain
actions are perceived to be right, and are approved accordingly as virtuous.
The most illiterate rustic would have told him simply, that to be honest or
to be grateful is right; and there he would stop, never having thought of
their useful tendency. Does not this evince, that men are directed by the
internal light of conscience to approve virtuous actions? Could our author
hope to escape a sneer, in contending that female chastity has no foundation
but a conviction of its utility?* That it is a virtue highly beneficial to society,
will readily be admitted. But when the chastity of a virtuous woman is
attacked, did he seriously think, that there is nothing to protect her innocence, but regard to public utility? Is there no such thing as a principle
of chastity, of honour, or of pride, to guard her in the critical minute?

An objection lies against this system, still more weighty. If utility be the
sole foundation of morality, it is to me evident, that duty and obligation
have no meaning that can distinguish them from benevolence, generosity,
or friendly affection. In the section on that head, duty is resolved into a
motive from interest, directing us to acquire those laudable qualities which
experience points out to be so useful. This confounds all, as no perception
differs more from another than that of duty from that of interest. That they
often appear in opposition is severely felt by the interested, when barred by
duty from doing what would redound much to their profit. From the beginning to the end of the Enquiry, Mr. Hume appears to have totally overlooked that innate sense of duty, that authority of conscience, which is a
law to man, regulating his conduct in society. Had he given more attention
to facts and less scope to invention he could not have erred. If there be ideas
corresponding to the words *duty, obligation, ought* and *should,* they undoubtedly imply something beyond an interested motive. If not, the miser
is under the same obligation to augment his stores, that the honest man is
to pay a debt or perform a promise.

* Page 66. [Hume argues that chastity, like justice, is an artificial virtue, based on
social utility (*An Enquiry concerning the Principles of Morals,* 4.5–7, pp. 100–101). Also
see the *Treatise,* 3.2.12. pp. 364–6.]

But now having followed this author through many intricate mazes, it appears to me demonstrable even from his own admission, that utility cannot be the foundation of morals. He fairly admits, that benevolence is in some measure the object of immediate approbation; but at the same time contends, "that at least a part of the merit of benevolence arises from its tendency to promote the interest of our species and to bestow happiness on human society."* I admit on my part, that not a part only, but the whole merit of benevolence arises from that tendency; and that the same holds of every social virtue. But this will not answer the author's intention of elevating utility above benevolence. On the contrary, the whole merit of utility arises evidently from benevolence. Is it not benevolence that interests me in the welfare of a fellow creature, that makes me rejoice with him in good fortune, and sympathise with him in affliction? Laying aside benevolence, it would not concern me whether my neighbours or even my relations, are happy or miserable. Here then, as in some former instances, the author has mistaken the effect for the cause. Actions done to promote the happiness of others, are approved: but is not benevolence the ground of the approbation? Supposing envy or malice to be the universal passion, utility would be odious in the sight of all men.

But though I am clear that the merit of utility is derived from benevolence, I am far from adopting Doctor Hutcheson's system, of morality being entirely founded on benevolence. Benevolence is justly entitled to a decisive vote in every action that is left to our own choice; but in none that concern right and wrong has it any authority. It would be iniquity in a judge to make benevolence his rule in any decision. Justice enforces payment of debt and performance of covenants, without regard to the circumstances of the person bound, whether rich or poor. Benevolence will not justify a man for a donation even to the most indigent, if his funds be not sufficient for every claim that can justly be made upon him. I repeat it again and again, that the true and solid foundation of morality is the moral sense, independent of which the terms *right* and *wrong, approbation* and *disapprobation, praise* and *blame,* would have no meaning when apply'd to human actions.

* Page 31. [*An Enquiry concerning the Principles of Morals,* 2.22, p. 82.]

I am not however for banishing utility out of the moral system. I admit, that by a reflex mental act, it may become an additional motive to justice and to every other moral action. Justice with regard to utility resembles food. Justice is useful, so is food; and nature has provided us with an appetite for both. But appetite, not utility, is the fundamental cause that moves us to do justice as well as to take food. Utility indeed, by a reflex act, may be an additional motive for both.

I conclude with observing, that man is a complex machine, complex no less in mind than in body. The only way to acquire knowledge of either, is carefully and patiently to investigate its various springs and movements. We are at least more likely to discover the truth in that way, than by seizing hastily a single principle, and erecting upon it an entire system. Morality lays claim to the first place among the sciences; and justly, because its tendency is to regulate our conduct. It therefore concerns all men to have the principles of that science firmly established, and their consequences accurately traced. In many branches of knowledge, we may err without much prejudice to ourselves or to others; but in the moral system, there is scarce an error but what is fatal.

Will the reader indulge me a few words more, to express some concern I feel for myself. The arguments urged in the Enquiry, appear inferior to the other productions of an author, who was justly esteemed the greatest philosopher of his time; and people will be apt to suspect, that I have disguised these arguments, in order for victory. The world will judge, as I have quoted chapter and verse. I am fond however of any apology I can make for Mr. Hume. That justice is an artificial virtue, was a favorite doctrine of his, early adopted, so as to become in him a sort of natural principle. And every one knows, that arguments upon a favourite opinion, commonly appear conclusive, while arguments against it are heard with a deaf ear, or rejected without examination. It is indeed mortifying, to find human reason so frequently led astray by partiality and prejudice, not only in religious matters, but in every science. Did controversial writers keep this bias always in view, they would be more moderate than they commonly are. Whatever prejudice I may have against the doctrines of the Enquiry, my conscience acquits me of any prejudice against the author. Our friendship was sincere while he lived, without ever a difference, except in matters of opinion. I never was addicted to controversy; and would have avoided the attacking a gentleman who had both my love and esteem, had it been consistent with the plan of the present work.

Liberty and Necessity

When we apply our thoughts to final causes, no subject more readily presents itself than the material world, which is stamped with the brightest characters of wisdom and goodness. The moral world, being less in view, hath been generally overlooked, though it yields not to the other in rich materials. Man's inward system will be found no less admirable, than the external system of which he makes a part. The subject is the more curious, that the traces of wisdom and design discernible in our internal frame, lie more out of common sight. They are touches, as it were, of a finer pencil and of a nicer hand, than are discovered in the material world. Thought is more subtile than motion; and more of exquisite art is displayed in the laws of voluntary action, than in the laws of mere matter.[i]

That nothing can happen without a cause, is a principle embraced by all men, the illiterate and ignorant as well as the learned. Nothing that happens is conceived as happening of itself, but as an *effect* produced by some other thing. However ignorant of the cause, we notwithstanding conclude, that every thing which happens must have a cause. We should perhaps be at a loss to deduce this proposition from any premises, by a chain of reasoning. But perception affords conviction, where reason leaves us in the dark. We perceive the proposition to be true. Curiosity is one of the earliest emotions that are discovered in children; and about nothing are they more curious, than to have causes and reasons given them, why such a thing happened or how it came about. Historians and politicians make it their chief concern, to trace the causes of actions, the most mysterious not excepted. Be an event ever so extraordinary, the sense of its being an effect, is not in the least weakened, even with the vulgar; who, rather than assign

97

no cause, recur to the operation of invisible powers. What is a cause with respect to its proper effect, is considered as an effect with respect to some prior cause, and so backward, without end. Events thus viewed in a chain of causes and effects, should naturally be considered, one would think, as necessary and fixed: for the relation betwixt a cause and its effect implies somewhat precise and determinate, and leads our thoughts to what must be, and cannot be otherways than it is.

That we have such a sense as is above described, cannot be controverted; and yet, when we search farther into human nature, a sense of chance or contingency in events seems to be no less deeply rooted in our nature than the former. This sense of chance or contingency is most conspicuous when we look forward to future events. Some things we indeed always consider as certain or necessary; such as, the revolution of seasons, and the rising and setting of the sun. These as experience teacheth, are regulated by fixed laws. But many things appear to us loose, fortuitous, uncertain; uncertain not only with respect to us on account of our ignorance of the cause, but uncertain in themselves, or not tied down and predetermined to fall out by any invariable law. We naturally make a distinction betwixt things that *must be,* and things that *may be,* or *may not be.* Thus, with respect to future events, we have a sense of chance, or of contingency, which seems to banish the other sense of the dependency of events upon precise and determinate causes.

When we consider in what view our own actions are perceived by the mind, there is somewhat equally strange and mysterious. It is admitted by all men, that we act from motives. The plain man, as well as the philosopher, perceives the connection betwixt an action and its motive to be so strong, that from this perception both of them reason with full confidence about the future actions of others. That an avaritious man will take every fair opportunity of acquiring riches, is as little doubted, as that rain and sunshine will make plants grow. The motive of gain is judged to operate as certainly and infallibly upon his temper, as heat and moisture upon the soil, each to produce its proper effect. If we be uncertain what part any particular man will act, the uncertainty ariseth not from our doubting whether he will act from a motive, for this is never called in question: it ariseth from our not being able to judge, what motive will prevail. If so, it should seem, that all the train of human actions would occur to the mind as necessary and fixed. Yet human actions do not always appear to us in that light. Previous to any particular action, we indeed always judge, that it will be the necessary result of some motive. But in a retrospect the judgment seems to vary. Hath a man done what is wrong and shameful? we accuse, and we condemn him for acting the wrong and shameful part. We conceive that he had power to act otherwise, and *ought* to have acted otherwise. Nay he himself gives the same impartial judgment of his conduct. The whole train of our perceptions, in a moment, accommodate themselves to the supposition of his being a free agent.

These are phaenomena in human nature of a singular kind; perceptions that clash with each other; every past event admitted to have a necessary cause, and yet many future events supposed contingent; every future action admitted to be necessary, and yet many actions, in an after view, judged free. Our perceptions are no doubt the test of truth; and the few exceptions that are discovered by reason or experience, serve the more to confirm the general rule. But the perceptions now laid open can be no test of truth; because, in contradictory propositions, truth cannot lie on both sides. There is no other way to get out of this labyrinth of doubts and difficulties, but to enter upon a strict survey both of the material and moral world, which may possibly lead to a discovery of what is really the truth. Let us then proceed with impartiality and attention, to inquire what we are to believe concerning contingency in events, and liberty or necessity in human actions: whether our perceptions can be reconciled to each other, and reconciled to truth; or whether there be not here some delusion.

Taking a view of the material world, we find all things there proceeding in a fixed and settled train of causes and effects. It is a point indisputable, that all the changes produced in matter and all the different modifications it assumes, are the result of fixed laws. Every effect is so precisely determined, that no other effect could, in such circumstances, have resulted from the operation of the cause: which holds even in the minutest changes of the different elements, as all philosophers admit. Casual and fluctuating as these seem, even their slightest variations are the result of pre-established laws. There is a chain of causes and effects which hang one upon another, running through this whole system; and not the smallest link of the chain can be broken, without altering the whole constitution of things, or suspending the regular operation of the laws of nature. Here then, in the material world, there is nothing that can be called *contingent;* nothing that is left loose; but every thing must be precisely what it is, and be found in that state in which we find it.

In the moral world, this necessary chain of causes and effects appears not so clearly.

> Man is the actor here. He is endued with will, and he acts from choice. He hath a power of beginning motion, which is subject to no mechanical laws; and therefore he is not under what is called physical necessity. He hath appetites and passions which prompt him to gratify them: but he is under no necessity of blindly submitting to their impulse. For reason hath a power of restraint. It suggests motives from the cool views of good and evil. He deliberates upon these. In consequence of his deliberation he chuseth: and here lies our liberty.[1]

Let us examine to what this liberty amounts. That motives have some influence in determining the mind, is certain; and that they have this influence in different degrees, is equally certain. The sense of honour and gratitude for example, are powerful motives with a man to serve a friend. Let the man's private interest concur; and the motives become more powerful. Add the certain prospect of poverty, shame, or bodily suffering, if he shall act a different part; and you leave him no choice; the motives to action become irresistible. Motives being once allowed to have a determining influence in any degree, it is easy to suppose the influence so augmented, whether of the same or of accumulated motives, as to leave little freedom to the mind, or rather none at all. In such a case, there is no denying that we are under a necessity to act. And though this arises from the constitution of the mind, not from external compulsion; yet in this case the consequence is no less certain, fixed, and unavoidable, than in that of external compulsion. So evident this is, that, in some instances, moral and physical necessity seem to coincide, or scarcely to be distinguished. A criminal walks to the

---

1. Here Kames quotes his own words, from Essay III, "Of Liberty and Necessity" (pp. 162–3) of the first edition of his *Essays* (for textual variations between the three editions, see Appendix).

scaffold in the midst of his guards. No man will deny that he is under an absolute necessity in this case. Why? because he knows, that if he refuse to go, they will drag him. I ask, Is this a physical or a moral necessity? The answer at first view is not obvious. And yet, strictly speaking, the necessity is only moral: for it is the force of a motive that determines the criminal to walk to the scaffold; to wit, that resistence is vain. The idea of necessity however in the mind of the spectators, when they view the criminal in this situation, is no less strong, than if they saw him bound and carried on a sledge. Nothing is more common, than to talk of an action which one must do, and cannot avoid. He was compelled to it, we say, and it was impossible he could act otherwise; when all the compulsion we mean, is only the application of some very strong motive to the mind. This shows, that, in the judgment of all men, a motive may, in certain circumstances, carry in it the power of rendering an action necessary. In other words, we expect such an action in consequence of such a motive, with equal confidence, as when we expect to see a stone fall to the ground when dropped from the hand.

> This, it will be said, may hold in some instances, but not in all. For, in the greater part of human actions, there is really a sense of liberty. When the mind hesitates betwixt two things, examines and compares, and at last resolves, is there any compulsion or necessity here?[2]

No compulsion, it is granted; but as to necessity, let us pause, and examine more accurately. The resolution being taken, the choice being made, upon what is it founded? Certainly upon some reason or motive, however silent or weak. No man in his senses ever made choice of one thing before another, without being able to assign a reason, weak or strong, for the preference. It would be a pregnant mark of idiocy, to say that one has come to a resolution and cannot say why. If this be an undoubted fact, it follows that the determination must result from that motive which has the greatest influence for the time; or from what appears the best and most eligible upon the whole. If motives be different with regard to strength and influence, which is plainly the case; it is involved in the very idea of the strongest motive, that it must have the strongest effect in determining the mind. This can

---

2. Another direct quotation from the first edition of the *Essays* (pp. 166–7).

no more be doubted, than that in a balance the greater weight must turn the scale.

Here perhaps we shall be interrupted. "Men are not always rational in their determinations: they often act from whim, passion, humor, motives loose and variable as the wind." This is admitted. But suppose the motive that determines the mind to be as whimsical and unreasonable as you please; its influence however is equally necessary with that of the most rational motive. An indolent man, for example, is incited to action, by the strongest considerations that reason, virtue, interest, can suggest. He wavers and hesitates: at last resists them all, and folds his arms. What is the cause of this odd choice? Is it that he is less under the power of motives than another man? Love of rest is his motive, his prevailing passion; which is as effectual to fix him in his place, as the love of glory or riches are to actuate the vain or the covetous. In short, if motives be not under our power or direction, which is confessedly the fact, we are necessary agents. In acting by blind impulse or instinct, we are obviously necessary agents: and with regard to matters that admit deliberation and choice, such is our constitution, that we cannot exert a single action, but with some view, aim, or purpose. And when two opposite motives present themselves, we have not the power of an arbitrary choice: we are necessarily determined to prefer the stronger motive.

It is true, that, in debating upon human liberty, a man may attempt to show that motives have no necessary influence, by eating perhaps the worst apple that is before him, or, in some such trifling matter, preferring an obviously less good to a greater. But is it not plain, that the humor of showing that he can act against motives, is the very motive of the whimsical preference?

Comparing the laws that govern human actions with those that govern the actions of matter, they will be found equally operative, and their effects equally necessary. Where the motives to any action are perfectly full, cogent, and clear, the sense of liberty, as we showed before, entirely vanisheth. In other cases, where the field of choice is wider, and where opposite motives counterbalance and work against each other, the mind fluctuates for a while, and feels itself more loose: but at last, must as necessarily be determined to the side of the most powerful motive, as the balance, after several vibrations, to the side of the preponderating weight. The laws of mind, and the laws of matter, are in this respect perfectly similar; though, in making the comparison, we are apt to deceive ourselves. In forming a notion of physical necessity, we seldom think of any force, but what hath visibly a full effect. A man in prison, or tied to a post, must remain there: if dragged along, he cannot resist. Whereas motives, which are very different, do not always produce sensible effects. Yet, when the comparison is accurately instituted, the very same thing holds in the actions of matter. A weak motive makes some impression: but, in opposition to one more powerful, it has no effect to determine the mind. In the precise same manner, a small force will not overcome a great resistance; nor an ounce in one scale, counterbalance a pound in the other. Comparing together the actions of mind and of matter, similar causes will in both equally produce similar effects.

But admitting all that hath been contended for, of the necessary influence of motives to bring on the choice or last judgment of the understanding, it is urged by Dr. Clarke, that man is still a free agent, because he hath a power of acting or beginning motion according to his will. In this he placeth human liberty, that motives are not physical efficient causes of motion.*[ii] Man is a free agent undoubtedly, because he acts as he wills; but he is equally a necessary agent, as being necessarily influenced by motives to act. The motive, according to his own concession, necessarily determines the will; and the will necessarily produces the action, unless it be obstructed by some foreign force. "But," says he, "it is only a moral necessity which is produced by motives; and a moral necessity is no necessity at all, being consistent with the highest liberty." The Doctor's error lies in opposing moral necessity to liberty. Man is a free agent, because he acts according to

---

* Vid. his Demonstration of the Being and Attributes, p. 565. fol. edit. and his answer to Collins *Passim*. [Kames quotes from Proposition X, "The Self-Existent Being, the Supreme Cause of all Things, must of Necessity have Infinite Powers," of Samuel Clarke's *A Demonstration of the Being and Attributes of God*, in *A Discourse concerning the Being and Attributes of God*, p. 98. Clarke engaged in a series of published exchanges with the freethinker Anthony Collins (1676–1729) over the question of divine will and human agency, and responded to Collins's *Philosophical Inquiry concerning Human Liberty* (1717) with his *Remarks upon a Book, Entituled, A Philosophical Enquiry concerning Human Liberty* (1717).]

his own will. He is at the same time a necessary agent, because his will is necessarily influenced by motives. These are perfectly consistent. The laws of action which respect the human mind, are as fixed as those which respect matter. The idea of *necessary, certain, unavoidable,* equally agrees to both.

One great source of confusion, in reflecting upon this subject, seems to be, our not distinguishing betwixt *necessity* and *constraint.* In common language, these are used as equivalent terms; but they ought to be distinguished when we treat of this subject. A person having a strong desire to escape, remains in prison because the doors are guarded. Finding his keepers gone, he makes his escape. His escape now is as necessary, *i.e.* as certain and infallible a consequence of the circumstances he finds himself in, as his confinement was before; though in the one case there is constraint, in the other none. When, being under no constraint, we act according to our inclination and choice, our actions are justly reckoned free. At the same time they are strictly necessary; because every inclination and choice is unavoidably caused or occasioned by the prevailing motive.

The preceding reasonings may perhaps make a stronger impression upon being reduced into a short argument, after the following manner. When a being acts merely by instinct and without any view to consequences, every one must see that it acts necessarily. Though not so obvious, the case comes to the same where an action is exerted in order to bring about some end or event. This end or event must be the object of desire; for no man in his senses who uses means in order to a certain end, but must desire the means to be effectual: if we do not desire to accomplish an event, we cannot possibly act in order to bring it about. Desire and action are then intimately connected; so intimately, that no action can be exerted where there is no antecedent desire: the event is first the object of desire, and then we act in order to bring it about. This being so, it follows clearly, that our actions cannot be free in any sense opposed to their being morally necessary. Our desires obviously are not under our own power, but are raised by means that depend not upon us. And if our desires are not under our power, neither can our actions be under our power. Liberty, as opposed to moral necessity, if it have any meaning, must signify a power to act in contradiction to desire; or, in other words, a power to act in contradiction to any view, purpose, or design, we can have in acting; which power, beside that no man was ever conscious of it, seems to be an absurdity altogether inconsistent with a rational being.

With regard to things supposed so equal as to found no preference of one to another, it is not necessary to enter into any intricate inquiry how the mind in such cases is directed. Though it should be admitted, that where there is no motive to influence the mind, it may act arbitrarily; this would not affect the preceding reasonings, which suppose the existence of a prevailing motive. Objects balanced one against another with perfect equality, if such are to be found, must be so few and in matters so trivial (as in the common instance of eggs) that they cannot have any considerable influence upon the chain of causes and effects. It may well admit of a doubt, whether the mind be in any case left altogether destitute of a motive to determine its choice betwixt two objects: for though the objects should in themselves be perfectly equal, yet various unobserved circumstances of fancy, custom, proximity of place, &c. may turn the scale in favour of one of the objects. In this state of suspense, betwixt two things equally balanced, the uneasiness one feels, searching and casting about for some ground of choice, proves, that to act altogether arbitrarily is unnatural, and that our constitution fits us to be determined by motives.

As there is scarce room for overdoing in explaining the doctrine of moral necessity, which in some particulars goes cross to vulgar notions, I shall endeavour to set it in a clear light, by opposing it to physical necessity. In the first place, a man under the influence of a physical cause is passive: he is acted upon, and doth not act. Under the influence of a moral cause, he himself acts; and the moral cause operates by influencing and determining him to act. Secondly, a physical cause is generally exerted against a man's inclination and will. If the force applied overcome his resistance, he must submit; and in this case, the necessity is involuntary: it is constraint or co-action.* On the other hand, moral necessity is always *voluntary*. A moral

---

* Physical necessity, however, is not always involuntary. Force may be applied to bring about an agreeable event. In this case the necessity is *voluntary*. A ship having in a storm lost its masts and rigging, is driven towards the port by a violent wind: the seamen being under the power of physical necessity, are entirely passive; but their desire is to be on shore. The necessity they are under, corresponds with their desire, and is thereby *vol-*

cause operates not by force or coaction, but by solicitation and persuasion. It applies to the judgment, and generally affords conviction. But whether or no, it never fails to succeed with the sensitive part of our nature, by raising desire; and when a man is under no restraint, he naturally and necessarily proceeds to action, in order to accomplish his desire. The action is performed as a means to an end. It is directed by will, and is in the strictest sense voluntary. It is at the same time necessary: for such is the nature of man, that desire always determines the will. The necessity here is of the same kind with that of being pleased with a beautiful object, or of being displeased with one that is ugly. But as this necessity is altogether voluntary, it is directly opposite to what arises from external force. Thirdly, physical necessity, except when voluntary which rarely happens, is extremely disagreeable. But moral necessity, which is always voluntary, is for that reason always agreeable. To nothing is human nature more averse than to constraint: on the other hand, our condition is always agreeable when we enjoy the freedom of our own will. Fourthly, a man impelled by a physical cause and acted upon involuntarily, must be sensible of the force and coaction, and consequently of the necessity he is under. A moral cause is in a very different condition. As it influences by persuasion, and not force, it may well be supposed to operate without discovering itself to be a necessary cause. And in fact that it so operates, is evident from constant experience. And hence the ignorance, almost universal, of our being necessary agents.

And this luckily suggests a comparison between moral necessity, and a power to act against motives, termed commonly *liberty of indifference*. To convince men that they are necessary agents, is I am sensible a difficult undertaking. Voluntary necessity is in the course of life never felt; and for that reason we find in common language no term for it. It is not otherways discoverable, but by a long chain of abstract reasoning. It is therefore known to philosophers only, who give it the name of *moral necessity*. Hence it is, that when we talk of necessity, the gross of mankind are apt to take the alarm; because they can form no idea of necessity, different from that of constraint, where the necessity is involuntary. We have thus natural prej-

---

untary. Elias was translated to heaven in a chariot of fire. The necessity was physical, but it was also voluntary. [The reference to Elias comes from 2 Kings 2:11.]

udice and prepossession to struggle with, which are not to be surmounted till the heart be prepared to receive a favourable impression. The comparison proposed will, I am hopeful, place moral necessity in a light to be generally relished. Moral necessity, as has been observed, is always agreeable. An action, provided it be voluntary, is not the less agreeable by being necessary: so far from it, that the necessity and agreeableness are inseparable, as proceeding from the same cause. An action is necessary, because it is directed by desire: it is at the same time agreeable, because it tends to the accomplishment of desire. And from this it clearly follows, that the greater the necessity is, the greater must also be the pleasure. And now to the other member of the comparison. It is difficult to form a conception of a power to act, without motives or any thing to influence the mind. But supposing such a power, it must be devoid of all pleasure or satisfaction, even when exercised without crossing any appetite or passion. It is still more difficult to form a conception of a power to act in contradiction to motives, or in other words in contradiction to desire. But such power, if it can exist, must be extremely disagreeable: for here a man acting in contradiction to his desires, must of course render himself miserable. In this particular, liberty of indifference resembles perfectly physical necessity: for when a man lies open to have his most rational and best-concerted schemes disappointed, it comes to the same in point of distress, whether the disappointment be occasioned by an internal or an external cause. Imagine a person constantly at my elbow, who contradicts me in every thing, would not I be a miserable being? Instead of such a person, imagine a power within the breast of every man, ready to cross all his inclinations, his most innocent desires, his firmest resolves, would any thing be wanting to render him the most unhappy of all beings?

But now a thought comes across the mind that demands attention. How hard is the lot of the human species, to be thus tied down, and fixed by motives; subjected by a necessary law to the choice of evil, if evil happen to be the prevailing motive, or if it mislead us under the form of our greatest interest or good! How happy to have had a free independent power of acting contrary to motives, when the prevailing motive hath a bad tendency! By this power we might have pushed our way to virtue and happiness, whatever motives were suggested by vice and folly to draw us back; or we might by arbitrary will have refrained from acting the bad part, though all the power of motives concurred to urge us on. So far well. But may not this arbitrary power be exerted against good motives as well as against bad ones? If it do good in restraining us from vice, may it not do ill in restraining us from virtue? and so shall we not be thrown loose altogether? At this rate, we could not rely on any man. Promises, oaths, vows, would be vain; for nothing can ever bind or fix one who is influenced by no motive. The distinction of characters would be at an end; for a person cannot have a character who hath no fixed nor uniform principle of action. Nay, moral virtue itself and all the force of law, rule, and obligation, would upon this hypothesis be nothing; for no creature can be the subject of rational or moral government, whose actions, by the constitution of its nature, are independent of motives, and whose will is capricious and arbitrary. To exhort, to instruct, to promise, to threaten, would be to no purpose. In short, such a creature, if such could exist, would be a most bizarre and unaccountable being; a mere absurdity in nature, whose existence could serve no end. Were we so constituted as always to be determined by the moral sense, even against the strongest countermotives; this would be consistent with human nature, because it would preserve entire the connection unalterably established betwixt the will and the prevailing motive. But to break this connection altogether; to introduce an unbounded arbitrary liberty in opposition to motives, would be, instead of amending, to deform and unhinge the human constitution. No reason have we therefore to regret, that we find the will necessarily subjected to motives; unless we would have man to be a whimsical and ridiculous being.[iii]

In the course of this reasoning, we have abstracted from all controversies about divine prescience and decree. Though from what hath been proved it appears, that the Divine Being decreed all future events: for he who gave such a nature to his creatures, and placed them in such circumstances, as that a certain train of actions must necessarily follow; did certainly resolve or decree, that events should fall out, and men should act as they do. Prescience indeed is not, properly speaking, any cause of events: for events do not happen because they are foreseen, but because they are to happen, they are capable of being foreseen. Though prescience doth not cause, yet it undoubtedly supposes, the certain futurition (as schoolmen speak) of events. And were there not causes that render the existence of future events certain, it would involve a contradiction to maintain, that future events could be certainly foreseen.[iv]

In *Sketches of the History of Man,* the argument here insisted on is brought within a narrow compass.

> With respect to instinctive actions, no man I presume thinks there is any freedom: an infant applies to the nipple, and a bird builds a nest, no less necessarily than a stone falls to the ground. With respect to voluntary actions, the necessity is the same, tho' less apparent at first view. The external action is determined by the will, the will is determined by desire, and desire by what is agreeable or disagreeable. Here is a chain of causes and effects, not one link of which is arbitrary, or under command of the agent. He cannot act but according to his will: he cannot will but according to his desire: he cannot desire but according to what is agreeable or disagreeable in the objects perceived. Nor do these qualities depend on his inclination or fancy: he has no power to make a beautiful woman appear ugly, nor to make a rotten carcase smell sweet.*

Thus, after a deep and diligent investigation, it is discovered, that moral necessity and prescience in the Deity are perfectly consistent with liberty or absolute freedom in acting; a seeming paradox which that acute and penetrating philosopher Mr. Locke despaired ever to explain. In a letter to Mr. Molyneux he writes,

> I own freely to you the weakness of my understanding, that though it be unquestionable that there is omnipotence and omniscience in God our Maker, and though I cannot have a clearer perception of any thing than that I am free; yet I cannot make freedom in man consistent with omnipotence and omniscience in God, though I am as fully persuaded of both as of any truth I most firmly assent to: and therefore I have long since given off the consideration of that question; resolving all into this short

---

* Vol. IV. p. 95. Edit. 2d. [From "Liberty and necessity considered with respect to morality," in Kames, *Sketches of the History of Man,* vol. 4, bk. 3, sketch 8. As Kames notes at the end of this sketch (p. 118), his discussion is an abridgement of the essay "Of Liberty and Necessity" from the *Essays,* parts of which were also published in the second edition (1767) of the *Principles of Equity* (1st ed. 1760).]

conclusion, That if it be possible for God to make a free agent, then man is free, though I see not the way of it.

On voit la liberté, cette esclave si fiere,
Par d'invisibles noeuds en ces lieux prisonniere;
Sous un joug inconnu, que rien ne peut briser,
Dieu fait l'assujétir sans la tyranniser;
A ses supremes loix d'autant mieux attachée,
Que sa chaine a ses yeux pour jamais est cachée.
Qu'en obeissant meme elle agit par son choix,
Et souvent aux destins pense donner des loix.
Voltaire Henriade.[3]

The sum of what is discovered concerning the impressions we have of contingency in events, and liberty in actions, is this. Comparing together the moral and the material world, every thing is as much the result of established laws in the one as in the other. There is nothing in the whole universe that can properly be called contingent, that may be, or may not be; nothing loose and fluctuating in any part of nature: but every motion in the material, and every action in the moral world, are directed by immutable laws; so that, whilst these laws remain in force, not the smallest

---

3. Locke to Molyneux, Jan. 1692–3, *Some Familiar Letters between Locke and several of his Friends,* in *The Works of John Locke,* 12th ed., 10 vols. (London, 1823), 8:304. William Molyneux (1656–1698), Anglo-Irish mathematician and astronomer, translated Descartes' *Meditations* into English as *Six metaphysical meditations wherein it is proved that there is a God and that mans mind is really distinct from his body* (London, 1680). Kames cites from part 7 of Voltaire's *La Henriade* (Rouen, France, 1723; English translation, 1728), an epic in ten verses that celebrates the struggles of the Protestant Henry of Navarre (Henri IV) against the Catholic League.

We see liberty, this slave so proud,
Held by invisible knots in these places that are like prisons.
Under an unknown yoke, that nothing can break,
God has subjugated her to his supreme laws,
but without tyranny,
The bond is all the more powerful because the chain
is forever hidden from her eyes,
She thinks she is acting out of free will but she's really obeying,
She thinks that she controls destiny.

link of the universal chain of causes and effects can be broken, nor any one thing be otherwise than it is.*

Against this system I know but of one objection that appears formidable. It is observed above, that though with respect to any future event we constantly judge that it will be the result of some motive, yet that after the event happens the judgement varies: looking back upon any shameful action, we condemn the author as having done wrong; have a conviction that he ought to have acted a better part; and the author himself has the same conviction. Is not this an appeal to every man's own conviction, that he is not a necessary agent; and can he be a necessary agent when he is conscious of the contrary? Let any man consider his own case when stung with remorse for having committed a gross crime: he will acknowledge his being convinced that he might and ought to have restrained his passion, that he is ashamed of himself and repents bitterly. I consider my own case. In a fit of remorse for having injured my best friend, conscience stares me in the face, and condemns me for a deed that even the most violent passion cannot excuse. "I was not deprived of my senses: I knew what I was doing; and yet yielded to an outragious passion, which I ought to have restrained." This objection is stated in the former editions;[4] and the only answer I could find was, that this sentiment relates to physical power only, "that I was compelled by no force, and that I could have acted a right part had I been so inclined." One is easily convinced of a favourite opinion; and in the heat

---

* As to an objection of making God the author of sin, which may seem to arise from our system, it is rather popular than philosophical. Sin, or moral turpitude, lies in the evil intention of him who commits it. It consists in some wrong or depraved affection supposed to be in the sinner. Now the intention of the Deity is unerringly good. The end purposed by him is order and general happiness; and there is the greatest reason to believe, that all events are so directed by him, as to work towards this end. In the present system of things, some moral disorders are indeed included. No doubt it is a considerable difficulty, how evil comes to be in the world, seeing God is perfectly good. But this difficulty is not peculiar to our doctrine; but recurs upon us at last with equal force, whatever hypothesis we embrace. For moral evil cannot exist, without being, at least, permitted by the Deity. And with regard to a first cause, PERMITTING is the same thing with CAUSING; since against his will nothing can possibly happen. All the schemes that have been contrived for answering this objection, are but the tortoise introduced to support the elephant. They put the difficulty a step further off, but never remove it.

4. In the first ed., pp. 197–9; in the second ed., p. 144.

of composition I was satisfied with that answer. But upon a long interval
the subject becoming in a measure new again, I perceived the answer to be
insufficient. After much perplexity, I discovered an answer, which I am con-
fident will be found solid and satisfactory. I take it for granted, that during
a fit of passion instigating one to perpetrate a lawless deed, there is not the
slightest notion of a power to resist; will being the necessary consequence
of desire, as the external act is of will. But no sooner does remorse make
its appearance, than we find it accompanied with the notion of a restraining
power. From the example now given, and from a thousand of the same
kind that may be recollected, there is reason to believe that the notion of
a restraining power constantly attends remorse; and so far they are connected. Further, that the connection is so entire as that the notion of a
restraining power never appears alone, will be evident from the following
example. A man who had long professed himself my friend, takes advantage
of the confidence I have in him, to corrupt my wife. Inflamed with revenge,
I put the infamous betrayer to death. This, it is true, is a crime prohibited
by the law of the land; but I cannot repent of it, nor have any remorse. My
constant reflection is, that not a man of spirit but would have done the
same; and that my revenge was not only just but unavoidable. This example
is given as a copy of human nature, representing what every man of feeling
would think on the like occasion. If so, it follows that where there is no
remorse, there is no notion of liberty or a restraining power after the deed
is committed more than before. Thus, we find that remorse and the notion
of a restraining power are constant companions; and in particular that the
latter never appears without the former. What remains for giving complete
satisfaction, is to make out that it is the nature of remorse to produce that
delusive notion. For this I refer to Elements of Criticism,* where is handled
the irregular influence of passion on our opinions and sentiments. All passions, especially those that are violent, are prone to their gratification. Remorse for an atrocious crime, makes the man odious in his own eyes: it
gratifies his remorse to find himself guilty; and to leave him without excuse,
the passion forces upon him a conviction that he might and ought to have

---

* Chap. 2. Part 5. [Kames refers the reader to his discussion of the "causes of fear and
anger" in *Elements of Criticism,* vol. 1, chap. 2, pt. I, sec. v.]

done otherways. If the unlawful act be so slight or so natural as to give no remorse, the man sees what he has done in its true light, without the disguise of passion. During the act he is not conscious of any restraining power; and as little after. Let any action of that kind be analised, and it will be found, that any notion of a power to act against motives, is intirely owing to the irregular influence of passion. So mighty indeed is its influence, as to force upon a man a sort of conviction of guilt, even where the fact done was accidental so as to admit no notion of a restraining power. A gentleman, directing his pistol to a troublesome cur biting his horse's heels, most unhappily lodged the ball in the breast of a young girl crossing the way. In his cool moments he was conscious of innocence; but at whatever time his imagination painted the sweet and beautiful creature lying dead at his feet, his tender and sensible heart stung him with a sort of remorse, and he could not help condemning himself as rash, impetuous, and in a degree criminal. If the reader wish more light on this curious subject, he will please to cast his eye on *Sketches of the History of Man.** What is here observed with respect to the author himself, is equally applicable to the bystanders. Remorse is gratified in the criminal by a conviction that it was in his power to have restrained his passion. The indignation of the bystanders is equally gratified, by thinking as the guilty person does. But with respect to any slight wrong that raises little or no indignation in others, there is nothing to bias them against truth, more than to bias the actor himself. And now having proved, I hope to the satisfaction of my readers, that this formidable objection is no better than a bugbear, and that any notion we have of a power to act against motives is a delusion of passion not of nature, I rest with entire satisfaction in the necessary chain of causes and effects, which I am thoroughly convinced to be the system of nature. [v]

The doctrine of universal necessity being thus laid open and proved to be the system of nature, we proceed to a most important speculation; which is to consider how far that system is consistent with our moral sentiments, and in particular with those of praise, blame, merit, demerit, guilt, &c. While we continue uncertain as to that point, we cannot have any just or

---

* Vol. IV. page 113. edition 2d. ["Liberty and necessity considered with respect to morality," in Kames, *Sketches,* vol. 4, bk. 3, sketch 8.]

accurate notion of morals. The doctrine of liberty and necessity is in that view worthy of great attention; and in that view chiefly was it undertaken. To find our actions governed by a law repugnant to the foregoing moral sentiments, which are natural and universal, would in the human constitution be a puzzling circumstance. It would argue a defect or inconsistence, not uncommon in works of art, but rare if at all to be found in any work of nature. And yet we have occasion to be alarmed, when we hear the advocates for liberty of indifference reason in the following manner.

> If human actions be necessary, and if we know them to be so, what ground can there be for reprehension and blame, for self condemnation and remorse? If a clock were sensible of its own motions, knowing that they proceed according to necessary laws, could it find fault with itself for striking wrong? Would it not rather blame the artist, who had ill-adjusted the wheels on which its movements depend? They urge accordingly, that upon the system of necessity, the moral constitution of our nature is totally overturned; that there is an end to all the operations of conscience about right and wrong; and that man is no longer a moral agent, nor the subject of praise or blame for what he does.

This is a strong attack upon human nature; and better a thousand times give up the system we have been contending for, than acknowledge that man is incapable of morality. But let us not rashly relinquish a system that is so well supported. Upon a narrower inspection, it may possibly be discovered, that the moral sense is concordant with necessity, and that the connection betwixt desire and will is no obstacle to approbation and disapprobation, praise and blame. To have a just conception of this matter, we must examine carefully by what particular circumstances these moral sentiments are occasioned. I observe, in the first place, that an action is always approved when it proceeds from a virtuous motive, and consequently hath a good aim or tendency. The connection betwixt the motive and the action, so far from diminishing, is the very circumstance that constitutes the morality of the action: the greater the influence of the motive, the greater the virtue of the actor, and the more warm our approbation. Do we not even praise one for modesty or sweetness of temper? The Deity is an object of the highest praise, for the very reason that he is necessarily good. On the other hand, an action is disapproved when it proceeds from a vitious motive; and the more influence the motive had on the agent, the greater his vice, and the more warm our disapprobation. We are so constituted, as to blame ourselves, even when we have the clearest conviction of inability to behave better. A coward is conscious that he has no heart to encounter danger, and that he will certainly turn his back upon the approach of an enemy. Though he cannot overcome this weakness, yet he accuses and blames himself: he cannot help censuring himself in this manner, more than he can help his weakness, or more than he can help being ashamed of it. Upon the same foundations are evidently built our notion of rewards and punishments. If virtue ought to be rewarded, the man hath the best claim who is virtuous by the constitution of his nature, and upon whom a vitious motive hath no influence. On the other hand, no man is more guilty or more deserving of punishment, than he who by his nature hath the strongest propensity to vice, and upon whom virtuous motives have little or no effect.

But in the foregoing instances it will be urged, that the man we praise or blame had it in his power to act a different part; that we praise him for a benevolent action, or blame him for one that is sordid, because such action was his choice when he could have abstained from it. I admit, that in all our moral sentiments it is understood that the person acts voluntarily, and according to the dictates of his own heart. A man, in doing what is worthy of praise or blame, must be free from external coaction, and at liberty to follow his own choice. This power or freedom, which is perfectly consistent with moral or voluntary necessity, is evidently the only power that morality requires. Supposing only a man to be free to act as he pleases, we currently praise or blame him for the part he acts, without requiring any other condition. We demand not that he should have a power to act in contradiction to his own desire and choice. The idea of such a power enters not into any of our moral sentiments: on the contrary, if the nature of any individual be either so good or so bad, as that he could not avoid being determined to the choice he made, he on that very account is the more praised or blamed.

We then find, that the moral sentiments have their full swing, without supposing liberty of indifference, or any thing like a power to act against our own will. Nor can I even conceive, that such a power, supposing it real, could add any spring or force to the moral sense. When a man commits a crime, let us suppose that he could have resisted the prevailing motive. Why then did he not resist? why did he yield to the vitious motive, and bring upon himself shame and misery? The answer must be, for no other can be given, That his disposition was bad, that he is a wretch, and deserves to be detested and abhorred. Here we clearly see, upon the present supposition as well as upon that of necessity that praise and blame rest ultimately upon the disposition or frame of mind; that a virtuous disposition is the only object of praise, and a vitious disposition the only object of blame. It is therefore a fond conceit, to espouse the chimerical system of liberty of indifference, as necessary to explain our moral sentiments. These sentiments are perfectly concordant with the system of voluntary necessity; and supposing liberty of indifference, we cannot even conceive how it should make man a more proper subject of moral sentiments, than in fact he is, considered as a necessary being.

I proceed one step farther; which is, to make out, that liberty of indifference, far from being implied in the moral sentiments of praise and blame, would in some measure cramp the moral sense, and blunt the sentiments arising from it. In order to put this matter in its true light, I shall state a case. A man tempted to betray his trust, deliberates, wavers, but at last rejects the offered bribe, and adheres to his duty. Another man, without the least deliberation, rejects with disdain the bribe, and considers the offer as a high injury. Which of these persons is the most virtuous and the most praise-worthy, no one is at a loss to say. A power of resisting the strongest motive, must imply a wavering and fluctuation of the mind, betwixt the motive, and the power of resistance; for, by the supposition, the mind has both to chuse on. If so, a man endued with liberty of indifference is justly represented by the person first described, fluctuating and wavering betwixt a virtuous and vitious motive; and upon that account the actions of a man endued with liberty of indifference, will, in the estimation of all mankind, be less praise or blame worthy, than the actions of a man who is unerringly directed by the strongest motive without wavering or fluctuating. And indeed, it would sound extremely harsh, that a good or an evil tendency, so slight as to leave power in the mind to resist it, should be an object of greater praise or blame, than a tendency so strong as to leave no power of resistance. Viewing the matter in this light, it evidently appears, that a power to act against motives, so far from being necessary to found praise or blame, would, if it really did exist, detract considerably from both.

Having showed that our moral sentiments are perfectly concordant with moral necessity; I urge, in the next place, that no other system of action can lay a better foundation for praise or blame, or for any moral sentiment, than the system of voluntary necessity doth. It is, I hope, made evident, that liberty of indifference or a power to act against motives, lays not so good a foundation; and yet I cannot imagine another system that will better answer the purpose. In judging of moral sentiments, an error is extremely apt to creep in. We have a clear conception, that a man under coaction or external force acts involuntarily, and can neither be praised nor blamed for what he doth. This reflection we unwarily apply to moral necessity, not adverting to the substantial difference betwixt a voluntary and involuntary action. A man in his own conscience is made accountable for every voluntary action: it is not regarded whether he had or had not a power of resistance. And it has been proved, that were that power to be regarded, so far from contributing to praise or blame, it would have no other effect but to lessen both.

The strong prepossession in favour of liberty of indifference, ariseth, I am sensible, from a laudable cause: it is conceived to be more consistent with our sentiments of morality, than the system of necessity is. This opinion is found to be erroneous. A man who is necessarily good or bad by the constitution of his nature, deserves more to be praised or blamed, than if he had a power of resisting all motives, and acting against them. And indeed as every action doth proceed from a virtuous or vitious temper as its primary cause; praise or blame must ultimately rest upon that cause, and not upon the external action, or the power of acting. This consideration ought to make us chearfully abandon a chimerical system, which at the same time is less concordant with the moral sense, than the system of necessity is.

And this leads me to enquire, whence is derived the delusive notion of liberty of indifference; for surely it could not be generally espoused without some foundation. It has been observed, that we have no intuitive perception or direct consciousness of our being necessary agents; and that this branch of our nature is hid from the generality of mankind. The knowledge of it, not being necessary for our well-being, is left to be gathered by reasoning and reflection. We are however intuitively conscious of freedom of action, and of a power existing in us to act according to our will and choice. This power is far from being the same with that of willing and chusing in an arbitrary manner; and yet, in superficial thinking, we are apt to confound these two powers, and to consider them as the same. Power indeed is with mankind a favourite idea, and we are prone to adopt any system which seems to extend it. The operations of the will, beside, are subtile and delicate; and, with the bulk of mankind, a power to chuse, and a power to act according to our choice, though essentially distinct, pass readily for being the same.

Having discovered, that the moral sense is perfectly concordant with moral or voluntary necessity, as also, that we have no such thing naturally as a sense of power to act in contradiction to our inclination and choice; I proceed to a more particular examination of the sense of contingency, in the view chiefly to discover, if possible, whether it have any deeper root in our nature, than the erroneous conviction of liberty of indifference. In our ordinary train of thinking, it is certain, that all events appear not to us as necessary. A multitude of events seem to be under our power to cause or to prevent; and we readily make a distinction betwixt events that are necessary, *i.e.* that must be, and events that are contingent, *i.e.* that may be or may not be. This distinction is void of truth; for all things that fall out either in the material or moral world, are, as we have seen, alike necessary, and alike the result of fixed laws. Yet whatever may be the conviction of a philosopher, the distinction betwixt things necessary and things contingent, possesses his common train of thought, as much as those of the most illiterate. We act universally upon that distinction: nay, it is in truth the cause of all the labour, care, and industry of mankind. I illustrate this doctrine by an example. Constant experience hath taught us, that death is a necessary event. The human frame is not made to last for ever in its present condition; and no man thinks of more than a temporary existence upon this globe. But the particular time of our death appears a contingent event: however certain it be, that the time and manner of a man's death is determined by a train of preceding causes, and is not less fixed than the hour of the sun's rising or setting; yet no person is affected by that doctrine. In the care of prolonging life, we are directed by the supposed contingency of the time of death; which, to a certain term of years, we consider as depending in a great measure on ourselves, by caution against accidents, due use of food, exercise, &c. These means are prosecuted with the same diligence, as if there were in fact no necessary train of causes to fix the period of life. In short, whoever attends to his own practical ideas, whoever reflects upon the meaning of the following words, which occur in all languages, of things *possible, contingent, that are in our power to cause or prevent;* whoever, I say, reflects upon these words, will clearly see, that they suggest certain perceptions or notions, repugnant to the doctrine above established of universal necessity.*

* This deviation of perception from truth, gave rise to the famous debate concerning things possible, among the ancient Stoics, who held the doctrine of universal necessity. Diodorus, as Cicero informs us in his book *De Fato,* cap. 7, held this opinion, *Id solum fieri posse, quod aut verum sit, aut futurum sit verum; at quicquid futurum sit, id dicit fieri necesse esse, et quicquid non sit futurum, id negat fieri posse:* that is, He maintained, there is nothing contingent in future events, nothing possible to happen, but that precise event which will happen. This no doubt, was carrying their system its due length: though, in this way of speaking, there is something that contradicts the preceptions of mankind. Chrysippus, on the other hand, maintained, that it is possible for future events to happen otherways than in fact they happen. This was inconsistent with his general system of necessity; and therefore, as Cicero gives us to understand, he was often imbarrassed in the debate with Diodorus: and Plutarch, in his book *De Repugnantiis Stoicorum,* exposes him for this inconsistency. But Chrysippus chose to follow his natural perceptions, in opposition to philosophy; holding, that Diodorus's doctrine of nothing being possible but what happens, is *ignava ratio,* tending to absolute inaction; *cui si pareamus,* as Cicero expresses it, *nihil omnino agamus in vita.* So early were philosophers sensible of the difficulty of reconciling speculation with perception, as to this doctrine of fate. [Cicero's account of the opinion of Diodorus: "For he says that only what either is true or will be true can happen, and he says that whatever is going to happen must necessarily happen, and that whatever will not happen cannot happen." Cicero, *On Fate* (*De Fato*), ed. and trans. R. W. Sharples (Warminster, England: Aris & Phillips, 1991), 7.13, pp. 64–5; 7.28, pp. 76–7. His characterization of *ignava ratio* ("lazy argument") reads: "If we obeyed this, we would do nothing at all in life." As an example of the inaction caused by lazy argument, Cicero writes that some followers of Diodorus maintain there is no point in calling a doctor when ill, since one is fated either to recover or not recover from the illness. Diodorus Cronus (fl. 3rd. c. B.C.) was a philosopher and dialectician known for his love of logical paradoxes. Chrysippus (ca. 280–207 B.C.) was a leading Stoic known for his book on logic. Plutarch (45–125 A.D.) attacked the doctrines of the Stoics in his *De Repugnantiis Stoicorum* ("On Stoic Self-Contradictions").]

So stands the fact, and the question is, Whence proceeds this delusive sense of contingency? Is it original, or can it otherwise be accounted for? Reflecting upon this subject, I find that uniform events are understood to be necessary, such as day and night, winter and summer, death, &c.; but that events in which there are any degrees of variety, such as the time of death, good or bad weather, &c. are generally understood to be contingent. Does our sense of contingency arise from the uncertainty of the event? Hardly so; for uncertainty cannot naturally have any other effect upon the mind, than to produce a consciousness of our ignorance. The sense of contingency, then, with respect to things uncertain, must be pronounced an original law in our nature. By this law we are made to conceive many future events as in themselves uncertain, and as having no determined cause of existence. Contingency in this view may justly be considered as a secondary quality, which hath no real existence in things; but, like other secondary qualities, is made to appear as an attribute of events, in order to serve the purposes of human life.

This sense of contingency in events, regards not only events in the material world, but also what arise from moral causes, or from the activity of man. The event of a pitched battle betwixt two armies equal in numbers and in discipline, every one deems to be in some measure contingent. When a man wavers in his resolutions, the course he will steer is reckoned a matter of chance or contingency. But how can the sense of contingency in this case be reconciled to the doctrine of our being necessary agents? A sense of necessity would, no doubt, be directly contradictory to the sense of contingency; and both could not subsist together. To make way for the sense of contingency, the necessary connection betwixt desire and will is kept out of sight; and by this contrivance it is, that we are not sensible of being necessary agents. The discovery that we are so, proceeds from a long train of reasoning; and the conviction that arises from a process of reasoning, is too faint to counterbalance an intuitive perception or original sense of contingency. [vi]

The Deity is the primary cause of all things. In his infinite mind he formed the great plan of government, which is carried on by laws fixed and immutable. These laws produce a regular train of causes and effects in the moral as well as material world, bringing about those events which are comprehended in the original plan, and admitting the possibility of none other.

This universe is a vast machine, winded up and set a-going: the several springs and wheels operate unerringly one upon another: the hand advanceth and the clock strikes, precisely as the artist had determined. Whoever hath just ideas, will see this to be the real theory of the universe; and that otherways there can be no general order, no whole, no plan, no means nor end in its administration. In this plan, man bears his part, and fulfils certain ends for which he was designed. He must be an actor, and must act with consciousness of spontaneity. He exercises thought and reason, and his nature is improved by the due use of these powers. Consequently, it is necessary, that he should have some notion of things depending upon himself to cause, that he may be led to a proper exercise of that activity for which he was designed. But as a sense of necessity would be a perpetual contradiction to that activity, it was well ordered, that his being a necessary agent should be hid from him. To have had his perceptions and ideas formed upon the plan of universal necessity, to have seen himself a part of that great machine, winded up and set a-going by the author of his nature; would have been inconsistent with the part that is allotted him to act. Then indeed the *ignava ratio,* the inactive doctrine of the Stoics, would have followed. Conceiving nothing to be contingent, or depending upon himself to cause, there would have been no room for forethought about futurity, nor for any sort of industry and care. He would have had no motives to action, but immediate sensations of pleasure and pain. He must have been formed like the brutes, who have no other principle of action but mere instinct. The few instincts he is at present endued with, would have been insufficient. He must have had an instinct to sow, another to reap; he must have had instincts to pursue every conveniency, and perform every office of life. In short, reason and thought could not have been exercised in the way they are, had not man been furnished with a sense of contingency, and been kept in ignorance of his being a necessary agent. Let the philosopher meditate in his closet upon abstract truth; let him be ever so much convinced of the settled necessary train of causes and effects, which leaves nothing, properly speaking, in his power; yet the moment he comes forth into the world, he acts as a free agent. And, what is wonderful, though in this he acts upon a false supposition, yet he is not thereby misled from the ends of action, but, on the contrary, fulfils them to better advantage. [vii]

So far the second edition, which, with respect to the present article, is

preserved entire as expressing the notion of chance and contingency hitherto universally admitted. But time, productive of many changes, has upon
the thinking part of mankind a great influence in detecting errors. It is now
my opinion, that there is no such thing in nature as a sense of chance or
contingency, such as is described above; that on the contrary our notions
of them are entirely consonant to the system of universal necessity, and
therefore not in any degree delusive. To clear that important subject, I lay
down a preliminary proposition which will have the voice of every thinking
person, namely, that nothing can happen without a cause. This proposition
is the work of nature, and familiar even among children, who are ever solicitous to learn, why such a thing happened, or how it came about. The
most singular events are not made an exception: rather than rest satisfied
without a cause, the vulgar commonly recur to invisible powers. It is indeed
true, that our conviction of a cause is not always equally entire. With respect
to events that happen regularly, such as summer, winter, rising and setting
of the sun, we have an entire conviction of a cause. It is less entire with
respect to irregular events, such as alterations in the weather; and least of
all entire with respect to events that are not only irregular but that seldom
fall out, such as a meteor, a water-spout, or an earthquake. But with respect
to no event whatever, does our conviction of a cause vanish so entirely, as
to give way to a notion of any thing happening without a cause. Chance is
applied to events that have happened: contingency, to future events. By the
expression that such a thing happened by chance, it cannot be meant that
it happened without a cause, or that chance was the cause; for no one ever
imagined that an effect can exist without a cause, or that chance can act
and produce effects. Nothing is or can be meant, but that we are ignorant
of the cause, and that for ought we know the event might have happened
or not happened. With respect to contingency, future events are said to be
contingent when they cannot be foreseen; not that they will happen without
a cause. Chance and contingency thus explained are entirely consistent with
the conviction of universal necessity: they are expressive of our ignorance
only, not of any looseness in the course of events. The first opportunity I
had of publishing this discovery, was in *Sketches of the History of Man;**

---

* Vol. IV. page 118. edition 2d. [*Sketches,* vol. 4, bk. 3, sketch 8.]

where it is more fully handled; particularly, that a firm conviction of universal necessity has no tendency to make us relax in our pursuits, either for our own good or for that of others; more than a delusive sense of contingency would have.* And here I finish the present Essay with the satisfaction of finding the system of universal necessity firmly established, and free from any delusive sense.

* It appears from Homer, that among the Greeks, an inquisitive and enlightened people, the doctrine of fate or destiny prevailed. Yet when a man's destiny was foretold, even by the most celebrated Oracle, it had no effect but to make him more diligent to evade the impending evil. Such authority have natural impressions, in opposition to abstract reasoning, and even to what is held divine authority.

Personal Identity[i]

Every man by nature has a sense of himself and of his own existence; which, for the most part, accompanies every thought and action. I say, for the most part, because this sense does not always operate. In a dead sleep we have no consciousness of self. And even some of our waking thoughts pass without it: during a reverie, the mind never thinks of itself. Without this sense, mankind would be in a perpetual reverie: ideas constantly floating in the mind without ever being connected with self. Neither would there be any notion of personal identity; for a man cannot consider himself to be the same person at different times, when he has no consciousness of himself at all.

This consciousness is of a lively kind. Self-preservation is every one's peculiar care; and the vivacity of that consciousness makes us attentive to our own interest, particularly to shun every appearance of danger: a man in a reverie has no attention to himself. It is remarkable, that one seldom falls asleep till this consciousness vanisheth: its vivacity preserves the mind in motion so as to bar sleep. A purling stream disposes to sleep: it fixes the attention both by sound and sight; and without creating any agitation in the mind, occupies it so much as to make it forget itself. The reading of some books, by similar means, produces the same effect.

The consciousness of self leads me to attribute self to others as I do to myself. When I talk to a person, I say *yourself.* When I talk of a person, I say *his self.* When I talk of a thing, I say *itself.*

I know not by what wrong bias many learned men have been led to think that nothing is to be believed but what can be demonstrated logically. How came they to overlook the evidence of their senses, internal and external, which in instances without number produces conviction superior to that of the strictest demonstration? The celebrated Des Cartes was a great mathematician; and so much accustomed to demonstration, that he would admit no truth but what could be demonstrated in form. So arrant a Quixote was he on this subject, that he was pleased to doubt even of his own existence, till he discovered that notable argument *cogito, ergo sum.*[1] Had he not as good reason to doubt of his thinking as of his existing? Strange! that in a long life the absurdity of this argument never occurred to him. A plain man would have informed him, that every human being has as thorough a conviction of his existence without reasoning, as the most expert mathematician can have with it.

So much for self. We proceed to personal identity. Animals are divided by nature into kinds or species, the individuals of each kind having uniformly the same external figure and internal disposition; but differing in both from the individuals of other kinds. Hence identity of kind in contradistinction to every other kind. Next, though the corporeal part of an animal is continually changing by perspiration and admission, yet it continues the same animal from birth to dissolution, the same with respect to its life, its faculties, its temper and disposition. Thus identity is predicated of an animal in contradistinction to every other animal. What is here said with respect to animals is equally applicable to plants.

Identity is also attributed to works of art, changes in the component parts notwithstanding. A ship may have been repaired at different times, till not a single original rope or plank be left. It is however held to be the same ship, not now from its component parts, but from the same idea being applied to it in all its changes. Law conforms itself to this sort of identity: a man is entitled to have a watch he had lost restored to him, considerable alterations in its constituent parts notwithstanding. The identity of a river cannot depend on the water, which is continually flowing; nor on the bed, which frequently changes, but on the same idea being invariably attributed to it in all its changes. The name of a ship, of a river, or of any work of art, tends to keep the mind steady in its idea of their identity. The identity of an animal or of a plant is the work of nature, independent of our ideas:

---

1. René Descartes, *Discourse on Method* (1637; reprint, trans. Donald A. Cress, Indianapolis: Hackett Publishing, 1998), pt. 4, p. 18.

the identity of a work of art through its different changes, depends intirely on our ideas.

Every one knows that there are different species of animals and plants, and can readily apply identity to one species in contradistinction to others. It is still more obvious to apply identity to an individual, in contradistinction to any other individual of whatever species. The means by which that knowledge is obtained, require to be explained, for they are not obvious. There is no difficulty with respect to works of art, the identity of which depends on our own ideas. But the identity of the works of nature is independent of our ideas, and is not obvious to any of our external senses. To explain our knowledge of that identity, I begin with the knowledge that every man hath of his own identity, as the simplest case. The consciousness that every man hath of himself and of his own existence, qualifies all his actions. *I* am eating, *I* am walking, *I* am speaking. This is so natural, that even children distinguish themselves from others. Now, if self qualify every present thought and action, it must also qualify every idea of memory; because that faculty recals to the mind things as they happened: *I* was present at the King's coronation; and, at a greater distance of time, *I* saw the first stone laid of the Ratcliff library at Oxford. It is thus that I am made acquainted with my personal identity; that is, with being the person who saw the things mentioned above, and every other thing recorded in my memory as said, done, or suffered by *me;* the same *person,* without regard to what changes my body may have undergone.

The same sense that by the help of memory discovers to me my own identity, discovers to me also the identity of other beings. A child who sees a dog of a certain shape and colour, knows it to be the same it saw yesterday. I am assured of my own identity by connecting every thing I thought and did with myself. The knowledge I have of the identity of other beings is from remembering their appearance to be the same at different times.

Our knowledge of the identity of a species is derived from the same sense. The eye serves us to distinguish a horse from a cow, as different individuals; but it can carry us no farther. It is nature that teaches us, that the horse belongs to one species and the cow to another. Other animals can distinguish one individual from another, as well as we can; but it is not probable, that brute animals have any conception of different species.

The knowledge I have of my personal identity, is what constitutes me a moral agent, accountable to God and to man for every action of my life. Were I kept ignorant of my personal identity, it would not be in my power to connect any of my past actions with myself: I could not think myself accountable for them, more than if done by another person. It would answer no good purpose, to reward me for a benevolent act or to punish me for a crime, if I could not connect them with myself as the author. The reward would be considered by me as foolish or whimsical: the punishment, as grossly unjust. Personal identity therefore is the corner-stone of morality, and of laws human and divine.

As I have a sense of my own identity, I have a conviction from the light of nature, that all of my own species have the same sense of their identity. From that conviction it is, that magistrates and judges have authority to reward and to punish.

Will the reader here indulge me a short episode, connected intimately with the principal subject? That man is finely adjusted internally as well as externally to his situation on this earth, is made evident from a thousand instances. I give one more, not a little interesting. Did every individual animal differ from every other in shape and nature, deplorable would be the condition of man. His experience of one would afford him no light with respect to others: he would be utterly at a loss to distinguish the noxious from the innocent, or to select what are proper for food and for other uses. But the author of nature leaves nothing disjointed in his works. He himself has taught man to know animals, and to bring under subjection such as can serve his purposes. The means employed for that important end, merit our attention. Animals are divided into kinds or species, differing in their internal character as well as external figure; and the individuals that compose a species have all of them the same character and figure. Unless we were made acquainted with these particulars, we would be left to starve in the midst of plenty. Experience evidently would be an instructor by far too slow: it would require ages to give us the perfect knowledge of animals by that means. Instruction is conveyed to us by an internal sense as above mentioned; a most compendious method of opening to us all the knowledge of animals that is necessary for our well-being.

We have an innate sense of a common nature, not only in our own species, but in every species of animals. And our conviction holds true; there being a remarkable uniformity in creatures of the same kind, and a disformity no less remarkable in creatures of different kinds.*

The nature and temper of one individual, a sheep for example or a horse, is soon discovered from information or from trial. The light of nature supplies what is farther necessary to be known. We conclude not only that this animal will continue the same for life, but that the whole species is of the same temper.

To return to our subject, Mr. Locke, writing on personal identity, has fallen short of his usual accuracy. He inadvertently jumbles together the identity that is nature's work with our knowledge of it. Nay, he expresses himself sometimes as if identity had no other foundation than that knowledge.† I am favoured by Doctor Reid with the following thoughts on personal identity.

All men agree, that personality is indivisible: a part of a person is an absurdity. A man who loses his estate, his health, an arm, or a leg, continues still to be the same person. My personal identity therefore is the continued existence of that indivisible thing which I call myself. I am not thought, I am not action, I am not feeling; but I think and act and feel. Thoughts, actions, feelings, change every moment; but that *self* to which they belong is permanent. If it be asked how I know that it is permanent, the answer is, that I know it from memory. Every thing I remember to have seen, or heard, or done, or suffered, convinces me that I existed at the time remembered. But though it is from memory that I have the knowledge of my personal identity, yet personal identity must exist in nature independent of memory; otherwise I would only be the same person as far as my memory serves me; and what would become of my existence during the intervals wherein my memory has failed me? My remembrance of any of my actions does not make me to be the person who did the action, but

* Sketches of Man, edition 2d, Vol. IV. page 20. [From the sketch on the "Principles and progress of morality," *Sketches,* vol. 4, bk. 3, sketch 2.]

† Chap. Identity and Diversity, from the 9th Section downward. [Locke, *An Essay Concerning Human Understanding,* II.xxvii.9–29, pp. 335–48.]

only makes me know that I was the person who did it. And yet it was Mr. Locke's opinion, that my remembrance of an action is what makes me to be the person who did it; a pregnant instance that even men of the greatest genius may sometimes fall into an absurdity. Is it not an obvious corollary from Mr. Locke's opinion, that he never was born: he could not remember his birth; and therefore was not the person born at such a place and at such a time.[2]

This subject leads to a thought, which will be more fully displayed in handling the veracity of our senses. Any doctrine that tends to a distrust of our senses, must land in absurd scepticism. If our senses be not admitted as the evidence of truth, I see not that we can be certain of any fact whatever: from what is now observed it appears, that we cannot be certain even of our own existence, nor of our being the same person at different times.

2. This letter has not survived.

Containing the Substance of a Pamphlet
Wrote in Defence of the Third Essay[1]

With respect to liberty and necessity, our author's doctrine may be comprised under the following heads. 1. That man is a rational being endued with liberty. 2. That his liberty consists in acting voluntarily, or according to his inclination and choice. 3. That his will is necessarily, that is infallibly and certainly, determined by motives; or, in the style of the schools, *voluntas necessario sequitur ultimum judicium intellectus practici.* 4. That, consequently, liberty of indifference, or an arbitrary power of acting without or against motives, is no part of human nature. 5. That though human actions proceed in a fixed train, this is owing to no blind fate, but to the predestination or decree of God, who is the first cause of all things.

Concerning these points, philosophers and divines may differ in opinion, and each side will impute error to the other; but, that by any of the church of Scotland such opinions should be censured as unsound or heterodox, shows great ignorance, considering that they are espoused by our first great reformers, and inculcated in all the most noted systems of theology, composed by calvinist divines and taught in our universities. With us it is a fundamental principle, That God from all eternity hath foreordained whatever comes to pass; that all events are immutably and necessarily fixed by the decree of God, and cannot happen in any other way than he hath predetermined. The most orthodox divines agree with our author, not only in his doctrine of necessity as founded on the decree of God; but likeways in distinguishing moral necessity which effects the mind

---

1. The pamphlet to which Kames refers was entitled *Objections against the Essays on Morality and Natural Religion Examined* (1756), written in response to a flurry of pamphlets condemning the first edition of the *Essays* as the work of a dangerous heretic.

only, from physical necessity which affects the body only; and they acquiesce in his explanation of moral necessity as produced by the operation of motives on the will. They hold with him, that liberty is opposed, not to necessity, but to constraint; that it consists not in indifference, but in spontaneity, or *lubentia rationalis;* [2] and that the will necessarily follows the last judgment of the understanding. They show, that none of the consequences follow that are endeavoured to be laid upon our author; but that virtue and vice, rewards and punishments, are consistent with a necessity of this sort. Thus, for instance, the great Calvin reasons in the following manner,

> Seeing we have often mentioned the distinction betwixt *necessity* and *constraint,* upon which this whole controversy turns, we must now explain it a little more accurately. They who defend free will in opposition to divine grace, maintain, that there can be neither virtue nor vice where there is necessity. We answer, That God is necessarily good; and that his goodness though necessary is not upon that account the less worthy of praise. Again, that the devil is necessarily wicked; and yet his wickedness is not the less criminal. Nor is this any invention of ours; for in the same manner St. Augustine and St. Bernard reason.————Our adversaries insist, That what is *voluntary,* cannot at the same time be *necessary.* We shew them, that both these qualities are found in the goodness of God. They pretend it to be absurd, that men should be blamed for actions they must unavoidably perform. By the instance above given, we show, that there is in this no absurdity.————They object again, That unless virtue and vice proceed from a free choice, according to their sense of freedom, there can be no reason either for inflicting punishments, or bestowing rewards. As to punishments, I answer, That they are justly inflicted on those who commit evil; because it makes no difference, whether their choice was free, *i.e.* arbitrary, or whether they were under the influence of bad motives; provided only they were *voluntary* in their guilt.————As to rewards there is certainly no absurdity in our saying, that these are bestowed rather according to the goodness of God, than the merit of men.

> *Calvin. Tractat. Theolog. p. 152. edit. Amstelod.* 1667.[3]

2. Rational spontaneity.

3. First published as Jean Calvin, *Tract. Theolog. & Comment.* (Geneva, 1576). For a more accessible version of this argument, see *Institutes of the Christian Religion in Two*

The learned Francis Turretine, Professor in Geneva, whose authority as an orthodox divine will be allowed to be of the greatest weight, examines this question fully in his *Institut. Theolog.* under the head *de Libero Arbitrio, vol.* 1. *p.* 728. to 737. and maintains the same doctrine with our author.[4] He represents it as the capital and fundamental heresy of the Pelagians and Arminians, that they hold liberty to consist in indifference, not in spontaneity; and that they maintain every kind of necessity to be inconsistent with liberty. With great accuracy and strength of reason, he considers the several kinds of necessity. He shows, that two of them, coaction, and physical necessity arising from the laws of matter, are destructive of liberty. But that rational or moral necessity, which arises from the constitution of the mind as necessarily determined by motives, and the necessity which arises from the divine decree, are perfectly consistent with liberty in its orthodox sense. He removes the objection against this doctrine of its making man a mere machine; and, much in the same manner with our author, shows, that upon the Arminian liberty of indifference, or an arbitrary power of counteracting all motives, man would be a most irrational and unaccountable being, to whom argument and reasoning, precept and command, would be addressed in vain. The following are his words, (*p.* 566. *vol.* 1.),

> There are only two kinds of necessity which are inconsistent with liberty; physical necessity, and the necessity of constraint. The other kinds of necessity, which arise either from the decree or influence of God, or from the object itself and the last judgment of the understanding, are so far from overthrowing liberty, that they rather establish it; because they do not constrain the will, but persuade it; and produce a voluntary choice in one that was before unwilling. For whatever a man does according to his inclination, with judgment and understanding and with the full consent of his will, it is impossible but he must do freely, although in another sense he does it necessarily. This holds, from whatever quarter we suppose the necessity laid upon him to arise; whether it be from the existence of the

Volumes, ed. John T. McNeill (Philadelphia: Westminster Press, 1960), vol. 1, II.iii.5, "Man sins of necessity but without compulsion," pp. 295–6.

4. François Turrettini (1623–1687), *Institutio theologiae elencticae,* 3 vols. (Geneva, 1679–1685).

thing itself, or from the motive effectually determining his will, or from the decree and concourse of the first cause.

Benedict Pictet, Turretine's successor in the chair of Geneva, and acknowledged in the universities of this country as an author of the soundest principles, establishes the same doctrine in so clear a manner, as that words cannot be more precise and express.

Before we discourse of free will we must explain the meaning of the term. By free will we understand nothing else, but a power of doing what we please, with judgment and understanding, without any external compulsion. To this free will two things are opposed. First, physical or natural necessity; such as we see in inanimate beings; for instance, the necessity by which fire burns. Next, the necessity of constraint; which arises from external violence, imposed against the inclination of him who suffers it; as when a man is hurried to prison, or to an idol-temple. But we must not oppose to free will that necessity of dependence on God which all creatures lie under, and from which no rational being can be exempted; nor that rational necessity which arises from the last judgment of the understanding; as when I necessarily chuse that which appears to me best; for my choice, though necessary, is notwithstanding free. Wherefore, all that is requisite to freedom is, that one should act spontaneously, and with understanding: which clearly follows from this, that God is the freest of all beings, and yet he is necessarily determined to good. The same holds of saints and angels. Liberty therefore does not consist in indifference: for if so, God would not be a free being; and the more man was determined to good, or the more perfect he was, the less liberty he would enjoy; which is absurd. This is further confirmed by the following reasoning. We all chuse what appears to us our chief good or happiness with entire liberty: for who is not hearty and voluntary in such choice? Yet to this choice we are determined by a strong and irresistible necessity: for no man has any freedom of indifference in this case. No man can wish himself miserable, or can chuse evil as such. Liberty therefore by no means consists in indifference.

Theolog. Christ. l. 4. cap. 6. § 4.[5]

---

5. Benedict Pictet (1655–1724), *Theologia Christiana*, 2 vols. (Geneva, 1696).

Of the modern Calvinist writers who agree with our author, we shall give one example, the Reverend Mr. Jonathan Edwards minister of Stockbridge in New England, in his late treatise, intitled, *A careful and strict inquiry into the modern prevailing notions of that freedom of will which is supposed to be essential to moral agency, virtue and vice, reward and punishment, praise and blame.* Published at Boston 1754.[6] The piety and orthodoxy of this author, it is presumed, none but Arminians will adventure to call in question. Nothing can be better calculated than this book to answer all the objections against our author's doctrine of moral necessity, to shew its consistency with reason and scripture, and the injustice of ascribing to it any bad tendency. To quote particular passages is unnecessary; for the whole book, from beginning to end, is one continued chain of argumentation in favour of this doctrine. He every where holds and maintains,

> That the will is in every case necessarily determined by the strongest motives, and that this moral necessity (*p.* 24.) may be as absolute as natural necessity; that is, that a moral effect may be as perfectly connected with its moral cause, as a natural effect is with its natural cause.

For, says he, (*p.* 22.), "The difference between these two does not lie so much in the nature of the connection, as in the two terms connected." He rejects the notion of liberty, as implying any *self-determining* power in the will, any *indifference* or *contingency, p.* 29.; and shews in several chapters, *p.* 135.–192. that those notions of liberty which the Arminians hold, are so far from being necessary to accountableness, to virtue or vice, to praise or blame, that, on the contrary, they are inconsistent with virtue, which must always suppose the determining power of motives.

6. Jonathan Edwards (1703–1758), *A Careful and Strict Inquiry into the Modern Prevailing Notions of That Freedom of Will, Which Is Supposed to Be Essential to Moral Agency, Virtue and Vice, Reward and Punishment, Praise and Blame* (Boston, 1754; London, 1762). Though Kames had initially hoped that his views would be supported by the American Calvinist minister, Edwards saw the matter very differently. In a letter to the Glasgow minister John Ervine, Edwards insisted that "it must be evidencet to every one, who has read both his Essay and my Inquiry, that our schemes are exceedingly different from each other." Edwards attached this letter to later editions of his *Inquiry* as an appendix entitled "Remarks on the Essays on the Principles of Morality and Natural Religion, in a Letter to a minister of the Church of Scotland."

He examines the passages of scripture that relate to this doctrine. He shews, that the acts of the will of the human soul of Christ were *necessarily holy,* yet virtuous, praise-worthy, and rewardable. He answers the objection to this doctrine of its making God the author of sin, exactly in the same way with our author, by distinguishing between the intention of God and the intention of the sinner.

Though no man, who either knows the character of this author or peruses his book, can entertain the least doubt of his zeal for religion; yet it appears, that in New England as well as elsewhere, the worthiest persons are liable to be calumniated and traduced. For Mr. Edwards, when concluding his book, observes (*p.* 285.)

> It is not unlikely that some who value themselves on the supposed rational principles of modern fashionable divinity, will have their indignation raised at the subject of this discourse, and will renew the usual exclamations about the *fate of the Heathens,* Hobbes's necessity, and making men mere machines; accumulating the terrible epithets of *fatal, inevitable, irresistible,* and it may be with the addition of *horrid* and *blasphemous;* and perhaps much skill may be used, to set the things which have been said in colours which shall be shocking to the imagination, and moving to the passions of those who have either too little capacity, or too much confidence of the opinions they have imbibed, and contempt of the contrary, to try the matter by any serious and circumspect examination; or some particular things may be picked out, which they think will sound harshest in the ears of the generality; and these may be glossed and descanted on with tart and contemptuous words, and from thence the whole treated with triumph and insult.

How unbecoming and indecent, such methods are, and how unlike the conduct of a fair and impartial inquirer after truth, the Reverend author fully shews; nor can I entertain any doubt that my readers will join with him in condemning such a spirit.

To relieve myself a little from the languid uniformity of a continued defence, I will upon this single occasion change hands, and try my fortune in making an attack. Let us approach a little nearer to this liberty of indifference, which in late times has become so mighty a favourite even with some who would be thought Calvinists, and let us examine whether it will bear a narrow inspection. Perhaps upon a cool survey, it will be found a favourite not worthy to be contended for. Liberty of indifference in chusing betwixt two things of equal importance, is abundantly palatable, and may pass without objection. But liberty of indifference is not confined to cases of this nature. It is asserted of man, that he has a power to will and act, without having any reason or motive whatever to influence his will. A thing still more extraordinary is asserted with equal assurance, that man has a power to will and act, not only without motives, but in direct contradiction to the strongest motives that can influence the mind. It might well be urged, that this doctrine is a bold attack upon the common sense of mankind; and not the less bold, that it is taken for granted without the least evidence, or so much as a single experiment to support it. Such a being there may possibly be as is described; but every man who has not a cause to defend, will bear witness that this is not his case. I venture to affirm, that when the proper questions are put to any plain man who is ignorant of the controversy, his answers to every one of them will be repugnant to liberty of indifference as above explained. But waving this consideration at present, my attack shall be made from a different quarter, by examining the consequences of such a power, supposing it for argument's sake to be inherent in man. In the essay upon liberty and necessity, it is inculcated at full length, that man endued with this power would be an absurd and unaccountable being: he could not be relied on: oaths and engagements would be but brittle ties; and therefore he would be quite unqualified for the social life. I add, that this power, which is imagined to exist in man in order to bestow on him the greater self-command, has in reality the contrary effect. At the instant perhaps of willing or acting, man, upon this supposition, must have a sway over himself, altogether arbitrary: but then, no measures adjusted before hand, not even the most prudent and sagacious, can have any influence: all may be overturned, no person can say why, at the instant of beginning action. The very moment before, no man can say what he will choose, or how he will act. It is evident from the nature of the thing, that even the Deity can have no foresight of actions that are altogether arbitrary, and independent of all connections internal or external.

I make a second attack, different from the former. I consider man as acting in the great theatre of the world, in which all things are governed by the providence of an almighty Being. As it appears to me, the directing influence of providence, is altogether excluded from human actions by this supposed liberty of indifference. The operations of matter are governed by steady laws, and thereby contribute unerringly to the great designs of providence. But to what rule can the actions of men be subjected, which are supposed to be altogether arbitrary, and under no control? They cannot be under the direction of the Deity; for that supposition effectually annihilates liberty of indifference. The influence of the Deity must be superior to all other motives in determining the will; and consequently, must have the effect to make man a necessary agent in the sense of moral necessity. Man then, by this supposed power, is withdrawn from under the government of providence, and left at large to the most bizarre and most absurd course of action, independent of motives from good or ill, independent of reason, and independent of every view, purpose, or end. Here is chance clearly introduced in its most ugly form, so far as human actions can have an influence. This displays a dismal scene, sufficient to raise horror in every one who has feeling. After this, let not the Arminians cry out against blind fatality; a very uncomfortable doctrine indeed. But is blind fatality worse than blind chance? Could I possibly be convinced of either, I should dread the falling into despair, and the being tempted to deny the being of a God.

But enough of this dismal scene. I return to a thought occasionally thrown out above, that liberty of indifference is an imaginary scheme, unsupported by facts, and of which no man was ever conscious. This leads me to say, that it never was embraced seriously in its true import by any man; not even by the most zealous Arminian. Those who espouse this doctrine, do certainly take up with words, neglecting to examine things as they truly are: for what man of plain sense ever imagined, that he can resolve and will, without being prompted by any consideration, good or bad, and without having any end or purpose in view? When a man acts, it is expected that he can say, what moves him. If he can give no account, every one considers him as a changeling or madman. As a consequence from this, I venture further to say, that the doctrine of moral necessity is that which is universally embraced by men of plain sense, whose minds are not warped by the tenets of a sect. This doctrine, I say, is universally embraced; though not carried its utmost length, nor seen in its full extent, except by the studious and contemplative. With regard to acting, every man indeed conceives himself to be free; because he is conscious that he acts voluntarily, and according to his own choice. He is however at the same time conscious, that he has not the power of chusing or willing arbitrarily or indifferently: his will is regulated by desire, which he is sensible is not under his arbitrary power. And if this be once admitted, the chain of moral necessity is established. For no plain man, at the time of the action, entertains the least doubt, that his will is influenced by desire; which puts a final end to liberty of indifference.

In the foregoing light to me appears unavoidably the celebrated doctrine of liberty of indifference: and when such is my conviction, I can as little avoid thinking that the author of the Essays has done well in contributing to banish the Arminian doctrine out of our Church. It is my serious opinion, that to embrace it with all its necessary consequences, is in effect introducing into this world, blind chance, confusion, and anarchy; which are the high road to Atheism. Far be it however from my thoughts, to accuse Arminians of Atheism, or of irreligion in any degree. I am sensible, that the Arminian doctrine has been and is espoused by many good and pious men. But this I must take the liberty to affirm, that these men stop short at the threshold, without pushing their way forward to behold the ugly appearances within doors. These appearances are now laid open to them. If the doctrine can be moulded into some new shape, to make it square with religion and morality, such improvement must be agreeable to every well-disposed mind, because of the comfort it will afford to those who adhere to liberty of indifference. But, without pretending to the gift of prophecy, I venture to fortel, that it will be extremely difficult to stop any where short of moral necessity; and that any solid reformation of the Arminian doctrine, must infallibly lead to the principles of Calvin, and of our other reformers.

ESSAYS

ON THE

PRINCIPLES

OF

MORALITY

AND

NATURAL RELIGION

PART II

Belief

Desiring, wishing, resolving, willing, believing, signify all of them simple mental acts that cannot be defined; and yet are understood by all the world, every man being familiarly acquainted with them passing daily in his own mind. When I say that I believe Caesar was murdered in the senate-house, that Ganganelli was a good Pope, or that the King of Britain has thirteen children, no person has any difficulty to comprehend my meaning: as little on the other hand, when I say that I do not believe in the Patagonians, nor in Mahomet's tomb being suspended in the air between two loadstones. Hence it is that no writer has thought it necessary to analyse belief, the author of the treatise on human nature excepted. He lays down two propositions, First, "that belief is not any separate action or perception of the mind, but only a certain manner of conceiving propositions." Next, "that belief making no alteration on the conception as to its parts and composition, must consist in the liveliness of the conception."[1] As every particular concerning the human mind, is of importance to those who are studious of human nature, these propositions shall be put upon trial. The first holds true in some instances, but far from holding true in all. This will appear by induction. I see a bird in the air, which I believe to be an eagle. My belief enters into my perception of the bird, and is not a separate act or perception. Take an opposite example. I see a horse feeding at a distance in an inclosure. My belief that the horse exists, enters into my perception of him. I also

---

1. Not verbatim, but Kames's own paraphrase of Hume's argument that "belief consists not in the nature and order of our ideas, but in the manner of their conception, and in their feeling to the mind" (see *Treatise*, 1.3.7–8).

143

believe him to be the same that gained the King's plate at Newmarket a month ago. My belief of that fact rests entirely on memory, and makes no part of my perception of the horse.

With respect to propositions, the same difference obtains. Take the following example, that any two sides of a triangle are longer than the third. My conception of this proposition, includes my belief, or more properly, knowledge of its truth. The same will hold in all self-evident propositions; but not in propositions that require evidence. Take for example the following proposition, that the three angles of a triangle are equal to two right angles. My knowledge of the truth of that proposition, cannot make a part of my conception of the proposition; because my knowledge comes after, upon perusing the demonstration.

The same difference appears in belief founded on testimony. An improbable fact is affirmed by one whose veracity is suspected: I believe not a word of it. The truth of the fact is afterward ascertained by undoubted evidence; and I believe it firmly. Yet my conception of the fact is precisely the same in both cases; and therefore my belief in the one case, and disbelief in the other, can neither of them make a part of my conception of the fact.

I have taken the more pains to analyse this proposition, not only as accurate definitions and descriptions are of great moment in philosophy, but as tending to cut down the second proposition, that which our author chiefly insists on as the foundation of his theory. It must be evident, that where belief is separate from the conception of the proposition, it cannot consist in the liveliness of that conception. But even where belief makes a part of the conception of the proposition, his argument appears extremely lame. Belief, he observes, making no alteration upon the conception as to its parts and composition, must consist in the liveliness of the conception. But why must it consist in liveliness, which is but one modification of the conception? Would not the argument conclude as justly, that it consists in a faint conception, or in any other modification? The argument has not a foot to stand on. Belief in reality differs as widely from liveliness of conception, as colour does from sound. Belief is relative to truth and falsehood, and makes a branch of knowledge: liveliness of conception has not the slightest relation to either. This is so evident that I am tempted to apply to our author the story of the blind man, who being asked his notion of colour, said that it resembled the sound of a trumpet. He is less excusable than the blind man, as belief ought to have been as well known to him, as colour to one who sees. But he had a system to defend; and nothing is more common among philosophers, than to sacrifice even common sense to a favourite system.

To distinguish reality from fiction, and truth from falsehood, is of the utmost importance to every human being. The means for making this distinction, are put into the hands of every person, though it requires a degree of understanding to apply the means for preventing error. Now, if by reducing belief to be merely a conception, whether lively or languid, man be rendered incapable of making the distinction, what better is he than a ship tossed about by every wind, without a pilot and without a rudder? But our author's doctrine carries him a great way farther. He must banish veracity along with belief; for laying aside either, the other is of no use. One great advantage of society is the communication of knowledge; by which every one may acquire the knowledge of all. But this source of knowledge would be entirely dried up, if men were not made by nature to believe what is reported to them by others. With what coolness and intrepidity do some writers lay violent hands upon that noble fabric the human mind!

In a system deviating so widely from truth, no just reasoning is to be expected, nor true delineation of human nature. It is urged by this author, that true history takes fast hold of the mind, and presents its objects in a more lively manner than any fabulous narration can do. Every man must judge for himself: I cannot admit this to be my case. History, no doubt, takes faster hold of the mind, than any fiction told in the plain historical stile. But can any man doubt who has taste, that poetry makes a stronger impression than history? Let a man of feeling attend the celebrated Garrick[2] in the character of Richard, or in that of King Lear; and he will find, that dramatic representations make strong and lively impressions, which history seldom comes up to. But let it be supposed, that history presents its objects in a more lively manner than can be done by dramatic or epic poetry; it will not therefore follow, that a lively idea is the same with belief. I read a

2. David Garrick (1717–1779), the most famous actor of his day, was also a dramatist, co-manager of the Drury Lane Theatre, and a friend of Samuel Johnson.

passage in Virgil: let it be the episode of Nisus and Euryalus. I read a passage in Livy, namely the sacking of Rome by the Gauls.[3] If I have a more lively idea of the latter story, I put it to my author to point out the cause of this effect. He surely will not affirm, that it is the force of expression or harmony of numbers: for in these particulars, the historian must yield to the poet. It is evident that no satisfactory account can be given, but that Livy's superior influence upon the conception, is the effect of his being a true historian. The most then that our author can make of his observation, supposing it to hold true, is, that the authority of the historian produceth belief, and that belief produceth a more lively idea than any fabulous narration can do. Truth indeed bestows a certain degree of vivacity upon our ideas. I cannot however admit, that history exceeds dramatic or epic poetry, in conveying a lively conception of facts; because it appears evident, that, in works of imagination, the want of truth is more than compensated by sentiment and language. Yet it is certain, that in an epic poem or in a tragedy intended merely for amusement, the finest descriptions, the most picturesque images, the most nervous expressions of the poet, or the most lively conceptions of the reader, will not on the whole contribute to produce belief.

Sometimes indeed, belief is the result of a lively impression. A dramatic representation is one instance, when it affects us so much as to draw off our attention from every other object, and even from ourselves. In this state, we do not consider the actor, but conceive him to be the very man whose character he assumes. We have that very man before our eyes. We perceive him as existing and acting, and believe him to be existing and acting. This belief however is but momentary. It vanisheth like a dream, as soon as we are roused to a consciousness of ourselves, and of the place we occupy. Nor is the lively impression, even in this case, the cause of belief, but only the occasion of it, by diverting the attention of the mind from itself and its situation. It is in some such manner, that the idea of a spectre in the dark, which fills the mind and diverts it from itself, is, by the force of imagination, converted into a reality. We think we see and hear it: we are convinced of it, and believe the matter to be so.

3. See Virgil, *Aeneid,* Book V; Livy, *History of Rome,* Book V.

With regard to the evidence of my own senses, though I am far from admitting, that the essence of belief consists in the vivacity of the impression, I so far agree with our author, that vivacity and belief, in this case, are always conjoined. A mountain I have once seen, I believe to be existing, though I am a thousand miles from it; and the image or idea I have of that mountain, is more lively and more distinct, than of any I can form merely by the force of imagination. But this is far from being the case, as above observed, of ideas raised in my mind by the force of language.

Belief arising from the evidence of others, rests upon a different foundation. Veracity, and a disposition to believe, are corresponding principles in the nature of man; and, in the main, these principles are so adjusted, that men are not often deceived. The disposition we have to believe, is qualified by the opinion we have of the witness, and the nature of the story he relates. But supposing a concurrence of all other circumstances to prompt our belief, yet if the speaker pretend only to amuse, without confining himself to truth, his narration will not, in the smallest degree, prompt our belief, let him enliven it with the strongest colours that poetry is master of.

I shall only add, that though our own senses and the testimony of others, are the proper causes of belief; yet that these causes are more or less efficacious, according to our present temper of mind. Hope and fear are influenced by passion: so is belief. Hope and fear relate to future events. If the event be agreeable, and the probability of its existence be great, our conception of its existence takes on a modification which is called *hope*. If the event be extremely agreeable, and the probability of its existing do greatly preponderate, our hope is increased proportionally, and sometimes is converted into a firm belief, that it will really happen. Upon weak minds, the delightfulness of the expected event will, of itself, have that effect. The imagination, fired with the prospect, augments the probability, till it convert it to a firm persuasion or belief. On the other hand, if fear get the ascendant, by a conceived improbability of the existence of the event, the mind desponds, and fear is converted into a firm belief that the event will not happen. The operations of the mind are quite similar, where the event in view is disagreeable.

I conclude this Essay with observing, that tho' our own senses and the testimony of others are the causes of belief, yet that the efficacy of these causes depends considerably on the present tone of mind. My belief that an agreeable event has happened, or will happen, rises above the probability when I am in high spirits. In low spirits my belief falls below it. Where the event is disagreeable, my belief rises above the probability if my spirits be low; and my belief falls below it, if my spirits be high.

Passion has still a stronger influence upon belief. As to which see Elements of Criticism chap. 2. part 5.[4]

---

4. *Elements of Criticism*, vol. 1, chap. 2, pt. v, treats of "the influence of passion with respect to our perceptions, opinions, and belief."

External Senses

An internal sense informs us of things passing within the mind, inclining, resolving, willing, reflecting, &c. By several external senses we discover things external. The latter is our present theme, as far as may tend to enforce the proof of a Deity.

For the sake of perspicuity, this Essay is divided into several sections. First, perceptions of the different external senses. Second, substance and qualities. Third, primary and secondary qualities. Fourth, veracity of the external senses.[i]

SECTION I

Perceptions of External Sense[ii]

The perceptions of the external senses differ widely one from another. I begin with the perceptions of touch and sight as the simplest. I close my eyes and lay a hand on my writing desk. I feel my hand resisted by a hard smooth body, of a certain figure. Viewing the same desk with my eyes, the figure appears the same, as far as the perceptions of these two senses correspond. But it is more material to be observed, that by each of these senses I am informed, that the desk exists independent of me, having certain properties or qualities equally independent. These senses serve evidently to inform me of things as they really exist.

The senses of hearing, smelling, and tasting, raise perceptions differing widely from these mentioned. A sound is produced in me by a certain vibration of the air striking the drum of my ear: a smell, by *effluvia* touching my nostrils: and a taste by a bit of matter touching my palate. With respect to these senses, it is not a little remarkable, that their perceptions have no resemblance to the causes that produced them; nor do they correspond to any thing existing independent of me. The beat of a drum produces nothing but a vibrating motion in the air; nor does any thing touch my ear but that vibration. The effect however is a perception of sound, which has not the slightest affinity either to the beat of the drum or vibration of the air; nor has it any existence but in my mind. A rose emits *effluvia* which touch my nostrils: the smell I perceive is neither in the rose nor in the *effluvia.* The sweetness I taste in sugar, is produced by the sugar; but in vain would one search for that quality in the sugar, more than in any other bit of matter. From this analysis it appears, that a sound, a smell, a taste, are not matter nor qualities of matter; but effects produced in a percipient. No mortal would without experience imagine, that such marvelous effects could be produced by causes in all appearance so inadequate, effects however that contribute in a high degree to our well-being.

SECTION II

Substance and Quality

As a just conception of the terms *substance* and *quality* is necessary in many branches of reasoning, particularly in reasoning about a Deity, and as the explanation given of these terms by Mr. Locke, our great master in logic, is extremely obscure, I shall endeavour to ascertain their meaning, to the satisfaction, I expect, of my reader.[1]

I cast my eye upon a tree, and perceive figure, extension, colour, and sometimes motion. Were these perceived as separate objects without relation to any other thing, I should never have any idea of substance. This possibly may be the condition of some animals; but the eye of man is more perfect. What we really perceive, is a tree of a certain figure, size, and colour. When I see motion, my perception is not of motion separately, but of a body moving. And so closely are these united, that we cannot even form a

1. See "Of Our Complex Ideas of Substances," in Locke, *Essay,* II.xxiii.

conception of motion, nor of colour, nor of figure, as independent existences, but as belonging to the tree and inhering in it. In short, the sense
of seeing is given us to perceive things as they really exist; and did it not
make us acquainted with things as they exist, we would be ill qualified for
living in this world. Now, when we abstract from particulars, and reason
in general, the things that have not a separate existence are termed *qualities,*
and the thing they belong to, body or *substance.* Thus the idea of substance,
as well as of qualities, is derived from sight. And the object so qualified, is
at the same time perceived as really existing, independent altogether of the
percipient.

A similar perception arises from the sense of feeling. Laying my hand
upon this table, I have a perception not only of smoothness, hardness, figure, and extension, but also of a thing I call *body,* of which the particulars
now mentioned are perceived as *qualities.* Smoothness, hardness, extension, and figure, are perceived, not as separate and unconnected existences,
but as inhering in and belonging to something I call *body,* which is really
existing, and which hath an independent and permanent existence. And it
is this body with its several qualities, which I express by the word *table.*

The foregoing analysis of the perceptions of sight and touch, will be best
illustrated by a comparison with the perceptions of the other senses. I hear
a sound, or I feel a smell. These are not perceived as the qualities or properties of any body, thing, or substance. They make their appearance in the
mind as simple existences; and do not suggest any perception of independency, nor permanent existence. Did seeing and feeling carry us no farther, we never could have the least conception of substance.

It is not a little surprising, that philosophers, who discourse so currently
of *qualities,* should affect so much doubt and hesitation about *substance;*
seeing these are relative ideas, and imply each other. For what other reason
do we call figure a quality, but that we perceive it, not as a separate existence,
but as belonging to something that is figured; and which thing we call *substance,* because it is not a property of any other thing, but is a thing which
subsists by itself, or hath an independent existence. Did we perceive figure
as we perceive sound, it would not be considered as a quality. In a word, a
quality is not intelligible, unless upon supposition of some other thing, of
which it is the quality. Sounds indeed, and smells, are also considered as

qualities. But this proceeds from habit, not from original perception. For, having once acquired the distinction betwixt a *thing* and its *qualities,* and finding sound and smell more to resemble *qualities* than *substances,* we readily come into the use of considering them as qualities.

Another observation hinted above occurs, with regard to those things which by the sight and touch are perceived as qualities; that we cannot form a conception of them, independent of the beings to which they belong. It is not in our power to separate, even in imagination, colour, figure, motion, and extension, from body or substance. There is no such thing as conceiving motion by itself, abstracted from some body which is in motion. Let us try ever so often, our attempts will be in vain, to form an idea of a triangle independent of a body which has that figure. We cannot conceive a body that is not figured; and we can as little conceive a figure without a body; for this would be to conceive a figure as having a separate existence, at the same time that we conceive it as having no separate existence; or to conceive it to be a quality, and not a quality. Thus it comes out, that *substance* makes a part, not only of every perception of sight and touch, but of every conception we can form of colour, figure, extension, and motion. Taking in the whole train of our ideas, there is not one more familiar to us, than that of *substance,* a being or thing which hath qualities.

When these things are considered, I cannot readily discover what wrong conception of the matter hath led Mr. Locke to talk so obscurely and indistinctly of the idea of substance. It is no wonder he should be difficulted to form an idea of substance in general, abstracted from all properties, when such abstraction is beyond our power: but nothing is more easy, than to form an idea of any particular substance with its properties. Yet this has some how escaped him. When he forms the idea of a horse or a stone, he admits nothing into the idea, but a collection of several simple ideas of sensible qualities.* "And because," says he,

> we cannot conceive how these qualities should subsist alone, nor one in another, we suppose them existing in and supported by some common subject, which support we denote by the name *substance;* though it be certain we have no clear or distinct idea of that thing we suppose a support.

* Book 2. chap. 22. [Locke, *Essay,* II.xxiii.4, p. 297.]

A single question would have unfolded the whole mystery. How comes it, that we cannot conceive qualities to subsist alone, nor one in another? Mr. Locke himself must have given the following answer, That the thing is not conceivable; because a property or quality cannot subsist without the thing to which it belongs; for if it did, that it would cease to be a property or quality. Why then does he make so faint an inference, as that we suppose qualities existing in and supported by some common subject? It is not a bare supposition: it is an essential part of the idea; it is necessarily suggested to us by sight and touch. He observes, that we have no clear nor distinct idea of substance. If he mean, that we have no clear nor distinct idea of substance abstracted from properties, the thing is so true, that we can form no idea of substance at all abstracted from properties. But it is also true, that we can form no idea of properties abstracted from substance. The ideas both of substance and of quality are perfectly in the same condition in this respect; which it is surprising philosophers should so little attend to. At the same time, we have clear and distinct ideas of many things as they exist, though perhaps we have not a complete idea of any one thing. We have such ideas of things as serve to all the useful purposes of life. It is true, our senses reach not beyond the external properties of beings. We have no direct perception of the essence and internal properties of any thing. These we discover from the effects produced. But had we senses to perceive directly the essence and internal properties of things, our idea of them would indeed be more full and complete, but not more clear and distinct, than at present. For, even upon that supposition, we could form no notion of substance, but by its properties, internal and external. To form an idea of a thing abstracted from all its properties, is impossible.

The following is the sum of what is above laid down. By sight and touch we have the perceptions of substance and body, as well as of qualities. It is not figure, extension, motion, that we perceive; but a thing figured, extended, and moving. As we cannot form an idea of substance abstracted from qualities, so we cannot form an idea of qualities abstracted from substance. They are relative ideas, and imply each other.

SECTION III

Primary and Secondary Qualities

Philosophers are pretty much agreed about primary qualities, that they are such as inhere in a body or substance, and exist with the body or substance intirely independent of us. According to that definition, primary qualities are objects of the senses of sight and touch, and of these only. Therefore secondary qualities, if these have any meaning, must be objects of the other senses: whether so or not, shall by and by be examined. According to these definitions, figure, size, solidity, and divisibility without end, are primary qualities. All of them belong to a substance or body; and are as much independent of us, as the substance or body itself. Holding gravity to be a tendency in every particle of matter to unite with every other particle, it may justly be considered as a primary quality: a tendency to motion, it is true, is properly a power; but a power to act is a property or quality, and may well be held a capital one. The *vis inertiae* is a power in matter to resist a change from rest to motion. The *vis incita* is another power, tending to make a body persevere in that degree of motion which is impressed upon it. These powers also may be added to the list of primary qualities. Colour at first view seems to be a primary quality, as we can as little conceive a body without colour as without figure. And yet, upon search we find nothing on the surface of a body but particles variously figured and combined, which have not the most distant resemblance to colour. These particles indeed, by reflecting rays of light on the eye, may produce a perception of colour in the beholder; but that perception cannot be a quality of the object, primary or secondary. Heat, whether a pleasant or painful feeling, cannot be in the fire, an inanimate body incapable of feeling. A power in fire to raise such a feeling, may indeed be classed among the primary qualities; and so may a power in a body to raise a perception of colour: but a cause ought not to be confounded with its effect.

According to the analysis here given, a sound, a smell, a taste, existing no where but in the mind of a percipient, cannot be qualities of a body, either primary or secondary. Mr. Locke however endeavours to make them secondary qualities by converting them into powers. "Colour, he says, is not a quality as it appears to be, but a power in matter to raise in us the perception of colour."* In the same manner, sweetness must be a power in sugar to raise a perception of sweetness, and sound must be a power in a drum to raise a perception of sound. But this account of secondary qualities is unsatisfactory, as evidently converting an effect into its cause. A mental perception, as observed above, can in no proper sense be held a quality of the object perceived. And could this perception be converted into a power inherent in the object perceived, it would be a primary quality, not a secondary.

These insuperable objections notwithstanding, all men agree to place the perceptions mentioned, not in the mind where they really exist, but in the bodies that produce them; and for that reason, and for that only, are they held to be secondary qualities. Nothing is more familiar among the learned as well as among the vulgar, than to conceive sweetness to be a quality of sugar, a fragrant smell to be a quality of the rose, and colour to be a quality of all bodies. Now if this illusion be the only foundation of secondary qualities, they must be defined perceptions in the mind of man, which by an illusion of nature are placed upon external objects.

Nature never goes out of the direct road in vain. This illusion must be contrived for some valuable purpose that cannot be obtained in the direct road. Consider what would be the face of nature did we perceive nothing around us but bodies and their primary qualities as they really exist, without any notion of what are termed secondary qualities. It is difficult to conceive a scence with which we are intirely unacquainted; but upon the slightest reflection it will appear cold and insipid. How little attractive would a beautiful woman be, were the pure red and white of her skin and her melodious accents, perceived to be no where but in the mind of her lover! Upon that supposition, how slight would be the influence of an orator or of a general harranguing his army! Conversation would be much less entertaining, were

* Book 2. chap. 8. § 10. [Not verbatim, but Kames's paraphrase of Locke's definition of secondary qualities as those which are "nothing in the Objects themselves, but Powers to produce various Sensations in us by their *primary Qualities, i.e.* by the Bulk, Figure, Texture, and Motion of their insensible parts, as Colours, Sounds, Tasts, *etc.*" (*Essay,* II.viii.10, p. 142).]

we conscious that the sounds we hear proceed not from the speaker. A rose would be little regarded, were it known that it has no fragrancy of smell. To sum up all in a single view, were this delusive curtain withdrawn, men, finding no pleasure but within, would be intirely occupied with internal objects, without paying any regard to their external causes. Society would be greatly relaxed, and selfish passions would prevail without any antagonist. It is much easier to conceive and to paint objects as they appear to us. We are placed as in a fairy land full of enchantments. Behold that flower-parterre, insipid in itself and void of ornament, yet cloathed apparently with splendid colours, in perfect harmony! It is a wonderful artifice to present objects to the eye in various attires, so as to be distinguished and remembered; and to paint on the fancy gay and lively, grand and striking, sober and melancholy scenes, whence many agreeable and affecting emotions arise. Yet all this beauty of colour is a mere illusion, a sort of enchantment. The illusion of sound has still greater influence. Listen to an orator pouring out instruction in all the harmony of sound, different tones suited to the variety of his subject. Listen to a musician ravishing the heart with his melodious strains. It is this illusion that makes the charm of conversation: thoughts passing from one to another, would have little influence, if the speaker did not command attention by variety of tones high and low. How sweet and how vivifying is the smell of a polished field producing the most fragrant flowers! In a word, this illusion is the cement of society, connecting men and things together in an amiable union.

I had almost forgot to add, that though pain and pleasure can exist no where but in the mind, yet the pain occasioned by any disorder of the body, is by this illusion placed on the part affected; by which we are directed to apply the cure to that part.

The relation that things have to each other, afford an instance of a similar illusion. Equality, uniformity, resemblance, proximity, are relations that depend not on us, but exist whether perceived or not; and upon that account may properly be termed primary relations. Propriety and impropriety, congruity and incongruity, are perceptions of an internal sense, having no existence in the objects perceived. But as these perceptions are, by an illusion of nature, placed in the objects and conceived as belonging to them, they may therefore be termed secondary relations.

SECTION IV

Veracity of the External Senses

The external senses serve two very different purposes, one to give information of things that concern us, and one to entertain us. With respect to the latter, handled in the section immediately foregoing, as enjoyment is intended not truth, it derogates not from our nature, that an illusion is happily employed for our good. A painter, who by the art of perspective, gives to a plain surface the appearance of hills and valleys, deserves praise for entertaining us, not blame as a deceiver. With respect to the former purpose, nature determines us to rely on the evidence of our senses; and they never deceive us when in a sound state. The senses chiefly intended to make us acquainted with things external, are sight and touch. These senses afford absolute conviction of the reality of their objects. By both we perceive external things existing independent of us. I see a white horse grazing in a field: I lift a book in the dark lying on my table. I can no more doubt of their existence than of my own. It is not even in my power to conceive that the Almighty can give me more satisfactory evidence. And the veracity of my perceptions is confirmed by constant experience. I see a tree of a certain shape and size. Advancing to it, I find it in its place by the resistance it makes to my body. I see it day after day, year after year; and find the object to be the same, with no variation but what the seasons and time produce. The tree is at last cut down: it is no longer seen nor felt.

The eye is nicely formed for seeing objects distinctly at the most convenient distance. A microscopic eye gives an accurate view of objects at hand, but reaches not distant objects: a telescopic eye enlarges our sphere of vision, but cannot take in minute objects. The eyes of the generality are accurately formed for a medium distance, that which is the most useful. It is true, that we see things differently at different distances and through different *media.* But that imperfection, if it can be termed so, is soon corrected by experience, and never betrays us into any hurtful error. By a diseased eye, we sometimes see things different from what they are in reality, as in a jaundice, which makes objects appear yellow; but even here the error appears upon the slightest reflection. In a word, there is nothing to which all men are more necessarily determined, than to put confidence in their senses. Their information is relied on; and we trust our lives and fortunes upon it, with perfect assurance. We entertain no doubt of their veracity, being so constituted as not to have it in our power to doubt.

When the veracity of our senses is thus founded on the necessity of our nature and confirmed by constant experience, it cannot but appear strange, that it should come into the thought of any man to call it in question. But the influence of novelty is great; and when a man of a bold genius, in spite of common sense, will strike out new paths to himself, it is not easy to foresee how far his airy metaphysical notions may carry him. A late author, who gives us a treatise concerning the principles of human knowledge, strikes at the root of the veracity of our senses, by denying the reality of external objects; and thereby paves the way to the most inveterate scepticism.[2] For what reliance can we have upon our senses, if they deceive us in a point so material? If we can be prevailed upon to doubt of the reality of external objects, the next step will be, to doubt of what passes in our own mind, of the reality of our ideas and perceptions; for we have not a clearer conviction of the one than of the other. And the last step will be, to doubt of our own existence; for it is shown in a former essay, that we have no certainty of this fact, but what depends upon sense and feeling.

It is reported, that Dr. Berkeley, the author of the above-mentioned treatise, was moved to adopt this whimsical opinion, to evade some arguments urged by materialists against the existence of the Deity. If so, he was in bad luck; for this doctrine, if it should not lead to universal scepticism, affords at least a shrewd argument in favour of Atheism. If I can only be conscious of what passes in my own mind, and if I cannot trust my senses when they give me notice of external and independent existences; it follows, that I am the only being in the world; at least, that I can have no evidence from my senses, of any other being, body or spirit. This is certainly an unwary concession; because it deprives us of our chief means for attaining knowledge of the Deity. Laying aside sense and feeling, this learned divine will find it

2. George Berkeley (1685–1753), *A Treatise Concerning the Principles of Human Knowledge* (1710; reprint, ed. Jonathan Dancy, New York: Oxford University Press, 1998).

a difficult task, to point out by what other means we discover the foregoing important truth. But of this more afterward.

Were there nothing else in view but to establish the reality of external objects, it would be scarce worth while to bestow much thought in solving metaphysical paradoxes against their existence, which are better confuted by common sense and experience. But as the foregoing doctrine appears to have very extensive consequences, and to strike at the root of the most valuable branches of human knowledge; an attempt to re-establish the veracity of our senses, by detecting the fallacy of the arguments that have been urged against it, may, it is hoped, not be unacceptable to the public. The attempt at any rate is necessary in this work; the main purpose of which is, to show, that our senses, external and internal, are the chief sources from whence the knowledge of the Deity is derived to us.

The author mentioned boldly denies the existence of matter, and the reality of the objects of external sense; contending, that there is nothing really existing without the mind of an intelligent being; in a word, reducing all to be a world of ideas. "It is an opinion strangely prevailing among men," says he, "that houses, mountains, rivers, and in a word all sensible objects have an existence, natural or real, distinct from their being perceived by the understanding." He ventures to call this a manifest contradiction; and his argument against the reality of these objects, is in the following words:

> The forementioned objects are things perceived by sense. We cannot perceive any thing but our own ideas or perceptions; therefore what we call men, houses, mountains, &c. can be nothing else but ideas or perceptions.[3]

This argument shall be examined afterward with the respect that is due to its author. It shall only be taken notice of by the way, that, supposing mankind to be under so strange a delusion as to mistake their ideas for men, houses, mountains, it will not follow, that there is in this any manifest contradiction, or any contradiction at all. For deception is a very different thing from contradiction. But he falls from this high pretension in the subsequent part of his work, to argue more consistently, "that, supposing solid, figured,

---

3. Berkeley, *Principles*, sec. 4, p. 104.

and moveable substances, to exist without the mind, yet we could never come to the knowledge of this."* Which is true, if our senses bear no testimony of the fact. And he adds,† "that, supposing no bodies to exist without the mind, we might have the very same reasons for supposing the existence of external bodies that we have now." Which may be true, supposing our senses to be fallacious.

The Doctor's fundamental proposition is, That we can perceive nothing but our own ideas or perceptions. Of this assertion he hath not even attempted a proof; though, in so bold an undertaking as that of annihilating the whole universe, his own mind excepted, he had no reason to hope, that an assertion so singular and so contradictory to common sense, would be taken upon his word. It may be true, that it is not easy to explain, nor even to comprehend, by what means we perceive external objects. But our ignorance is in most cases a very lame argument against fact. At this rate, he may take upon him equally to deny many operations in the material world, which have not hitherto been explained by him or others. At the same time, it is perhaps as difficult to explain the manner of perceiving our own ideas, or the impressions made upon us, as to explain the manner of perceiving external objects. The Doctor beside ought to have considered, that by this bold doctrine he sets bounds to the power of nature, or of the Author of nature. If it was in the power of the Almighty to bestow upon man a faculty of perceiving external objects, he has done it. We have indeed no conception how external objects could be more clearly manifested to us than in fact they are. Therefore the Doctor was in the right to assert, that a faculty in man to perceive external objects would be a contradiction, and consequently a privilege not in the power of the Deity to bestow upon him. He perceived the necessity of carrying his argument so far: sensible however that this was not to be made out, he never once attempts to point at any thing like a contradiction. And if he cannot prove it to be a contradiction, the question is at an end: for supposing only the fact to be possible, we have the very highest evidence of its reality that our nature is capable of, namely the testimony of our senses.

* Sect. 18. [Berkeley, *Principles,* p. 109.]
† Sect. 20. [Ibid.]

It hath been urged in support of this doctrine, that nothing is present to the mind but the impressions made upon it; and that it cannot be conscious of any thing but what is present. This difficulty is easily solved. For the proposition, "That we cannot be conscious of any thing but what is present to the mind, or passes within it," is taken for granted, as if it were self-evident: and yet the direct contrary is an evident fact, that we are conscious of many things which are not present to the mind; that is, which are not, like perceptions and ideas, within the mind. Nor is there any difficulty to conceive, that an impression may be made upon us by an external object, so as to raise a direct perception of the external object itself. When we attend to the operations of the external senses, we discover that external objects make not impressions all of them in the same manner. In some instances we feel the impression, and are conscious of it as an impression. In others, being quite unconscious of the impression, we perceive only the external object. And to give full satisfaction to the reader upon the present subject, it may perhaps not be fruitless, briefly to run over the operations of the several external senses, by which the mind is made conscious of external objects, and of their properties.

And, first, with regard to the sense of smelling, which gives us no notice of external existences. Here the operation is of the simplest kind. It is no more but an impression made at the organ, which makes me perceive a smell. Experience, it is true, and habit, lead me to ascribe it to some external thing as its cause. But that this connection is the child of experience only, will be evident from the following considerations; that when a new smell is perceived, we are utterly at a loss what cause to ascribe it to; and that when a child feels a smell, it is not led to ascribe it to any cause whatever.

In the senses of tasting and touching, we are conscious not only of the impression made at the organ, but also of the body that makes the impression. When I lay my hand upon this table, the impression is of a hard smooth body that resists the motion of my hand. In this impression, there is nothing to create the least suspicion of fallacy. The body acts where it is, and it acts merely by resistance. We have, from that sense, the fullest and clearest perception of external existences that can be conceived, subject to no doubt, ambiguity, nor even cavil. And this perception must at the same time, support the veracity of our other senses, when they give us notice of external existences.

What remains is the sense of seeing, which it is presumed the Doctor had chiefly in view, when he argues against the reality of external existences. Here there occurs a difficulty, which possibly has had weight with our author, tho' not once mentioned by him. It is, that no being can act but where it is; and that a body at a distance cannot act upon the mind, more than the mind upon it. This appears to evince the necessity of some intermediate means in the act of vision; and one is suggested by a fact. The image of a visible object is painted upon the retina of the eye; which puts the operation of vision, in one respect, upon the same footing with that of touching, both being performed by means of an impression made at the organ. There is indeed this difference, that the impression of touch is felt, whereas the impression of sight is not felt: we are not conscious of any impression, but singly of the object itself that makes the impression.

And here a curious circumstance presents itself to view. Though an impression probably is made upon the mind by means of the image painted upon the retina, whereby the external object is perceived; yet nature hath concealed this impression from us in order to remove all ambiguity, and to give us a distinct perception of the object itself, and of that only. In touching and tasting, the impression made at the organ creates no confusion nor ambiguity, the body that makes the impression being perceived as operating where it really is. But were the impression of a visible object perceived as made on the retina, which is the organ of sight, all objects must be seen as within the eye. It is doubted among naturalists, whether outness or distance be at all discoverable by sight, and whether that appearance be not the effect of experience. But bodies and their operations are so closely connected in place, that were we conscious of an organic impression at the retina, the mind would have a constant propensity to place the body there also; which would be a circumstance extremely perplexing in the act of vision, as setting feeling and experience in perpetual opposition; enough to poison all the pleasure we enjoy by that noble sense.

In so short-sighted a creature as man, it is the worst reason in the world for denying any well-attested fact, that we cannot account how it is brought about. We cannot explain how the intervention of rays of light, lays open to our view the beings and things around us: but it is great arrogance, to pretend to doubt of the fact upon that account, for it is in effect maintaining, that there is nothing in nature but what we can explain.

The perception of objects at a distance by intervention of rays of light, involves no inconsistency nor impossibility: and unless that could be asserted, we have no reason to call in question the evidence of the perception. And after all, this particular step of the operation of vision, is not more difficult to be conceived or accounted for, than the other steps, of which no man entertains a doubt. It is perhaps not easy to explain how the image of an external body is painted upon the *retina tunica;* and no person can explain how that image is communicated to the mind. Why then should we hesitate about the last step, to wit, the perception of external objects, more than about the two former, when they are all equally supported by unexceptionable evidence? The whole operation of vision far surpasses human knowledge; but not more than the operation of magnetism, electricity, and a thousand other natural appearances: our ignorance of the cause, ought not to make us suspect deceit in the one, more than in the other.

Whether our perception of external objects correspond to truth, or whether it be a mere illusion, is a question that cannot be ascertained one way or other by reasoning. But it is ascertained by a higher degree of evidence, to wit, intuitive conviction, which admits not the slightest doubt of the veracity of our senses. It is clear, that supposing the reality of external objects, we can form no conception of their being displayed to us in a more lively and convincing manner, than in fact is done. Why then call a thing in doubt, of which we have as good evidence as human nature is capable of receiving? But we cannot call it in doubt, otherways than in speculation, and even then but for a moment. We have a thorough conviction of the reality of external objects: it rises to the highest certainty; and we act in consequence of it with the greatest security of not being deceived. Nor are we in fact deceived. When we put the matter to a trial, every experiment answers to our perceptions, and confirms us more and more in our belief.

I close this Essay with a comparison between the evidence of our senses and that of human testimony. That we ought not to give credit to any man's testimony because some men fail in veracity, would be a very lame argument. The only effect such instances have, or ought to have, is to correct our propensity to believe, and to bring on a habit of suspending belief till circumstances be examined. The evidence of our senses rises undoubtedly much above that of human testimony: and if we put trust in the latter after many instances of being deceived, we have better reason to put trust in the former, were the instances of being deceived equally numerous; which is plainly not the fact. When people are in sound health of mind and body, they are very seldom misled by their senses.

Different Theories of Vision[1]

The sense of seeing is one of the most simple and distinct of all that belong to man. And yet by many philosophers it has been rendered so intricate, as to tempt plain people to a diffidence and distrust of it. The present Essay is intended to point out the errors of these philosophers, and to restore the sense of seeing to the authority it justly possesses in human nature, with respect to veracity. I have a further view, which is to put writers on their guard against attempting subjects beyond the sphere of human knowledge, of which I shall have occasion to give several mortifying instances, even in this narrow subject, the theory of vision,—scarce more excusable than the attempt made by the inhabitants of Shinar to erect a tower *whose top should reach into heaven.*[2] Moderation is proper for man, no less in reasoning than in behaviour. Man, tho' the chief of the terrestrial creation, is limited in the powers of his mind, as much as in those of his body. When he struggles to pass these limits, he acts and thinks in vain; and meets with nothing but disappointment and disgrace.

The connection between soul and body, and their manner of acting upon each other, are hid from us; and for ever will remain hid: we cannot form even the slightest conjecture how mind acts on matter, or matter on mind. And yet, writers talk familiarly on that mystery, as if they had been

1. This essay is new to the third edition.
2. Shinar refers to a region of Babylonia (in modern-day southern Iraq), where the Tower of Babel was built (Genesis 11:1–9).

admitted to the councils of the Almighty in the formation of man.* A collection of all the strange and incoherent stuff that has been written on that subject, would fill a large volume. In the different theories of the sense of seeing adopted by writers of note, will be found, if I be not grossly mistaken, many rash attempts to build the tower of Babel; and to these I shall confine myself as being connected with the present work.

One capital error that all the writers on that subject have fallen into, is, to apply to mind axioms peculiar to matter. It holds true in matter, that one body cannot act upon another at a distance, nor be acted upon but by what is in contact with it. Extension in length, breadth, and thickness enters into every idea we can form of matter; and every thing that is so extended, is in our conception matter. Therefore, if mind or spirit be different from matter, which all admit, it cannot be so extended; consequently cannot occupy space, nor have any relation to place. Now, as local situation is implied in the axioms mentioned, there can be no foundation for applying them to mind, which has no local situation. The actions of the soul and body on each other, must be governed by laws intirely different from what govern the mutual actions of matter. As these laws are beyond the bounds of human knowledge, every attempt to explore them must prove abortive and be absurd. Writers however, by applying inadvertently to mind the axioms mentioned peculiar to matter, have been led into a labyrinth of metaphysical jargon, of the brain being the local situation of the soul, of phantasms or images carried along the nerves into the brain, where, being in contact with the soul, they make impressions upon it, &c. &c.

I begin with Aristotle's account of vision. Taking it for granted that mind and matter cannot act upon each other at a distance, he is reduced to hold, that of every external object there is in the mind of the beholder a phantasm or species, having the form of the object without the matter, like the impression of a seal upon wax; and that by these, external objects are made

* Quam bellum est velle confiteri potius nescire quod nescias, quam ista effutientem nauseare, atque ipsum displicere I Cic. de Natur. Deor. l. 1. ["And tell me this: are we also to assume that the gods bear the names which we allot to them?" Cicero, *On the Nature of the Gods* (*De Natura Deorum*), trans. P. G. Walsh (Oxford: Clarendon Press, 1997), I.84, p. 32.]

visible.[3] His followers add, that these phantasms or species, sent from external objects, make impressions on the passive intellect, which are perceived by the active intellect. This account of vision differs not from that of Epicurus, which is, that external objects send forth, constantly and in every direction, slender ghosts or films of themselves, which striking the mind are the means of perception.[4] Had these philosophers instead of films and phantasms, stumbled on rays of light passing from the object to the eye of the spectator, they would have been nearer the truth. But they may well be excused, as they were groping in the dark and had no knowledge of pictures on the *retinae*. But they ought not so easily to be excused for stopping short at the first step: they could not expect to give satisfaction, but by explaining how it comes that these films and phantasms, of which the mind is not conscious, are however the means of seeing distant objects. Doctor Porterfield is the only writer who attempts to supply that defect. His words are,

> The mind in seeing is subject to a law, whereby it traces back its own sensations from the *sensorium* to the *retinae,* and from thence along perpendicular lines to the object itself; and thence concludes, that what it perceives is the external object, and not in the mind.*

What does one think of sensations having a local situation in the brain or *sensorium,* and of being traced back along imaginary perpendicular lines? Have these words any meaning?

3. See Aristotle, *On the Soul,* trans. J. A. Smith, *The Complete Works of Aristotle,* ed. Jonathan Barnes (Princeton: Princeton University Press, 1984), 2.7.

4. As described by Lucretius in his *De rerum natura* ("On the Nature of Things"), Epicurus (341–270 B.C.) put forth an atomistic theory of vision, according to which objects emit tiny particles (*eidola*) which retain the shape of the bodies from which they emanate, and which enter the eye to cause visual sensation.

* Medical Essays, vol. 3. p. 228 [William Porterfield, "An essay concerning the motions of our eyes. Part I. Of their external motions" (1737) in *Medical Essays and Observations, Published by a Society in Edinburgh,* 5 vols., 5th ed. (London and Edinburgh, 1771). The *Medical Essays* were published by the Philosophical Society of Edinburgh, to which both Kames and Porterfield belonged. William Porterfield (1695–1771), Professor of Medicine at the University of Edinburgh, was a leading authority on the senses and the author of *A Treatise on the Eye* (1759).]

Here it will be observed, that neither Aristotle nor Epicurus make any doubt of seeing the external objects themselves: they only pretend to explain by what means these objects, though at a distance, are perceived. Des Cartes, adhering more rigidly to the axiom that objects at a distance cannot act upon us, denies that we have any perception of such objects, maintaining, that the objects we perceive are not external, but images or ideas in the mind. From which premises he concludes, that the existence of external objects cannot be known to us, otherwise than by a process of reasoning, inferring it from these images or ideas.[5] Locke adopting this doctrine holds,

> that we cannot perceive, remember, nor imagine any thing, but by having an idea or image of it in the mind; that we are conscious of ideas or images, and of nothing else; consequently, that we can have no knowledge of things external, but what we acquire from reasoning on ideas or images.[6]

He accordingly employs a whole chapter to make out by reasoning the existence of external objects. Doctor Porterfield, adhering to this doctrine, expresses himself in very strong terms.

> How body acts upon mind, or mind upon body, I know not; but this I am very certain of, that nothing can act or be acted upon where it is not. And therefore our mind can never perceive any thing but its own proper modifications, and the various states and conditions of the *sensorium* to which it is present. When I look at the sun or moon, it is impossible that these bodies, so far distant from my mind, can with any propriety of speech be said to act upon it. To imagine that things can act where they are not present, is as absurd as to imagine that they can be where they are not. These bodies do indeed emit light, which falling upon the *retina* does excite certain agitations in the *sensorium;* and it is these agitations alone which can any way act upon the mind. So that it is not the sun or moon in the heavens which our mind perceives, but only their image or repre-

5. Descartes argued that while the senses provide us with useful information concerning the material world, they cannot give us reliable knowledge about the real nature of things.

6. Not verbatim, but Kames's paraphrase of Locke's argument that the senses furnish the soul "with ideas to think on." By "compounding those Ideas, and reflecting on its own Operations," writes Locke, "it increases its Stock, as well as Facility, in remembring, imagining, reasoning, and other modes of thinking" (*Essay,* II.i.20, p. 116).

sentation impressed upon the *sensorium.* How the soul sees these images, or how it receives those ideas from such agitations in the *sensorium,* I know not; but I am sure it can never perceive the external bodies themselves to which it is not present.*

With respect to this theory, it cannot escape observation, that in two particulars it contradicts the testimony of our senses; first in denying that we see external objects; and next in affirming that we perceive images in the mind, which no man ever perceived. It may be further observed, that supposing these particulars to hold true, yet this account of vision remains wofully imperfect. We acknowledge pictures on the *retinae;* but how these pictures are conveyed to the brain, no man can justly say. Next, supposing them conveyed, no man can account how they should raise a perception in the mind. And admitting the perception, it ought naturally to be of the pictures; and yet we have not the slightest consciousness of these pictures.

But waving these observations, there occurs an argument founded on a stuborn fact directly inconsistent with this theory. The three philosophers last mentioned agree in maintaining, that as external objects are hid from our eye-sight, our belief of them must depend on a process of reasoning. Their reasonings have been found insufficient by two acute philosophers, Berkeley and Hume, as shall by and by be mentioned. But supposing them solid, what must be the condition of a great plurality, who are incapable of abstruse reasoning? they must remain utterly ignorant of external objects. Yet the direct contrary is vouched by the testimony of all men; these philosophers excepted, who renounce the evidence of their senses for the sake of a favourite opinion. Even children have as lively a conviction of external objects as the most acute reasoners. In fact, objects of sight are perceived so clearly, as that we cannot even conceive that the Author of our nature could have made them more clear, or have given us a more satisfactory conviction of them. The means by which this is done, are beyond the sphere of human knowledge: we do not therefore pretend to say how it is done: we only say that it is done.

Misled by the same error of applying to mind axioms that hold true of matter only, two philosophers, Berkeley and Hume, have given us theories

* Medical Essays, vol. 3. p. 220.

still more wild. The former, taking it for granted that mind and matter cannot act upon each other at a distance, and perceiving the insufficiency of the arguments urged by Des Cartes and Locke for the existence of matter, has ventured bluntly to deny its existence. The latter, observing Berkeley's reason for denying the existence of matter to be equally conclusive against the existence of mind, has with great intrepidity discarded both, giving quarter to nothing but to phantasms or ideas, floating in the great void without inhering in any subject or *substratum;* an absurdity farther distant from common sense than ever entered into the imagination of any other writer.

Upon our supposed inability to see objects at a distance, is grafted a difficulty that has puzzled many a philosopher, how it comes that with two eyes external objects appear single only. Supposing that external objects are not visible to us, and that we perceive nothing but the representative pictures in the *retinae,* it seems highly presumable, that the two perceptions raised by these two pictures should to every external object give the appearance of being double. Gassendus and Porta could not imagine any solution of the difficulty, but to contradict an evident fact, asserting that though both eyes are open, yet we only see with one at a time.[7]

The great Newton, sensible of the difficulty arising from the two pictures, endeavours to remove it in the following words.

> Are not the species of objects seen with both eyes united where the optic
> nerves meet before they come into the brain, the fibres on the right side
> of both nerves uniting there, and after union going thence into the brain
> in the nerve which is on the right side of the head, and the fibres on the
> left side of both nerves uniting in the same place, and after union going
> into the brain in the nerve which is on the left side of the head, and these

7. Pierre Gassendi (1592–1655), French Catholic priest, philosopher, astronomer, and mathematician, best known for his attempt to reconcile Epicurus with Christianity (*Syntagma Philosophicum,* 1658) and for his experiments in astronomy (he was the first to observe the planetary transit of Mercury). Giambattista della Porta (c. 1535–1615), an Italian natural philosopher with interests both in magic and in optics, described his experiments with the *camera obscura* in his *Magia Naturalis* (1558; English trans., *Natural Magick,* 1658) and discussed binocular vision in *De refractione, optices parte* ("On Refraction, the Division of Light"), which was published in 1593.

two nerves meeting in the brain in such a manner that their fibres make but one entire species or picture, half of which on the right side of the *sensorium* comes from the right side of both eyes through the right side of both optic nerves to the place where the nerves meet, and from thence on the right side of the head into the brain, and the other half on the left side of the *sensorium* comes in like manner from the left side of both eyes? For the optic nerves of such animals as look the same way with both eyes (of men, dogs, sheep, oxen, *&c.*) meet before they come into the brain; but the optic nerves of such animals as do not look the same way with both eyes (as of fishes and of the camelion) do not meet, if I am rightly informed.*

The difficulty is attempted to be solved by uniting in the brain the two pictures, in order to produce a single perception. But whether this be fact or even probable, is what we can never know. One thing we know to be fact, that the external object appears single, even where the optic nerves happen not to be united. In a case reported by Vesalius, the optic nerves did not meet: yet the intimate companions of the man when alive, declared, that he never complained of any defect of sight, nor of objects appearing to him double. But what I chiefly remark here is, that Sir Isaac transgresses the bounds of human knowledge, in saying that the pictures in the *retinae* are carried along the optic nerves and united in the brain. Hypotheses may be thrown out at pleasure; but if they be of things surpassing our knowledge where we have no data either to verify or refute, they are no better than castles in the air. If the greatest philosopher ever existed be liable to this censure, it ought to be a most serious admonition to all others. Will the reader indulge me to observe further, that this hypothesis has not even a plausible appearance. I can well conceive a picture with the canvass, to be carried from place to place; but it is past my conception, how a painting can be detached from the *retinae* more than a painting from the canvass; or how in that detached state it can be carried to the brain, either entire or in halves. But supposing a picture formed in the brain, it must be different

---

* 15th Query subjoined to his optics. [Sir Isaac Newton (1642–1727), *Opticks: Or, a Treatise of the Reflexions, Refractions, Inflexions and Colours of Light* (London, 1704), pp. 320–1.]

from those in the *retinae;* and how this is done is not said, nor how this new picture can raise a perception of the external object. Here we are left in utter darkness, where light is the most wanted. It may even be doubted, whether the pictures in the *retinae* contribute to vision. Their existence is no proof; because they are necessarily produced by rays of light acting on the eyes, precisely as on a *camera obscura;* and the same picture appears in an eye, even when separated from the body. This censure may be thought too severe; but where truth and reality are concerned, no partiality to any opinion ought to be admitted, not even to that of a Newton.*

Dr. Briggs taking it for granted with Sir Isaac, that two separate pictures in the brain must occasion the external object to appear double, endeavours to unite them in the following manner,

* The framing systems upon conjectures beyond the bounds of human knowledge, is far from being rare among philosophers. Take the following notable instance from Avicen an Arabian philosopher. His opinion is, that man may be formed out of the earth without father or mother, in the following manner.

> A piece of matter being in a fermentation by the mixture of four qualities; hot, cold, dry, moist, there arise some bubbles; in the midst of which there is a little bubble full of a spirituous and aërial substance; into which by the command of God a spirit is infused. Opposite to this bubble there arises another bubble divided into three receptacles by thin membranes, filled with an aërial substance; and in these are placed certain faculties subject to the governing spirit, and appointed to communicate every thing to that spirit. The first mentioned bubble by its flaming heat is formed into a conical figure like fire; by which means the thick body about it becomes of the same figure, being solid flesh covered with a thick membrane, which is what we call the heart. Now considering the great waste of moisture from so much heat, some part must be formed to supply that waste. This spirit is endued with a sense both of what is convenient for it and what is hurtful, so as to attract the one and repel the other. For these services there are two parts formed, namely the brain and the liver. The first presides over all things relating to sense; the latter over all things relating to nutrition.

This is an epitome of much indigested stuff imagined by Arabian doctors on this subject. [The physician and philosopher Avicenna or Ibn Sina (980–1037), a central figure in medieval Islamic philosophy whose influence extended to the West, most notably to Thomas Aquinas, who commented extensively on Avicenna's *al-Shifa* ("On the Soul").]

that the fibres of the optic nerves passing from corresponding points of the *retinae* to the *thalami nervorum opticorum,* having the same length, the same tension, and a similar situation, must have the same tone, and therefore that their vibrations excited by the impression of the rays of light, will, like unisons in music, present one image to the mind; but that fibres passing from parts of the *retinae* that do not correspond, having different tensions and tones, must have discordant vibrations, which present different images to the mind.[8]

An inference from an object of sound to one of sight can never hold, as there is no resemblance between objects of different senses upon which to form any sort of comparison. I can readily conceive, that fibres having the same tone must produce similar sounds, or if you please the same sound; and that fibres having different tones must produce dissimilar sounds; but that fibres, whether having the same or different tones, should produce pictures, is to me utterly inconceivable. What else have we here but sounding words that have no meaning? I need scarce add, that the doctor's comparison overturns his theory, instead of supporting it. Two sounds are perceived as different, whether concordant or discordant. Two sounds in unison make not an exception; for unisons produce harmony, and there is no harmony in a single sound.

Dr. Porterfield composed an ingenious treatise on vision, in which the present subject is handled at great length.[9] He differs from both Sir Isaac and Dr. Briggs; for he admits that the two pictures on the *retinae* are by motion propagated along the fibres of the optic nerves to the brain, so as to raise two perceptions in the mind; and that the mind traces back these perceptions from the *sensorium* to the *retinae,* and from thence to the object perceived. Here the two perceptions are kept distinct through the whole process till the ultimate step; and he gives the following reason for the objects appearing single in place of double. "By an original law of our nature,

---

8. William Briggs (1642–1704), who discovered the optic papilla (or optic disk, also known as the "blind spot"), was the author of *Ophthalmographia* (Cambridge, 1676; London, 1685) and *Nova visionis theoria* (1685).

9. William Porterfield, *A treatise on the eye, the manner and phaenomena of vision,* 2 vols. (London: A. Miller, and Edinburgh: G. Hamilton and J. Balfour, 1759).

we perceive visible objects in their true place; and consequently, an object seen with each eye in its true place at the same time, must appear single."

Here it is taken for granted, that we see external objects, and that we see them with both eyes in the same place; inadvertently it must be acknowledged, as it flatly contradicts what he had been all along inculcating, that external objects are not visible otherwise than in imagination. It was incumbent on the Doctor to account for single vision upon his own theory; and yet he accounts for it on an opposite theory. It is true, that two bodies cannot occupy the same place at the same time; but they may occupy it in imagination, and ten thousand more. Had the Doctor adhered to his own theory, to wit, that we know nothing of external objects but by reasoning from ideas or images in the mind, every argument must have led him to conclude with Sir Isaac and Doctor Briggs, that the two pictures in the *retinae* ought to produce the appearance of a double external object. This of itself is a confutation of the Doctor's theory, as in fact objects are never seen double when the eyes are in a sound state.

But it will afford a more satisfactory confutation, to examine what the result must be, from seeing external objects themselves and not their images. To pave the way, I shall premise an account of the other external senses that have double organs. I lay my two hands on a globe: an impression is made upon each hand, nay upon each finger, every one of which impressions must be felt by the mind. There is here no coincidence of place; and yet the object is not felt double. In hearing, an impression is made on the drum of each ear, which one would naturally think should raise in the mind two perceptions of sound; yet in fact we hear but one sound. The effect is similar with respect to smell from effluvia taken in at the two nostrils. There must be here some cause, that prevents a multiplication in appearance of the same object. Sir Isaac Newton and Doctor Briggs with respect to vision, explain this difficulty by uniting the two pictures into one, to produce a single perception only. With respect to the other senses, we are left in the dark; for it is not said that this explanation is applicable to any of them. Doctor Smith in his optics attributes single vision entirely to custom; which in effect is maintaining, that in childhood we see double, hear double, feel double, and smell double. This solution I cannot acquiesce in. If we commence life with double perceptions, they, instead of being altered by custom, will be confirmed by it. But perhaps the Doctor's meaning is, that in time the perceiving the same object double being discovered to be an error, we learn to correct the error and to perceive the object single only as it is in reality. This supposed struggle between perception and reflection and the complete victory obtained by the latter, must be the work of time and ripe years; which could not escape remembrance. But as no man can say that he ever had such remembrance, it is a demonstration that there never existed such a struggle.

All the writers on this subject take it for granted, that two perceptions must necessarily make the external object appear double; and they have reason to do so, supposing external objects not to be perceived but their ideas or images only. Sir Isaac Newton endeavours to reduce the two pictures in the eyes to a single picture in the brain, producing consequently but a single perception. Doctor Briggs attempts the same in a different way. Doctor Porterfield admits two perceptions; but in effect reduces them to one, when the object is seen with both eyes in the same place. But upon supposition of the real fact that the external objects themselves are perceived, the question is, why should two perceptions produce necessarily an appearance of two objects? Let us give attention to that question. If the external object could not be known but by a chain of reasoning, the conclusion from the double perception would naturally be that the external object should appear double. But the case differs widely where the external object is seen, and perhaps known. My little dog has a collar with my name inscribed: it has long been my companion; and I cannot mistake it for another. Viewing it with one eye, I know the creature: viewing it with the other, it is the same. What is there here but the seeing the same object at different times? Viewing now my dog with both eyes at once, it is still the same dog: the two perceptions are indeed varied as they now coincide in time; but what else can be the effect of this coincidence but a sight of the dog as formerly? I look to my dog, lay both hands upon him, and at the same time hear him bark. In this experiment, my perceptions are many and various; but as they are only different perceptions of the same object, they have no tendency to give it the appearance of more than one.

It is extremely true, that for ought we know of vision, our eyes might have been so framed, as to make an object appear double with one eye, instead of appearing single with two. But this would be a delusion, which cannot be imputed to the Author of our nature. He has provided us with the sense of seeing to perceive objects as they exist; and so effectually has he prevented delusion, that when by a distorted eye an object appears double, means are afforded to detect the error. Of the five senses, four have double organs, that if one be rendered useless, its office may be supplied by the other. These organs produce indeed two perceptions; but being perceptions of the same object, they cannot have the effect to make it appear double. No person thinks it necessary to explain, why an object repeatedly perceived in succession appears single: why not the same in simultaneous perceptions? In hearing, smelling, and touching, the object never appears double: why should it appear double in seeing? I am not satisfied with Dr. Porterfield's explanation of single vision, in which it is taken for granted that the external object itself is seen by each eye separately; for though the two apparent objects must be blended when seen in the same place, it is however natural to think, that there should still remain an impression and conviction of two objects. But be this as it may, the Doctor undoubtedly errs in affirming that each eye has a separate object. Both eyes have but one object, evident from this, that the external object never appears double whether seen successively by one eye, or by both at once. And as the object appears single, his solution of blending two objects together does not hold. There can remain no doubt that the account given in this Essay of single vision is solid, when it is equally applicable to every one of the other senses that have double organs; whereas the Doctor's explanation holds only in vision. In short, we are so constituted as to have a firm conviction of the reality of external objects from the perceptions of sight; and by the same constitution, we have a firm conviction of the Identity of an object, from a pair of organs as from a single organ. Is it above the power of the Almighty to make us perceive things as they really exist? In fact he has done so; and what better evidence can be required, than that when our eyes are found, an object is never seen double. Thus, a difficulty that has puzzled many a sage philosopher, turns out to be no difficulty at all.

Philosophers may exert their utmost powers to explain vision; but all in vain, for it is beyond the limits of human knowledge. There are difficulties in accounting for the other senses, no less puzzling. A sound, a smell, a taste, has not the slightest relation to the cause that produces it. This is set forth in the Essay immediately foregoing. Here is more work for a curious enquirer, attempting to transgress the limits of human knowledge. These things I do not pretend to explain; but humbly rest satisfied with the small portion of knowledge that is bestowed on me, because universal knowledge is not given to human beings.

I conclude with repeating what is observed above, that the connection between soul and body and their way of acting upon each other, are hid from us; and for ever will remain hid. Our senses not only guide us in acting, but are the means of manifold enjoyments. Their salutary effects are known to all; but by what means these effects are produced, is known to none. But we suffer not by our ignorance, as it gives no obstruction to the operation of our senses. We know from experience, that in vision, representations of the external object are painted on the *retinae* of our two eyes; but in what manner these pictures contribute to vision or whether they at all contribute, we know not. One thing only is certain, that our perception is not of the pictures but of the object itself. And after all, why are these great philosophers, in explaining vision, more bold than in explaining other actions of the mind on the body. It is not pretended that the circulation of the blood can be explained from any power in matter; and as little walking, or breathing, or moving the hand on a musical instrument. In these instances, and in many others that might be mentioned, the soul is the first mover; and writers venture not to say how the body is moved by the soul. Why then such intricate and obscure theories concerning vision? The seeing external bodies as they are, is an operation as simple as any of these now mentioned.

Matter and Spirit[1]

Whatever is extended in length, breadth, thickness, is termed *matter*. Hence, it is an essential property of every particle of matter to occupy space, and to exclude every other particle from that space. As we have no notion of spirit but as opposed to matter, spirit and immaterial substance pass as synonimous terms. The property therefore of extension, or length, breadth and thickness, cannot be attributed to spirit. Nor does it enter into our conception of spirit, that it must exclude other beings either matter or spirit from occupying the same place.

From any notion we can form of matter, there is no reason to think that it is necessarily passive or inert. None of its properties, as far as we know, is inconsistent with its being endued with a power of motion; and that it is possessed of various powers, we have the best evidence that can be expected, namely experience. Gravity is a power inherent in every particle of matter; and so is the *vis inertiae* and the *vis incita*. Magnitism, electricity, elasticity, and a great variety of elective attractions, belong to some kinds of matter only. When we ascend to organized bodies, the powers of matter multiply upon us. How many powers are requisite for the life even of the humblest vegetable! Advancing to animals, we find not only life, sense, and spontaneous motion, but the power of thinking, and in the more elevated animals even the power of reflecting. Many brute animals show evident symptoms of sagacity and reasoning.

Mr. Locke accordingly, in his answer to the bishop of Worcester, maintains "that the omnipotent Being can give to certain systems of created

---

1. This essay is new to the third edition.

sensible matter some degrees of sense, perception, and thought."[2] This he has clearly made out, first, by showing that there is no inconsistency between our conception of matter and a power to think; and next, that in fact he has bestowed a power of thinking on many animals. There appears to me no way of evading the force of this argument, but by proving that animals are composed of two distinct substances, soul and body, that thinking is confined to the soul, and that matter is incapable of thinking. This proof has indeed often been attempted, but with very bad success. That matter is capable of acting, appears to me clear from instances without number. Now, as thinking is a species of action, it will be hard to prove, that matter, which can exert actions of one kind, is incapable to exert actions of another kind. I know of no data upon which that proof can be founded.

When we talk of soul and body in the same animal, of their union, and of the means by which they operate on each other, all is supposition and conjecture, without the possibility of any sort of evidence on the one side or on the other. It is a mystery to us; and will for ever remain a mystery, as human knowledge reaches not so far. Were I to indulge a conjecture, it would be, that the inferior animals are but organized matter, having powers for procreation and preservation, not even excepting the power of thinking as far as necessary to their well-being; but that man, the noblest exertion of Omnipotence upon this earth, is composed of two separate substances, one matter, the other soul or spirit; and that all his noblest faculties inhere in the latter. That the latter can subsist independent of the former, is a fact for which we are indebted to Revelation, being far beyond the reach of human investigation.

I proceed now to an analysis of human actions, without venturing to say, whether they all proceed from the mind, or partly from the body.

2. *Locke's Reply to the Right Reverend the Lord Bishop of Worcester's Answer to his Letter* (1697). In 1696, Edward Stillingfleet, Bishop of Worcester (1635–1699), published *A Discourse in Vindication of the Doctrine of the Trinity,* in which he attacked the theological implications of Locke's ideas about substance. This prompted a published controversy that was cut off by Stillingfleet's death in 1699. In his *Reply,* the second of his responses to Stillingfleet, Locke reiterates and defends a point made in the *Essay,* where he wrote that he saw "no contradiction in it, that the first eternal thinking Being or omnipotent Spirit should, if he pleased, give to certain systems of created senseless matter, put together as he thinks fit, some degrees of sense, perception, and thought" (IV.iii.6, p. 541).

Human actions are of two kinds, actions that put the body in motion, and actions that contribute to the acquisition of knowledge.

Actions of the former kind are exerted, some constantly, some at intervals. The motion of the heart, circulation of the blood, and others essential to life, require constant action. In moving the hands or head, in speaking, walking, and in other voluntary motions, we act at intervals. These actions are for the most part attended with consciousness: actions necessary for life, are exerted without any consciousness.

Actions necessary for life, require no illustration. But the other kind have drawn less attention than they merit. In order to external motion, the body is commonly prepared for it by direction of the mind. In dancing on the slack rope, it is by internal direction that the body is kept in equilibrio. When an external motion happens unexpectedly, it is always painful: in walking on a smooth road, I put my foot inadvertently into a hole, a violent shock ensues, which would not have happened had I been prepared: I walk down stairs with facility; but if I set my foot on a plain, expecting another step, the shock is considerable: when the motion of a horse in trotting is regular, the rider, accommodating his body to the expected motion, is carried smoothly; but if a horse, having a bad ear, move irregularly, the rider is jolted by motions different from what he expected.

Voluntary actions are commonly directed by the will, not always. Every motion of the fingers, in playing on a violin or harpsicord, is in a learner preceded by an act of will: but an artist moves his fingers with no less accuracy than celerity, without affording time for the will to interpose. An act of will is necessary at the commencement only: the train proceeds by habit without any new act of will. In learning to knit a stocking, every motion of the needle requires strict attention; but by practice a girl of nine or ten, without once looking on her work, moves the needle so swiftly as to escape the eye.

Of the actions that contribute to the acquisition of knowledge, thinking is the chief. It is a celebrated question among philosophers, whether the mind always thinks. Des Cartes, who, overlooking the works of nature, formed a world to his own taste, makes the essence of the soul to consist in thinking; not adverting that it is denied to man to dive into the essence of any thing. Locke, more justly, holds thinking to be only an action of the soul; and by many feeble arguments endeavours to prove, that the soul does not always think; adding, that we are not always conscious of thinking, and "that it is hard to conceive that any thing should think and not be conscious of it."[3] One thing is certain, that thinking must precede the consciousness of it; but that consciousness must necessarily follow, is a proposition not entitled to our assent till it be proved. I find not however that any writer has ever attempted a proof. It is observed above, that actions essential to life are directed without our being conscious of them. And if such actions, which are of the first importance, can be exerted without consciousness, I cannot see that the action of thinking must necessarily be an exception.

I do not pretend to form an opinion whether we always think or not: to determine that question requires more knowledge than is given to man. But I venture to give my opinion, that we sometimes think without being conscious of it. From long experience I am induced to believe, that we frequently think and reason during sleep, without knowing any thing of the matter. I have facts at hand to make this probable: my only concern is, that I have no other evidence to give but my own. If the reader however listen with patience, he probably will find more truth in the proposition than at first he may be apt to imagine. Frequently have I gone to bed at night, with various ideas floating in my mind without order, relative to some intricate point I had been studying. After a sound sleep, perhaps without a dream, the subject has presented itself to me perfectly well arranged. I must hold this as a proof of the proposition, unless it be made out, that this could happen during sleep without thinking. I never shall forget an incident that happened to me in attending an intimate friend in his last moments. Hanging over him and watching the concluding scene, the fatigue of suspense made me retire to another room. At that awful time, occurred to me a very difficult problem in law, which I had studied a month or two before, but without success; and to my utter astonishment the solution appeared instantaneously, without an intervening thought. I put in writing three short propositions, so complete that I had no occasion after to alter a word. There is a singular fact that even to this day I cannot reflect upon without surprise. After perusing a work deeply metaphysical, with the

3. Locke, *Essay,* II.i.ii, p. 110.

author at my elbow ready to clear every doubt, my notions remained extremely obscure. Convinced of my inability, I laid aside the book, firmly resolved never to think of it again. More than six months after, curiosity prompted me to examine what had puzzled me so much. I scarce expect to be believed when I inform the reader, that I understood every word, even so clearly as directly to take down in writing every point which I doubted of. The paper being put into the author's hand, he brought it back a few days after, and acknowledged that my corrections were right. Once I was seized with a fever, which brought me to the gates of death. The moment the fever left me, I recollected a question concerning architecture, which I had been studying before I fell ill, but without being able to make any thing of it. I dictated to my secretary what filled four pages of paper, which I approved of upon a revisal after my health was restored. I have often experienced a similar effect with respect to music. After hearing a new tune without being able to carry away a note of it, it has occurred to me complete at the distance of days. The first time I took particular notice of this, was in humming a tune from end to end, wondering where I had heard it. With difficulty I recollected, that more than a fortnight before I had heard it in such a place, and that I could not then join two bars together.

The foregoing particulars suggested to me what I have practised many years. In studying a knotty point, if the solution do not soon occur, the student begins to fret, and the longer he thinks, the less capable he is of thinking. As this has frequently been my case, my practice now is to stop short after collecting the circumstances, trusting the rest to nature. At any spare moment I resume the subject, sometimes with success, sometimes without. But soon or late, the solution seldom fails to start up, often when I am thinking of something else, or scarce thinking at all. These facts are incapable of any proof but from my own testimony. But as nature is fundamentally the same in all, I have reason to believe, that my experience is not singular with respect to such facts: and I with confidence appeal to the experience of others, willing to stand or fall by their testimony.

I am confirmed in the opinion of the mind's thinking during sleep, from several facts that I cannot otherways explain. People commonly rise at their usual time in the morning, however late they have been in going to rest. If a man, having a journey in view, purposes to rise an hour or two before his usual time, he awakes at that hour, perhaps from a sound sleep. How can this be accounted for, unless on supposition of some internal operation directing the external act? A man's rest is not disturbed by any noise he is accustomed to; but he awakes instantly upon being told, even in a low voice, that it is time to rise. To what cause are we to ascribe the first idea that presents itself to the mind after a profound sleep; an idea perhaps very different from what is suggested by the surrounding objects? Every effect must have a cause; and I cannot imagine any cause, other than the continuation during sleep of a train of ideas passing in the mind without consciousness.

These facts have the appearance of bringing to light a latent power in man, hitherto little thought of. If the opinion above suggested appear well founded from repeated experiments, may not the studious lay hold even of their sleeping hours for enlarging their fund of knowledge? By the method above suggested, we may without fatigue double the time of study.

ESSAY V

Power, Cause and Effect

As all things on this globe are in a continual flux, much activity and new productions without end, man would be ill fitted for his station, were he kept in ignorance of the laws that govern animate and inanimate beings. Without some notion of power in himself and in others, he would rival in ignorance the lowest of the brute creation, and be utterly at a loss how to regulate his conduct. But he is not left imperfect with respect to this branch of knowledge, more than with respect to others that contribute to his well-being. The idea of power is familiar even with children. When they see a play-thing, a never-failing question is, Who made it, or who brought it here? How that idea is acquired, has however puzzled some philosophers, one in particular who shall be introduced by and by. Power is indeed not discernable by any external sense: we cannot see power, nor hear it, nor smell it, nor taste it, nor touch it. Neither can the idea be derived from experience, which, being barely a repetition of known facts, cannot produce a new object, nor a new idea. It may give information, that certain known objects are always conjoined, such as fire and heat, the sun and light; but such conjunction is far from being the same with the idea of power.

Power is a simple idea, and therefore incapable of being defined; but no person can be at a loss about it; for it is suggested to the mind by every external action. A being may be so formed, as to have no consciousness of *itself* nor of what it does; but every human being is conscious of itself, and of its actions as proceeding from itself. A man cannot throw a stone without being conscious that it is he himself who makes the stone move; which imports that he has a power to produce that effect. A child who is learning to walk, reflects very early that it *can* walk; which in other words is saying,

185

that it has a power to walk. *I can, I am able, I have a power,* are terms perfectly synonimous. A young boy tells his mother, that he is going to the garden, to pull a flower, or to eat gooseberries. Does not this import knowledge in the boy that he can go, or that he has a power to go? A resolution imports, in the very nature of it, a power to act. In short, there is not in the whole circle of our ideas one more familiar than that of power.

The author of the treatise of human nature has employed a world of reasoning, in searching for the foundation of our idea of power, and of necessary connection. And, after all his anxious researches, he can make no more of it, but,

> That the idea of necessary connection, *alias power* or *energy,* arises from a number of instances, of one thing always following another, which connects them in the imagination; whereby we can readily foretel the existence of the one from the appearance of the other.

And he pronounces, "That this connection can never be suggested from any one of these instances, surveyed in all possible lights and positions."* Thus, he places the essence of power or necessary connection upon that propensity which custom produces to pass from an object to the idea of its usual attendant. And from these premises, he draws a conclusion of a very extraordinary nature, and which he himself acknowledges to be not a little paradoxical. His words are:

> upon the whole, necessity is something that exists in the mind, not in objects; nor is it possible for us even to form the most distant idea of it, considered as a quality in bodies. The efficacy or energy in causes, is neither placed in the causes themselves, nor in the Deity, nor in the concurrence of these two principles; but belongs entirely to the soul, which considers the union of two or more objects in all past instances. It is here that the real power of causes is placed, along with their connection and necessity.†

---

* Philosophical Essays, Essay 7. [David Hume, *An Enquiry Concerning Human Understanding* (first published as *Philosophical Essays concerning Human Understanding* in 1748), ed. Tom L. Beauchamp (Oxford: Oxford University Press, 1999), 7.28, pp. 144–5.]

† Treatise of Human Nature, vol. 1. p. 290, 291. [Hume, *Treatise,* I.4.14.23, p. 112.]

He may well admit this doctrine to be a violent paradox; because it wages war with the common sense of mankind. We cannot put this in a stronger light than our author himself does, in forming an objection against his own doctrine.

> What! the efficacy of causes lie in the determination of the mind! as if causes did not operate entirely independent of the mind, and would not continue their operation, even though there was no mind existent to contemplate them, or reason concerning them. This is to reverse the order of nature, and to make that secondary which is really primary. To every operation there is a power proportioned; and this power must be placed on the body that operates. If we remove the power from one cause, we must ascribe it to another. But to remove it from all causes, and bestow it on a being that is no ways related to the cause or effect, but by perceiving them, is a gross absurdity, and contrary to the most certain principles of human reason.*

To what a cruel situation does a man reduce himself, when he is led unhappily to adopt a system inconsistent with common sense. Even his own conviction of a gross absurdity, is not sufficient to convert him. Upon such reasoners demonstration itself makes no impression; yet nothing is more clear, than that the very sight of a body in motion suggests to the mind the idea of power.

And to show, that our author's account of this matter comes far short of truth, it will be plain, from one or two instances, that though a constant connection of two objects, may by custom produce a similar connection in the imagination; yet that a constant connection, whether in the imagination or betwixt the objects themselves, doth by no means come up to our idea of power. Far from it. In a garrison, the soldiers constantly turn out at a certain beat of the drum. The gates of the town are opened and shut regularly, as the clock points at a certain hour. These connected facts are observed by a child, are associated in his mind, and the association becomes habitual during a long life. The man however, if not a changeling, never imagines the beat of the drum to be the cause of the motion of the soldiers;

---

* Pag. 294. [Ibid., 1.4.14.26, p. 113.]

nor the pointing of the clock to a certain hour, to be the cause of the opening or shutting of the gates. He perceives the cause of these operations to
be very different; and is not led into any mistake by the above-mentioned
circumstances, however closely connected. Let us put another instance, still
more apposite. Such is the human constitution, that we act necessarily upon
motives. The prospect of victuals makes a hungry man accelerate his pace:
respect to an ancient family moves him to take a wife: an object of distress
prompts him to lay out his money, or venture his person. Yet no man dreams
a motive to be the cause of action; though here is not only a constant, but
a necessary connection.*

The reader will take notice, that this author founds the idea of power
upon instances of one thing always following another, which connects them
in the imagination. According to that account, our idea of power includes
two objects, one going before, another following. But what is to be said
with respect to a single object, as where we see a man walking? Here there
is no connection of one thing following another. It ought therefore to be
admitted, that the idea of power is independent of that connection; otherwise, when a man is seen walking, it must be maintained that we have no
idea of his having a power to walk. We have a conviction of power from
every action, even of the simplest kind. Every man is conscious of having
himself a power to act; and he readily transfers the idea to other beings,
animate and inanimate.

I have still more to urge, though very little necessary, which is, to quote
our author against himself. Though in his Philosophical Essays he continues to maintain, "That necessity exists only in the mind, not in objects; and
that it is not possible for us even to form the most distant idea of it, considered as a quality in bodies;"[1] yet, in the course of the argument, he more
than once discovers, that he himself is possessed of an idea of *power*, considered as a quality in bodies. Thus, he observes,† "That nature conceals

---

* A thought or idea, it is obvious, cannot be the cause of action, cannot, of itself,
produce motion. It is the mind itself that is the agent. Its power indeed is so regulated
as that it cannot be exerted but by means of certain motives present to it.

   1. That is, Hume continues to maintain what he had already argued in the above-
quoted passage, which comes from the *Treatise* (1.3.14.22, pp. 111–12).

   † London edition, p. 58. [*An Enquiry concerning Human Understanding*, 4.16, p. 113.]

from us those powers and principles on which the influence of objects entirely depends." And of these powers and principles he gives several apt instances; such as, a power or quality in bread to nourish; a power by which bodies persevere in motion. This is not only owning an idea of power as a quality in bodies, but also owning the reality of this power. In another passage,* he observes, "That the particular powers by which all natural operations are performed, never appear to the senses"; and "that experience does not lead us to the knowledge of the secret power by which one object produces another." What leads us to the knowledge of this secret power, is not at present the question. But here is the author's own acknowledgment, that he hath an idea of a power in one object to produce another; for he certainly will not say that he is here making use of words without having any ideas annexed to them. In one passage in particular,† he talks distinctly and explicitly of "a power in one object, by which it infallibly produces the other, and operates with the greatest certainty, and strongest necessity." No person can give a description of power, considered as a quality in bodies, in more apt or more clear terms. So difficult it is to stifle or to disguise natural perceptions and sentiments.‡

Having thus ascertained the reality of our idea of power, as a quality of bodies, and traced it to its proper source, I shall close this Essay with some observations upon causes and their effects. That we cannot discover power in any object, otherways than by seeing it exert its power, is above observed. Therefore, we can never discover any object to be a cause, otherways than from the effect produced. But with regard to things caused or produced, the case is different. For we know an object to be an effect, when the cause is not seen. No one is at a loss to say, that a table or a chair is an effect produced: a child will ask who made it? We know from the light of nature every event, every new object, to be an effect or production, and consequently to have a cause. Hence the maxim, "That nothing can fall out,

* Page 72. [Ibid, 5.3–4, pp. 120–1.]
† Page 121. [Ibid., 7.2.27, p. 144.]
‡ Naturam expellas furca, tamen usque recurret. ["You may drive out Nature with a pitchfork, yet she will ever hurry back." Horace, *Epistles. Satires. Arts Poetica,* trans. H. Rushton Fairclough, Loeb Classical Library, No. 194 (Harvard: Harvard University Press, 1926), Epistles, 1.10.]

nothing begin to exist, without a cause"; in other words, "That every thing which begins to exist, must have a cause." This maxim cannot be the result of experience, for it is applied to unknown objects and singular events as readily as to the most familiar. Mr. Locke endeavours to evince it by an argument. "Whatever, says he, is produced without any cause, is produced by *nothing,* or in other words has *nothing* for its cause. But *nothing* cannot be a cause more than it can be *something*."[2] This is a plain begging of the question, for the argument proceeds on the supposition of a cause being necessary. Doctor Clarke has an argument that lies open to the same objection. "Every thing must have a cause; for if any thing wanted a cause, it would produce itself, that is, exist before it existed, which is impossible."[3] Thus, any sort of argument, however frail, passes current even with acute philosophers, when applied to prove a proposition that they before knew to be true. At the same time, they have not adverted that these arguments, supposing them to be strict demonstration, cannot reach children and rustics, who however are far from being ignorant of this maxim. And were there no more, the futility of these arguments is of itself sufficient to show, that the maxim must be founded upon conviction derived from the light of nature.

Further, the sense of any object as an effect leads us to infer a cause proportioned to it. If the object be an effect properly adapted to some end, we infer an intelligent designing cause. If the effect be some good end brought about by proper means, we infer a designing and benevolent cause. Nor is it in our power, by any sort of constraint, to vary these inferences. It may be in our power to conceive, but it is not in our power to believe, that a fine painting, a pathetic poem, or a beautiful piece of architecture, can ever be the effect of chance, or of blind fatality. It may be possible, for

2. Not a direct quote, and probably a mistaken attribution. Perhaps Kames had in mind Locke's statement that "whatever is considered by us, to conduce or operate, to the producing any particular simple Idea, or Collection of simple Ideas, whether Substance, or Mode, which did not before exist, hath thereby in our Minds the relation of a Cause" (*Essay,* II.xxvi.1, p. 324). In the first edition of his *Essays* (p. 295), however, Kames cited the above as "a universal maxim" without linking it to Locke.

3. Kames paraphrases the argument found in Proposition XI of Clarke's *A Discourse concerning the Being and Attributes of God.*

ought we know to the contrary, that a blind and undesigning cause may be productive of excellent effects. But we have intuitive conviction, that every object which appears beautiful as adapted to an end or purpose, is the effect of a designing cause; and that every object which appears beautiful as fitted to a good end or purpose, is the effect of a designing and benevolent cause. We are so constituted, that we cannot entertain a doubt of this, if we would. And as far as we gather from experience, we are not deceived.

Knowledge of Future Events

While we are tied to this globe, some knowledge of the beings around us
and of their operations, is necessary; because, without it, we should be utterly at a loss how to conduct ourselves. But that knowledge is not sufficient
for our well-being, and scarce for our preservation. It is likeways necessary,
that we have some knowledge of future events; for about these we are mostly
employed. A man will not sow, if he hath not a prospect of reaping: he will
not build a house, if he hath not some security, that it will stand firm for
years. Man is possessed of that valuable branch of knowledge: he can fortel
future events. There is no doubt of the fact. The difficulty only is, how that
knowledge is acquired. It is indeed an established maxim, That the course
of nature continues uniformly the same; and that things will be as they have
been: but, from what premises we draw this conclusion, is not obvious.
Uniformity in the operations of nature with regard to time past, is discovered by experience; but of future time having no experience, the maxim
cannot be derived from that source. Neither will reason help us out. It is
true, the production of one thing by another, even in a single instance, infers
a power; and that power is necessarily connected with its effect. But as
power is internal, not discoverable but by the effects produced, we can never
by any chain of reasoning, conclude power to be in any body, except in the
instant of operation. The power, for ought we know, may end at that instant. We cannot so much as conclude by any deduction of reason, that
this earth, the sun, or any one being, will exist tomorrow. And, supposing
their future existence to be discoverable by reason, we are not so much
acquainted with the nature or essence of any thing, as to discover a necessary
connection betwixt it and its powers, that the one subsisting, the other must

also subsist. There is nothing more easily conceived, than that the most active being shall at once be deprived of all its activity: and a thing that may be conceived, can never be proved inconsistent or impossible. An appeal to past experience, will not carry us through. The sun has afforded us light and heat from the beginning of the world. But what reason have we to conclude, that its power of giving light and heat must continue; when it is as easy to conceive powers to be limited in point of time, as to conceive them perpetual? If we have recourse to the wisdom and goodness of a Supreme Being, establishing permanent general laws; the difficulty is, that we have no *data,* from whence to conclude, in the way of reasoning, that these general laws must continue invariably the same without end. It is true, the conclusion is actually made, but it must be referred to some other source; for reasoning will not aid us, more than experience, to draw any one conclusion from past to future events. It is certain however, that the uniformity of nature's operations, is a maxim admitted by all men. Though altogether unassisted either by reason or experience, we never have the least hesitation to conclude, that things will be as they have been; even so firmly as to trust our lives and fortunes upon that conclusion. I shall endeavour to trace out the principle upon which this important conclusion is founded. And this subject will afford a fresh instance of the admirable correspondence that is discovered betwixt the nature of man and his external circumstances. If our conviction of the uniformity of nature be not founded upon reason nor experience, it can have no foundation but the light of nature. We are so constituted, as necessarily to transfer our past experience to futurity; and we have an innate conviction of the constancy and uniformity of nature. Our knowledge here is intuitive, and is more firm and solid than any conclusion from reasoning can be. This conviction must arise from an internal sense, because it evidently hath no relation to any of our external senses. And an argument which hath been more than once stated in the foregoing Essays, will be found decisive upon this point. Let us suppose a being destitute of this sense: such a being will never be able to transfer its past experience to futurity. Every event, however conformable to past experience, will come equally unexpected to this being, as new and rare events do to us; though possibly without the same surprise.

This sense of constancy and uniformity in the works of nature, is not confined to the subject above handled, but displays itself remarkably upon many other objects. We have a conviction of a common nature in beings that are similar in their appearance. We expect a likeness in their constituent parts, in their appetites, and in their conduct. We not only lay our account with uniformity of behaviour in the same individual, but in all the individuals of the same species. This sense hath such influence, as even to make us hope for constancy and uniformity, where experience would lead us to the opposite conclusion. The rich man never thinks of poverty, nor the distressed of relief. Even in this variable climate, we cannot readily bring ourselves to believe, that good or bad weather will have an end. Nay, it governs our notions in law-matters, and is the foundation of the maxim, "That alteration or change of circumstances is not presumed." Influenced by the same sense, every man acquires a certain uniformity of manner, which spreads itself upon his thoughts, words, and actions. In our younger years, its effect is not remarkable, being opposed by a variety of passions, which, as they have different and sometimes opposite tendencies, occasion a fluctuation in our conduct. But as soon as the heat of youth is over, it seldom fails to bring on a punctual regularity in our way of living, which is remarked in most old people.

Analogy is one of the most common sources of reasoning; the force of which is universally admitted. The conviction of every argument founded on analogy, ariseth from this very sense of uniformity. Things similar in some particulars, are presumed to be similar in every particular.

In a word, as the bulk of our views and actions have a future aim, some knowledge of future events is necessary, that we may adapt our views and actions to natural events. To this end, the Author of our nature hath done two things: he hath established a constancy and uniformity in the operations of nature; and he hath given us an intuitive conviction of this constancy and uniformity, and that things will be as they have been.

Dread of Supernatural Powers in the Dark

A very slight view of human nature is sufficient to convince us, that we were not dropt here by accident. This earth is fitted for man, and man is fitted for inhabiting this earth. By our senses we have an intuitive knowledge of the things that surround us, at least of those things, by which we may be affected. We can discover objects at a distance. We discern them in their connection of cause and effect; and their future operations are laid open, as well as their present. But in this grand apparatus of senses external and internal, by which the secrets of nature are disclosed to us, one seems to be with-held; though in appearance the most useful of all: and that is, a sense to discern what things are noxious, what are friendly. The most poisonous fruits have sometimes the fairest colours; and savage animals partake of beauty with the tame and harmless. And by the most extensive induction it will be found, that man hath no original sense of what is salutary to him, and what is hurtful.

It is natural to inquire why this sense is with-held, when it appears to be the design of nature, to furnish us plentifully with senses for the discovery of useful truths. It is too bold an undertaking in man, to dive into the secrets of his Maker. We ought to rest contented with the numerous instances we have of good order and good purpose; which must afford us a rational conviction, that good order and good purpose take place universally. At the same time, a rational conjecture may be formed of this matter. We have a conviction, that there is nothing redundant or superfluous in the operations of nature: different means are never afforded us to bring about the same end. Experience, as far as it can go, is given us for acquiring knowledge;

and sense only, where experience cannot aid us. Sense is with-held in the present case, because the knowledge of what is harmful, and what beneficial, may be obtained by experience. And this suggests a final cause, not a little interesting. Man by his nature is made for an active life, and his felicity depends greatly on it. To excite activity, we are left to gather knowledge from experience, and sense is only afforded where experience can give us no instruction.

Man then is placed in this world, amidst a great variety of objects, the nature and tendency of which are unknown to him, otherways than by experience. In this situation, he would be in perpetual danger, had he not some faithful monitor to keep him constantly upon the watch against harm. This monitor is the propensity he hath to be afraid of new objects; such especially as have no peculiar beauty to raise desire. A child, to whom all nature is strange, dreads the approach of every object; and even the face of man is frightful to it. The same timidity and suspicion may be observed in travellers, who converse with strangers, and meet with unknown appearances. Upon the first sight of an herb or fruit, we apprehend the worst, and suspect it to be noxious. An unknown animal is immediately conceived to be dangerous. The more rare phaenomena of nature, the causes of which are unknown to the vulgar, never fail to strike them with terror. From this induction it is clear, that we dread unknown objects: they are always surveyed with an emotion of fear, till experience discover them to be harmless.

This dread of unknown objects is thought to be inherent in all sensible beings; but chiefly in the weak and defenceless. The more feeble and delicate the creature is, the more shy and timorous it is observed to be. No creature is by nature more feeble and delicate than man; and this principle is to him of admirable use, to balance the principle of curiosity, which is prevalent in man above all other creatures; and which, indulged without control, would often betray him into fatal accidents.

The dread of unknown objects fires the imagination to magnify their supposed evil qualities. For it is a well-known truth, that passion hath great influence on the imagination. The less we know of a new object, the greater liberty we have to dress it in frightful colours. The object is conceived to have all the dreadful qualities that imagination can invent; and the same terror is raised, as if these qualities were real, not imaginary.

If the new and unknown object have any thing dreadful in its appearance, this circumstance, joined with our natural propensity to dread unknown objects, will raise terror even in the most resolute. If the evils dreaded from such objects, be known neither in quality nor degree; the imagination, being under no restraint, figures the greatest evils, both in kind and magnitude, that can be conceived. If no immediate harm ensue, the mind, by the impulse it hath received, transports itself into futurity, and imagines the strange forms to be presages of direful calamities. Hence it is, that the uncommon phaenomena of nature, such as comets, eclipses, earthquakes, are by the vulgar held as forerunners of dreadful events.

The most common instance of our dread of unknown objects, is the fear that seizes many young persons in the dark; a phaenomenon that has not been clearly accounted for. Light disposeth the mind to chearfulness and consequently to courage. Darkness, by depressing the mind, disposeth it to fear. Any object alarms the mind, when it is already prepared by darkness to receive impressions of fear. An object seen in the dark but obscurely, leaves the heated imagination at liberty to bestow upon it the most dreadful appearance. This phantom of the imagination, conceived as a reality, unhinges the mind, and throws it into a fit of distraction. The imagination, now heated to the highest degree, multiplies the dreadful appearances to the utmost bounds of its conception. The object becomes a spectre, a devil, a hobgoblin, something more terrible than ever was seen or described.

A very few accidents of this kind, having so powerful an effect, are sufficient to introduce an association between darkness and malignant powers. And when once this association is formed, there is no occasion for the appearance of an object to create terror. Frightful ideas croud into the mind, and augment the fear occasioned by darkness. The imagination becomes ungovernable, and converts these ideas into real appearances.

That the terror occasioned by darkness is entirely owing to the imagination, will be evident from a single reflection, that in company no such effect is produced. A companion can afford no security against super-natural powers. But a companion hath the same effect with sunshine to chear the mind, and preserve it from gloominess and despondence. The imagination is kept within bounds, and under due subjection to sense and reason.*

* Buffon, tome 6th of his Natural History, octavo, endeavours to account for the dread of spectres in the dark from the indistinct appearances of objects. A small bush at hand is imagined a great tree placed at a distance, and a fly passing near the eye is imagined a monstrous bird at a great distance. But that author has not adverted, that the dread of spectres is greatest in utter darkness, when no object can be seen either distinctly or confusedly. [Buffon suggests that while reports of specters in the dark are commonly attributed to the imagination, they may refer to actual objects the perception of which is distorted by our inability to judge distance and proportion in the dark. Thus, "the conception of spectres is founded in nature, and, contrary to what philosophers believe, their appearance does not depend solely on imagination." Georges Louis Leclerc, comte de Buffon (1707–1788), "Du sens de la Vue" ("Of the Sense of Sight") in De L'Homme, vols. 2 and 3 of Histoire naturelle, générale et particulière, 15 vols. (Paris, 1749), vol. 3, pp. 319–20. Published between 1749 and 1804, Buffon's encyclopedic work covered the natural history of the earth, man, the quadrupeds, birds, and minerals, and eventually reached 44 volumes (with 35 volumes published by 1788, an additional volume in press at the time of Buffon's death, and 8 volumes prepared by assistants and published in 1804).]

Knowledge of the Deity

The arguments *a priori* for the existence and attributes of the Deity, are urged, with the greatest shew of reason, in the sermons preached at Boyle's lectures.[1] But these sermons, though they command my attention, never reach my heart: on the contrary, they always give me a sensible uneasiness; the cause of which I imagine I can now explain. Such deep metaphysical reasoning, supposing it to be conclusive, is surely not fitted for the vulgar and illiterate. Is then our Maker known to none but to persons of great study and deep thinking? Is a vail thrown over the eyes of the rest of mankind? This thought always returned upon me, and gave me pain. If there really exist a Being who made and who governs the world, and if it be his purpose to display himself to his rational creatures; it is not accountable that he should stop short at a very small part of mankind. At the same time, to found our knowledge of the Deity upon reasoning solely, is not agreeable to the analogy of nature. We depend not on abstract reasoning, nor indeed on any reasoning, for unfolding our duty to our fellow creatures: it is engraved upon the table of our hearts. We adapt our actions to the course of nature, by mere instinct, without reasoning, or even experience. Therefore, if analogy can be relied on, it ought to be thought that God will discover himself to us, in some such manner as may take in all mankind, the vulgar and illiterate as well as the deep-thinking philosopher.

If these abstruse arguments be relished by the learned and speculative, it is so far well. I cannot help acknowledging, that they afford me no conviction; at least no solid and permanent conviction. We know little about

---

1. That is, Samuel Clarke's *Discourse concerning the Being and Attributes of God.*

the nature of things, but what we learn from a strict attention to our own nature. That nothing can begin to exist without a cause, is sufficiently evident from sense.* But that this can be demonstrated by any argument *a priori,* drawn from the nature of things, I have not observed.† And if demonstration fail us in the very outsetting, we cannot hope for its assistance in the subsequent steps. But if this difficulty shall be surmounted, we have another to struggle with. Admitting that something has existed from all eternity, I find no *data* to determine *a priori,* whether this world has existed from all eternity, in a constant succession of causes and effects; or whether it is an effect produced by an almighty power. It is indeed hard to conceive a world, eternal and self-existent, where all things are carried on by blind fate, without design or intelligence. And yet I can find no demonstration to the contrary. If we can form any obscure notion of a single being existing from all eternity, is it more difficult to form a notion of a succession of beings, existing from all eternity, or a notion of a perpetual succession of causes and effects?

Mr. Locke‡ admits that we have no innate idea of God; but insists that the existence of God can be demonstrated; and the following is his demonstration.

> Whatever had a beginning must be produced by something else: but man, an intelligent being, had a beginning; and therefore must have been produced by some powerful intelligent Being: and if that powerful intelligent Being had no beginning, he must have existed from all eternity; and it is that Being we term God.

This is a very infirm demonstration. It rests intirely upon the foundation of man having had a beginning, which is not self-evident. It includes no absurdity to suppose that this earth with all the beings upon it, cogitative and incogitative, may have existed from all eternity. This argument could not have passed as a demonstration with so consummate a logician as Mr. Locke, but for an antecedent conviction of a self-existent intelligent Being

* See the Essay of Power.
† See the same Essay.
‡ Book 4. chap. 10. ["Of Our Knowledge of the Existence of a God," in Locke, *Essay,* IV.x.]

who made and governs the world. And with respect to any known truth, nothing is more common than to hold a few lame *ergos* to be a strict demonstration.

When we think of eternity and of an eternal Being, difficulties press on every side. But these difficulties are occasioned by the limited capacity of the mind of man. We cannot comprehend an eternity of existence: it is an object too bulky: it eludes our grasp. The mind is like the eye: it cannot take in an object that is very great or very little. This plainly is the source of our difficulties, when we attempt speculations so remote from common apprehension. Abstract reasoning upon such a subject, must lead into endless perplexities. It is indeed less difficult to conceive one eternal unchangeable Being who made the world, than to conceive a blind chain of causes and effects. At least, we are disposed to the former, as being more agreeable to the imagination. But as we cannot find any inconsistency in the latter supposition, we cannot justly say that it is demonstrably false.

Give me leave to add, that to bring out such abstruse and intricate speculations into any clear light, is at any rate scarce to be expected. And if, after the utmost straining, they remain obscure and unaffecting, it is evident to me, that they must have a bad tendency. Persons of a peevish and gloomy cast of mind, finding no conviction from that quarter, will be fortified in their propension to believe that all things happen by blind chance; that there is no wisdom, order, nor harmony, in the government of this world; and consequently, that there is no God.

Being therefore little solicitous about arguments *a priori* for the existence of a Deity, which are not proportioned to the capacity of man, I apply myself with zeal and chearfulness, to search for the Deity in his works; for by these we must discover him, if he have thought proper to make himself known. And the better to manage the inquiry, I shall endeavour to make out three propositions; 1*st,* That if there exist a Being who is the Maker and Governor of the world, it seems to be a necessary part of his government, that he should make himself known to his intelligent creatures. 2*dly,* That in fact he hath done so. And, 3*dly,* That to compass this end, a method is employed entirely suited to our nature, and the same by which many other truths of the greatest importance are laid open to us.

There certainly cannot be a more discouraging thought to man, than that the world was formed by a fortuitous concourse of atoms, and that all things are carried on by blind impulse. Upon that supposition, he can have no security for his life; nor for his continuing to be an intelligent creature, even for a moment. Things have been carried on with regularity and order: but chance may, in an instant, throw all things into horrid confusion. We can have no comfort in virtue, when it is a work of mere chance; nor can we justify our reliance upon the faith of others, when the nature of man rests upon so precarious a foundation. Every thing must appear gloomy, dismal, and disjointed, without a Deity to unite this world of beings into one beautiful and harmonious system. These considerations, and many more that will occur upon the first reflection, afford a very strong conviction, if there be a wise and good Being who superintends the affairs of this world, that he will not conceal himself from his rational creatures. Can any thing be more desirable or more substantially useful, than to know that there is a Being, from whom no secrets are hid, to whom our good works are acceptable, and even the good purposes of our hearts; and whose government, directed by wisdom and benevolence, ought to make us rest secure, that nothing doth nor will fall out but according to good order? This sentiment, rooted in the mind, is an antidote to all misfortune. Without it, life is at best but a confused and gloomy scene.

And this leads to a different consideration, which makes our knowledge of a benevolent Deity of the greatest importance to us. Though natural and moral evil are far from prevailing in this world, yet so much of both is scattered over the face of things, as to create some degree of doubt, whether there may not be a mixture of chance or of ill-will in the government of this world. But once supposing the superintendency of a good Being, these evils are no longer considered as such. A man restrains himself from unlawful pleasures, though the restraint gives him pain. But then he does not consider this pain as an evil to repine at: he submits to it voluntarily and with satisfaction, as one doth to grief for the loss of a friend; being conscious that it is *right* and *fit* for him to be so affected. In the same manner, he submits to all the evils of this life. Having confidence in the good government of the Deity, he is persuaded that every thing happens for the best; and therefore that it is his duty to submit to whatever happens. This unfolds a scene so enlivening and so productive of chearfulness and good humour, that we cannot readily think, if there be a benevolent Deity, that he would with-hold from his creatures so invaluable a blessing.

Man, at the same time, by his taste for beauty, regularity, and order, is fitted for contemplating the wisdom and goodness displayed in the frame and government of this world. These are proper objects of admiration and joy. It is not agreeable to the ordinary course of nature, that man should be endued with an affection, without having a proper object to bestow it upon. And as the providence of the Deity is the highest object of this affection, it would be unnatural, that man should be kept in ignorance of it.

These, I admit, are but probable reasons for believing, that if there exist a benevolent Deity, it must be his intention to manifest himself to his creatures: but they carry a high degree of probability, which leaves little room for doubt. At the same time, though it should be our fate to search in vain for this object of our affection, we ought not however to despair, and in that despair to conclude there is no God. Let us but reflect, that he hath not manifested himself to all his creatures. The brutes certainly know nothing of him. And should we be disappointed in this search, all we can conclude is, that, for good and wise purposes which we cannot dive into, he hath thought proper to with-hold himself also from us. We certainly have no reason to convert our ignorance into an argument against his existence. Our ignorance brings us only a step lower, and puts us so far upon a footing with the brute creation.

The second and important branch of our disquisition is, to ascertain that there is a Deity, and that he hath manifested himself to us. I request only attention of my reader, and not any unreasonable concession. In a former Essay,* two propositions are made out. The first is, That every thing that hath a beginning, is perceived as a *production* or *effect,* which necessarily involves the idea of a *cause.* The second, That whatever of contrivance or usefulness is discovered in the effect, is necessarily attributed to the cause. Considering a house, garden, picture, or statue, in itself, it is perceived as beautiful. If we attend to these objects as things having a beginning, we perceive them to be effects, involving the idea of a cause. Natural objects, such as plants and animals, are also perceived as effects, or as the production

* Power, Cause and Effect.

of some cause. The question will always recur, How came it here? Who made it? What is the cause of its existence? We are so accustomed to human arts, that every work of design and use will be attributed to man, if it exceed not his known powers. Nor do effects above the power of man unhinge our notion of a cause: they only lead the mind to a more powerful cause.

With respect to the second proposition, that we attribute to the cause whatever of contrivance or usefulness is discovered in the effect, attend to any useful machine, such as a plough or a fire-engine, we necessarily infer that the contriver was a man of skill, and probably public spirited. With respect to works of nature, so much art and usefulness are discovered in the various plants covering the surface of this globe, as necessarily to make us infer them to be the production of some cause, benevolent as well as powerful and intelligent. The scene opens more and more, when, passing from plants to animals, we come to man, the most wonderful of all the works of nature. And when at last we take in at one view the material and moral worlds, full of harmony, order, and beauty, happily adjusted to answer great and glorious purposes; there is in this grand production necessarily involved the conviction of a cause, unbounded in power, intelligence, and goodness.*

Thus it is, that the Deity hath manifested himself to us by principles wrought into our nature, which infallibly operate upon viewing objects in their relation of cause and effect. We discover external objects by their qualities of colour, figure, size, and motion. In the perception of these qualities, connected after a certain manner, is comprehended the perception of the substance or thing, to which these qualities belong. At the same time, we perceive this substance or thing supposing it to have had a beginning, to be an effect produced by some cause; and we perceive the powers and properties of this cause, from its effects. If there be an aptitude in the effect to some end, we attribute to the cause intelligence and design. If the effect

---

* See the Greenlander's Argument, Sketches of the History of Man, edit. 2d. vol. 4. p. 196. [In his sketch on the "Principles and progress of theology" (Sketches, vol. 4, bk. 3, sketch 3), Kames cites a conversation between a Danish missionary and a Greenlander (taken from David Crantz's History of Greenland, 1767) in order to show that "savage" peoples have intimations of a knowledge of the Deity.]

produced be something that is good in itself, or that hath a tendency to some good end or purpose, we attribute goodness to the cause, as well as intelligence and design: and this we do, not by any process of reasoning, but by the light of nature. The Deity hath not left his existence to be gathered from slippery and far-fetched arguments. We need but open our eyes, to receive impressions of him almost from every thing we perceive. We discover his being and attributes in the same manner as we discover external objects, namely by the evidence of our senses. And none but they who deny the existence of matter against the evidence of their senses, can seriously and deliberately deny the existence of the Deity. In fine, there is a wonderful harmony established betwixt our senses, internal and external, and the course of nature. We rely on our senses, for the existence of external objects, and their past, present, and future operations. We rely on these senses by the necessity of our nature; and upon experience find ourselves not deceived. Our conviction of the Deity, is as distinct and authoritative as that of external objects. And though here we have not experience to appeal to, the want of experience can never afford an argument against any proposition, where, from the nature of the thing, there can be no experience. It is sufficient for conviction, that our senses correspond to the truth of things, wherever there is an opportunity to try them by experience; and therefore we can have no cause to doubt of our senses in any case, where they are not contradicted by experience.

So far the Deity is discoverable, by every person who goes but one step beyond the surface of things, and their mere existence. We may indeed behold the earth in its gayest dress, the heavens in all their glory, without having any perception other than that of beauty, something in these objects that pleases and delights us. Many pass their lives, brutishly involved in corporeal pleasures, without having any perception, at least any strong or permanent perception, of the Deity. But the Deity cannot be long hid from those who are accustomed to any degree of reflection. No sooner are we prepared to relish beauties of the second and third class;* no sooner do we acquire a taste for regularity, order, design, and good purpose, than we begin to perceive the Deity in the beauty of the operations of nature. Savages,

* See the Essay upon the Foundation and Principles of Morality, chap. 2.

who have no consistent rule of conduct, who act by the blind impulse of passion and appetite, and who have only a glimmering of the moral sense, are but ill qualified to discover the Deity in his works. If they have little or no perception of a just tenor of life, of the dignity of behaviour, or of the beauty of action, how should they perceive the beauty of the works of creation, or the admirable harmony of all the parts, in the great system of things? Society teaches mankind self-denial, and improves the moral sense. Disciplined in society, the taste for order and regularity unfolds itself by degrees: the social affections gain the ascendant; and the morality of actions takes firm hold of the mind. In this improved state, the beauty of the creation makes a strong impression; and we can never cease admiring the excellency of that Cause, who is the author of so many beautiful effects.*

Hitherto we have gone no farther, than to point out the means by which we discover the Deity, and his attributes of power, wisdom, and goodness. So far are we carried, by those principles in our nature which discover the connection betwixt cause and effect, and from the effect discover the powers and properties of the cause. But there is one attribute of the Supreme Being, of the most essential kind, which remains to be unfolded. It is what commonly passeth under the name of *self-existence,* that he must have existed for ever; and, consequently, that he cannot be considered as an effect, to require a cause of his existence; but, without being caused, that, mediately or immediately, he is the Cause of all other things. If all beings had a beginning, there must have been a time when the world was an absolute void; upon which supposition, it is intuitively certain, that nothing ever could have come into existence. This proposition we perceive to be true; and our

---

* These are thy glorious works, Parent of good,
    Almighty! Thine this universal frame,
    Thus wondrous fair. Thyself how wondrous then?
    Unspeakable! who sit'st above these heavens,
    To us invisible, or dimly seen
    In these thy [lowest] works; yet these declare
    Thy goodness, beyond thought, and power divine.
                         MILTON.

[John Milton, *Paradise Lost* (1674), ed. Scott Elledge (New York: W. W. Norton, 1993), bk. 5:153–9.]

perception affords us, in this case, a more solid conviction than any demonstration can do. One being, therefore, must have existed from all eternity: who, as he is not an effect or production, cannot be indebted for his existence to any other being.

That there must be one eternal self-existing Being, is a capital point. What only remains is to consider, whether this world with all it contains was created by that Being; or whether the world itself be that one eternal self-existent Being. The latter opinion is maintained by several writers, ancient and modern. And supposing their eternal and self-existent world to be endued with an intelligent mind, uniting the various parts into one great whole, and directing the great chain of causes and effects, I perceive not any absurdity in the supposition, as far as my reason can carry me. But as this governing mind would be the Deity, the very Being we are in quest of, the supposition is rejected by these writers; who hold, that this world, devoid of intelligence, is governed by blind fatality, or perhaps by chance. Chance, in the sense here given it, must be exploded, as it is made out above, that the term signifies nothing but our ignorance of a cause.* And as for blind fatality, the intelligence and foresight displayed in the government of the world, is clearly inconsistent with that opinion. The numberless effects daily falling out, that bespeak power, wisdom, and benevolence in their cause, afford to us intuitive conviction of the world being governed by a powerful, wise, and benevolent Being. The light of nature leads us to that conclusion, and permits us not to entertain the slightest doubt of it.† Therefore, supposing this world to be eternal and self-existent, there must be notwithstanding an independent cause which governs all, and that cause is God. At the same time, I am far from admitting the world, this earth at least, to be eternal. The following argument appears to me conclusive against that opinion. Whatever is frequently changing must be an effect; because if it never had a beginning, all the changes it is susceptible of must have happened millions of ages ago. This earth, the surface at least, is continually changing, the hills gradually mouldering down to the valleys, the sea incroaching on the land, and the land on the sea, the latter growing

---

* Essay Liberty and Necessity, page 122.
† See Essay on Power, Cause and Effect, at the end.

salter and salter, &c. &c. Therefore it cannot be eternal. It will not enervate this argument, that these changes may be the effect of earthquakes, deluges, or other extraordinary events; for every grand revolution as well as every minute change must have happened long ago, if this earth had no beginning.

The bulk of mankind in forming their notion of a Deity, do not include the attribute of self-existence: a man must be accustomed to abstract reasoning, who of himself discovers this truth. But it is not difficult to explain it to others, after it is discovered. And it deserves well to be inculcated; for without it our knowledge of the Deity must be extremely imperfect. His other attributes of power, wisdom, and goodness, are in some measure communicated to his creatures; but his attribute of self-existence makes the strongest opposition imaginable betwixt him and his creatures.

The third point, namely, the means employed by the Deity to make himself known to us, require very little explanation after what is laid down above. The essence of the Deity is far beyond the reach of our comprehension. Were he to exhibit himself to us in broad day-light, he could not be reached by any of our external senses. Spirit cannot be reached by any of them; and the attributes of self-existence, wisdom, goodness, and power, are purely intellectual. By means indeed of that sense which discovers causes from their effects, he hath manifested himself to us in a satisfactory manner, liable to no doubt nor error. And after all, what further evidence can we desire, when the evidence we have of his existence is little inferior to that we have of our own existence? Our senses serve us for evidence in both.* Our own existence indeed is, of all facts, that which concerns us the most; and therefore of our own existence we ought to have the highest certainty. Next to it, we have not, as it appears to me, a greater certainty of any matter of fact, than of the existence of the Deity. It is equal to the certainty we have of external objects, and of the constancy and uniformity of the operations of nature, upon the faith of which our whole schemes of life are adjusted.

The arguments *a posteriori* that have been urged for the being and attributes of the Deity, are generally defective. There is always wanting one

---

* See the Essay Personal Identity.

link of the chain, to wit, that sense upon which is founded our knowledge of causes and their effects. But the calm perceptions, turning habitual by frequent repetition, are apt to be overlooked in our reasonings. Many a proposition is rendered obscure by much laboured argument, for the truth of which we need but appeal to our own senses. Thus, we are told, that the frame and order of the world, the wisdom and goodness displayed in every part of it, are an evident demonstration of the being of a God. These, I acknowledge, afford full conviction. But, laying aside sense and perception, I should be utterly at a loss to conclude from reasoning, the existence of any one thing from that of another. In particular, by what process of reasoning can we demonstrate it to be true, That order and beauty must proceed from a designing cause? The idea of an effect involves indeed the idea of a cause; but does reason make out, that the thing we name an *effect,* may not exist of itself, as well as what we name a *cause?* If it be urged, that human works, where means are apparently adjusted to an end and beauty and order discovered, are always known to be the effects of intelligence and design: I admit this to be true, as far as I have experience. But where experience fails me, I desire to know by what step, what link in the chain of reasoning, am I to connect my past experience with the future. If it be said, that nature prompts us to judge of similar instances, by former experience; this is giving up reason and demonstration, to appeal to that very sense, on the evidence of which this truth must entirely rest. All the arguments *a posteriori* may be resolved into this principle: which probably influenced the writers who handle the present subject; though, I must be allowed to say, it hath not been explained, nor perhaps sufficiently understood by them; whereby all of them have been led into the error of stating as demonstrative reasoning, what is truly an appeal to our senses. They reason, for example, upon the equality of males and females; and hold the infinite odds against this equality to be a demonstration that matters cannot be carried on by chance. This, considered merely as reasoning, does not conclude; for events are infinite in their variety. But though reason cannot afford demonstration in this case, sense and perception afford conviction. The equality of males and females, is one of the many instances which we know and perceive to be effects of a designing cause; and of which we can no more entertain a doubt, than of our own existence. The same sense that unfolds to us the connection of causes and their effects in the most common events, discovers this whole universe to stand in the relation of an effect to a supreme cause.

To substitute sense in place of reason and demonstration, may seem to put the evidence of the Deity upon too low a footing. On the contrary, intuition affords a higher degree of conviction than any reasoning can do. Human reason is commonly overvalued by philosophers. It affords very little aid in making original discoveries. The comparing things together, and directing our inferences from sense and experience, are its proper province. Reason indeed gives its aid, in our inquiries concerning the Deity: it enlarges our views of final causes, and of the prevalence of wisdom and goodness. But the application of the argument from final causes to prove the existence of a Deity, and the force of our conclusion from beautiful and orderly effects to a designing cause, are not from reason, but from an internal light, which shows things in their relation of cause and effect. These conclusions rest entirely upon sense; and it is surprising, that writers should overlook what is so natural, and so obvious. But the pride of man's heart, makes him desire to extend his discoveries by dint of reasoning, which is his own work. There is merit in acuteness and penetration; and we are better pleased to assume merit to ourselves, than humbly to acknowledge, that, to the most important discoveries, we are directly led by the hand of the Almighty.*

Having unfolded that principle upon which I would rest the most important of all truths, objections must not be overlooked. To these I shall give their utmost weight; which ought to be done in every controversy, and which becomes more strictly a duty, in handling a subject where truth is of the utmost importance.

One objection may be, that the foregoing argument from which we con-

---

* To prevent mistakes, it is proper to be observed, that, in a lax sense, reason comprehends intuition, as well as the power of drawing conclusions from premises. But here it is used in its strict and proper sense, as opposed to intuition. By intuition we perceive certain propositions to be true, precisely as by sight we perceive certain things to exist. Other propositions require a chain of comparisons and intermediate steps, before we arrive at the conclusion; by which we perceive, either demonstrably or probably, the proposition to be true. Hence it is clear, that intuitive knowledge, which is acquired by a single act of perception, must stand higher in the scale of conviction, than any reasoning can do that requires a plurality of perceptions. The more complex any process is by which we acquire knowledge, the greater is the chance of error; and consequently the less entire our conviction.

clude the eternity and self-existence of one Being who made this world, doth not necessarily infer the conclusion; because it will equally conclude for an eternal succession of beings deriving their existence from each other. In matters so profound, it is difficult to form notions with any degree of accuracy. It is observed above, that it is much for man to grasp in his thought an eternal Being, whose existence cannot admit the supposition of a cause. To talk, as some of our metaphysical writers do, of an absolute necessity in the nature of the Being as the cause of his existence, is mere jargon. For we can conceive nothing more clearly, than that the cause must go before the effect, and that the cause cannot possibly be in the effect. But however difficult it may be to conceive one eternal Being, without a cause of its existence; it is no less difficult to conceive an eternal succession of beings, deriving their existence from each other: for though every link be supposed a production, the chain itself exists without a cause, as well as one eternal Being does. Therefore an eternal succession of beings is not a more natural supposition, than one eternal self-existent Being. And taking it in a different light, it will appear a supposition much less natural, or rather altogether unnatural. Succession in existence, implying the successive annihilation of individuals, is indeed a very natural conception. But then it is intimately connected with frail and dependent beings; and cannot, without the utmost violence to the conception, be applied to the Maker of all things, to whom we naturally ascribe perpetual existence, and every other perfection. And therefore, as this hypothesis of a perpetual succession, when applied to the Deity, is destitute of any support from reason and is contradicted by nature, there can be no reason for adopting it.

The noted proposition, That *primos in orbe Deos fecit timor*,[2] may be objected; as it will be thought unphilosophical, to multiply causes for our belief of a Deity, when fear alone must have that effect. For my part, I have little doubt of the truth of the proposition taken in its proper sense, that fear is the foundation of our belief of invisible malevolent powers; for evidently fear can never be the cause of our belief of a benevolent Deity. There is unfolded in another Essay,* the cause of our dread of malevolent invisible powers. And I am persuaded, that nothing has been more hurtful to reli-

---

2. "Fear first created gods in the world." Originally from *Thebaid* (3.661), an epic poem composed by Statius circa 80–92 A.D.

* Dread of Supernatural Powers in the Dark.

gion, than an irregular propensity in our nature to dread such powers. Superficial thinkers are apt to confound these phantoms of the imagination, with the objects of our true and genuine perceptions: and finding so little reality in the former, they are apt to conclude the latter also to be a fiction. Man in his original savage state, is a shy and timorous animal, dreading every new object, and attributing every extraordinary event to some invisible malevolent power. Led at the same time by mere appetite, he hath little idea of regularity and order, of the morality of actions, or of the beauty of nature. In this state he multiplies his invisible malevolent powers, without entertaining any notion of a supreme Being, the Creator of all things. As man ripens in society and is benefited by the good-will of others, his dread of new objects gradually lessens. He begins to perceive regularity and order in the course of nature. He becomes sharp-sighted, in discovering causes from effects, and effects from causes. He ascends gradually through the different orders of beings and their operations, till he discovers the Deity, who is the cause of all things. When we run over the history of man, it will be found to hold true, that savages, who are the most possessed with the opinion of evil spirits, are extremely deficient in the knowledge of a Deity; and that as all civilized nations, without exception, entertain the firm belief of a Deity, so the dread of evil spirits wears out in every nation, in proportion to their gradual advances in social intercourse.

And this leads to a reflection, which cannot fail to touch every thinking person. Man in a savage state, is hurried on by every gust of passion, and by every phantom of the imagination. His powers and faculties are improved by education and good culture; he acquires deep knowledge in the nature of things, and learns to distinguish truth from falsehood. And as he increaseth in knowledge and in the discerning faculties, his conviction of a Deity becomes proportionally more clear and authoritative. The universal conviction of a Deity, which hath spread through all civilized nations, cannot possibly be without a foundation in our nature. To insist that it may, is to insist that an effect may be without an adequate cause. Reason cannot be an adequate cause; because our reasonings upon this subject, must at best be abstruse, and beyond the comprehension of the generality of mankind. Our knowledge therefore of the Deity, must be founded on intuition and perception, which are common to mankind. And it is agreeable to the analogy of nature, that God should discover himself to his rational creatures after this manner.

If this subject be involved in any degree of obscurity, writers are to blame, who, in a matter of so great importance, ought to give no quarter to inaccuracy of thought or expression. But it is an error common among writers, to substitute reason in place of intuitive perception. Sense working silently and without effort, is generally overlooked: and we must find a reason for every thing we judge to be true, without considering that every sort of reasoning must be founded on axioms or principles that are intuitively certain. Instances of this wrong bias are not unfrequent even in mathematics, the most perfect of all sciences. In the first Book of Euclid, more than one self-evident proposition are brought under the form of a demonstration.[3] It is by the same wrong bias, that the principles of morality have been involved in obscurity by several writers. The qualities of right and wrong in human actions, are known to us intuitively by means of the moral sense; and far from being discoverable by reason, they are axioms or principles upon which every reasoning upon moral subjects must be founded. I need no better instance of this observation, than Doctor Clarke's demonstration, as it is termed, of the unalterable obligation of moral duty, mentioned above, page 67, which consists in words merely without any distinct meaning, or rather without any meaning.[4] And even after the long neglected anatomy of the mind came to be more the subject of inquiry than formerly, the moral sense was not soon recognized. Hutcheson discovered a sense of beauty and deformity in things, and particularly in human actions; but he was mistaken in holding that sense to be the moral sense. The sense of right and wrong in actions passed unobserved by that author, though it is what ought only to be termed the moral sense, as being the director of our con-

3. Euclid's *Elements* follows a syllogistic model, in which each geometrical proposition is justified by its own demonstration.

4. "That, from the Eternal and Necessary Differences of Things, there naturally and necessarily arise certain Moral Obligations, which are of themselves incumbent on all Rational Creatures, antecedent to all positive Institution and to all expectation of Reward or Punishment," Proposition I of Clarke's *Discourse concerning the Unchangeable Obligations of Natural Religion*. See above, Part I, essay II, footnote 9, for Kames's previous citation.

duct, informing us what we ought to do, and what we ought not to do. In the same way, our knowledge of the Deity has been involved in much obscurity. Writers reason without end about a Deity and his attributes, overlooking the light of nature, by which we discover the Deity not only from his works, insisted on above, but from an innate perception of his existence, made evident in Sketches of the History of Man, which makes a branch of our nature, no less evidently than does the sense of right and wrong in actions.

With respect to the deification of heroes, which was the practice in the first stages of society, it is a common opinion, that, in the eagerness of a too forward gratitude to those who had in any degree contributed to the better accommodation of life, their countrymen no sooner saw them removed by death from the society of men than they exalted them to that of the gods. I cannot relish this conjecture. The notions of immortality among savages are generally obscure; and when a man is cut off by a natural or violent death, he is not conceived to be still alive, far less to be translated into a higher order of beings. It is true, that among savages, where every new invention makes a shining figure, a man who contributes in any measure to the accommodation of society, is honoured during his life, and remembred after his death; and to honour the memory of such men, feasts and ceremonies have been instituted. It is not reasonable to believe, that at first the matter was carried any further. That among savages the first notions of supernatural powers arose from fear, is extremely probable. In the gradual improvement of society, regularity, order, and good design, came in some obscure manner to be recognized in the affairs of this world; and this naturally suggested the superintendance of benevolent powers, perhaps of the sun or moon, those exalted and illustrious beings. This apparently was the first dawn of internal conviction with respect to the Deity. So far is certain, that Polytheism was recognized before the unity of the Deity was discovered by our more enlightened faculties. In this first stage of religion, superior beings, according to the notions entertained of them, were much limited in power, as well as in benevolence. Men could not strain their thoughts to conceive much more power or benevolence than existed in their own species. Such confined and groveling notions favoured the system of Polytheism; for we are apt to supply by numbers what is wanting in energy: and as fear had multiplied the number of malevolent powers, hope was no less fruitful with respect to those who were supposed benevolent. Then it was, and no sooner, that good men, held in remembrance by solemn institutions, were, in the fond imagination of their countrymen, advanced a step higher, and converted into genii, or tutelary deities. They were still supposed to superintend the affairs of mankind, and in their exalted state to continue that good-will to their country which was so remarkable during their existence in the human shape. These appear to be the natural gradations of the mind in its progress toward the Deity.

Having settled the belief of a Deity upon its proper basis, we shall proceed to take a general view of the attributes which belong to that great Being. And, first,

Unity of the Deity

With regard to this and all the other attributes of the Deity, it ought to be no discouraging reflection, that we cannot attain an adequate idea of them. The Deity is too grand an object to be comprehended in any perfect manner by the human mind. We have not words nor ideas which any way correspond to the manner of his existence. Did even some good angel undertake to be our instructor, we would still be at a loss to form a distinct conception of it. Power, intelligence, and goodness, are attributes which we can comprehend. But with regard to the nature of the Deity in general and the manner of his existence, we must be satisfied in this mortal state to remain in the dark. The attribute of *Unity*, is, what of all we have the least certainty about by the light of nature. It is not inconsistent, that there should be two or more beings of the very highest order, whose essence and actions may be so regulated by the nature of the beings themselves, as to be altogether concordant. In truth, the nature of the Divine Being is so far out of our reach, that we must be absolutely at a loss to apply to it *unity* or *multiplicity*. This property is applicable to individual things; but we know not that it is applicable to the Deity. Yet if we may venture to judge of a matter so remote, we ought to conclude in favour of *unity*. We perceive the necessity of one eternal Being; and it is sufficient, that there is not the smallest foundation from sense or reason, to suppose more than one.

Power and Intelligence of the Deity

These two attributes I join together, because the same reflection is applicable to both. The wisdom and power necessarily supposed in the creation and government of this world, are so far beyond the reach of our comprehension, that they may justly be styled *infinite*. We can ascribe no bounds to either: and we have no other notion of *infinite,* but that to which we can ascribe no bounds.

Benevolence of the Deity

The mixed nature of the events that fall under our observation, seems to point out a mixed cause, partly good and partly ill. The author of *Philosophical Essays concerning human understanding,* in his eleventh essay, *Of the practical consequences of natural religion,* puts in the mouth of an Epicurean philosopher a very shrewd argument against the benevolence of the Deity. The sum is what follows:

> If the cause be known only by the effect, we never ought to assign to it any qualities, beyond what are precisely requisite to produce the effect. Allowing, therefore, God to be the author of the existence and order of the universe; it follows, that he possesses that precise degree of power, intelligence, and benevolence, which appears in his workmanship.

And hence, from the present scene of things, apparently so full of ill and disorder, it is concluded, "That we have no foundation for ascribing any attribute to the Deity, but what is precisely commensurate with the imperfection of this world." With regard to mankind, he reasons differently.

> In works of human art and contrivance, it is admitted, that we can advance from the effect to the cause, and returning back from the cause, that we conclude new effects, which have not yet existed. Thus, for instance, from the sight of a half-finished building, surrounded with heaps of stones and mortar, and all the instruments of masonry, we naturally conclude, that the building will be finished, and receive all the farther improvements which art can bestow upon it. But the foundation of this reasoning is plainly, that man is a being whom we know by experience, and whose

motives and designs we are acquainted with, which enables us to draw many inferences, concerning what may be expected from him. But did we know man only from the single work or production which we examine, we could not argue in this manner; because our knowledge of all the qualities which we ascribe to him, being, upon that supposition, derived from the work or production, it is impossible they could point any thing farther, or be the foundation of any new inference.[4]

Supposing reason to be our only guide in these matters, which is supposed in this argument, it appears to be just. By no inference of reason, can I conclude any power or benevolence in the cause, beyond what is displayed in the effect. But this is no wonderful discovery. The philosopher might have carried his argument a greater length: he might have observed, even with regard to a man I am perfectly acquainted with, that I cannot conclude by any chain of reasoning, that he will finish the house he has begun. It is to no purpose to urge his temper and disposition; for from what principle of reason can I infer, that these will continue the same as formerly? He might further have observed, that the difficulty is greater with regard to a man I know nothing of, supposing him to have begun the building. For what foundation have I in reason to transfer the qualities of the persons I am acquainted with to a stranger, which surely is not performed by any process of reasoning? There is still a wider step; which is, that reason will not support me in attributing to the Deity even that precise degree of power, intelligence and benevolence, which appears in his workmanship. I find no inconsistency in supposing, that a blind and undesigning cause may be productive of excellent effects: it will I presume be difficult to produce a demonstration to the contrary. And supposing, at the instant of operation, the Deity to have been endued with these properties, can we make out, by any argument *a priori,* that they are still subsisting in him? Nay, this same philosopher might have gone a great way farther, by observing, when any thing comes into existence, that, by no process of reasoning, can we so much as infer any cause of its existence.

But happily for man, where reason fails him, sense and intuition come to his assistance. By means of principles implanted in our nature, we are

5. Hume, *An Enquiry concerning Human Understanding,* 11.13, p. 190; 11.25, p. 195.

enabled to make the foregoing conclusions and inferences; as at full length is made out in some of the foregoing Essays. More particularly, power discovered in any object, is intuitively perceived to be a permanent quality, like figure or extension.* Upon this account, power discovered by a single effect, is considered as sufficient to produce the like effects, without end. Further, great power may be discovered from a small effect; which holds even in bodily strength, as where an action is performed readily and without effort. This is equally remarkable in wisdom and intelligence: a very short argument may unfold correctness of judgment, and a deep reach. The same holds in art and skill: examining a slight piece of workmanship done with taste, we readily observe, that the artist was equal to a greater task. But it is most of all remarkable in the quality of benevolence: even from a single effect produced by an unknown cause, which appears adapted to some good purpose, we necessarily attribute to this cause benevolence, as well as power and wisdom.† The perception is indeed but weak, when it ariseth from a single effect; but still it is a perception of pure benevolence, without any mixture of malice; for such contradictory qualities are not readily ascribed to the same cause. There indeed may be a difficulty, where the effect is of a mixed nature, partly ill partly good; or where a variety of effects, having these opposite characters, proceed from the same cause. Such intricate cases cannot fail to embarrass us; but as we must form some sentiment, we ascribe benevolence or malevolence to the cause, from the prevalence of the one or other quality in the effects. If evil make the greater figure, we perceive the cause to be malevolent, notwithstanding opposite instances of goodness. If, upon the whole, goodness be supereminent, we perceive the cause to be benevolent; and are not moved by the cross instances of evil, which for ought we know may be necessary for producing on the whole the greatest quantity of good. In a word, it is the tendency of our nature to reject a mixed character made up of benevolence and malevolence, unless where it is necessarily pressed home upon us by an equality of opposite effects; and in every subject that cannot be reached by the reasoning faculty, we justly

* Essay Knowledge of Future Events.
† Essay Power, at the close.

rely on the tendency of our nature, as the best proof the subject can admit of.

Such are the conclusions that we can draw; not indeed from reason, but from intuitive perception. So little are we acquainted with the essence or nature of things, that we cannot establish these conclusions upon any argument *a priori*. Nor would it be of great benefit to mankind, to have these conclusions demonstrated to them; few having either leisure or talents to comprehend such profound speculations. It is more wisely ordered, that they appear to us intuitively certain.

This is a solid foundation for our conviction of the benevolence of the Deity. If, from a single effect, pure benevolence in the cause can be perceived; what doubt can there be of the pure benevolence of the Deity, when we survey his works, pregnant with good-will to mankind? Innumerable instances of things wisely adapted to good purposes, give us the strongest conviction of the goodness as well as wisdom of the Deity; which is joined with the firmest persuasion of constancy and uniformity in his operations. A few cross instances cannot make us waver. When we know so little of nature, it would be surprising indeed, if we should be able to account for every event and its final tendency. Unless we were let into the counsels of the Almighty, we can never hope to unravel all the mysteries of the creation.

I shall add some other considerations to confirm our belief of the pure benevolence of the Deity. And first, the independent and all-sufficient nature of the Deity, sets him above all suspicion of being liable either to envy, or to the pursuit of any interest, other than the general interest of his creatures. Wants, weakness, and opposition of interests, are the causes of ill-will among men. From all such influences the Deity is exempted. And therefore, unless we suppose him less perfect than the creatures he hath made, we cannot suppose that there is any degree of malice in his nature.

There is a second consideration, which hath always afforded me great satisfaction. Did natural evil prevail in reality, as much as it doth in appearance, we must expect, that the enlargement of natural knowledge should daily discover new instances of bad, as well as of good intention. But the fact is directly otherways. Our discoveries ascertain us more and more of the benevolence of the Deity, by unfolding beautiful final causes without number; while the appearances of ill intention gradually vanish, like a mist when the sun breaks out. Many things are now found to be curious in their contrivance and productive of good effects, which formerly appeared useless, or perhaps of ill tendency. And, in the gradual progress of learning, we have the strongest reason to expect, that many more discoveries of the kind will be made. This very consideration, had we nothing else to rely on, ought to make us rest with assurance upon the intuitive conviction we have of the benevolence of the Deity; without giving way to the perplexity of a few cross appearances, which, in matters so far beyond our comprehension, ought rationally to be ascribed to our own ignorance, not to any malevolence in the Deity. In the progress of learning, the time may come, we have great reason to hope it will come, when all doubts and perplexities of this kind shall be fully cleared up.

I satisfy myself with suggesting but one other consideration, That inferring a mixed nature in the Deity from events which cannot be clearly reconciled to benevolence, is, at best, new-moulding the Manichean system, by substituting in place of it, one really less plausible. For I can with greater facility form a conception of two opposite powers governing the universe, than of one power endued with great goodness and great malevolence, principles so repugnant to each other.

It thus appears, that our conviction of the attribute of pure benevolence hath a wide and solid foundation. It is impressed upon us by intuitive perception, by every discovery we make in the science of nature, and by every argument suggested by reason and reflection. There is but one objection of any weight that can be moved against it, arising from the difficulty of accounting for natural and moral evil. It is observed above, that the objection, however it may puzzle, ought not to shake our faith in this attribute; because an argument from ignorance can never be a convincing argument in any case. This therefore, in its strongest light, appears but in the shape of a difficulty, not of a solid objection. At the same time, as the utmost labour of thought is well bestowed upon a subject so interesting, I shall proceed to some reflections, which may tend to satisfy us, that the instances commonly given of natural and moral evil, are not so inconsistent with pure benevolence, as at first sight may be imagined.

One preliminary point must be settled, which I presume will be admitted without much hesitation. It certainly will not be thought inconsistent in any degree with the pure benevolence of the Deity, that the world is filled with an endless variety of creatures, gradually ascending in the scale of being, from the most groveling to the most glorious. To think that this affords an argument against pure benevolence, is in effect to think, that all inanimate beings ought to be endued with life and motion, and that all animate beings ought to be angels. If at first view it shall be thought, that infinite power and goodness cannot stop short of absolute perfection in their operations, and that the work of creation must be confined to the highest order of beings, in the highest perfection; this thought will soon be corrected, by considering, that by this supposition a great void is left, which, according to the present system of things, is filled with beings, and with life and motion. And, supposing the world to be replenished with the highest order of beings created in the highest degree of perfection, it is certainly an act of more extensive benevolence, to complete the work of creation by the addition of an infinity of creatures less perfect, than to leave a great blank betwixt beings of the highest order and nothing.

The imperfection then of a created being, abstractly considered, impeaches none of the attributes of the Deity, whether power, wisdom, or benevolence. And if so, neither can pain abstractly considered be an impeachment, as far as it is the natural and necessary consequence of imperfection. The government of the world is carried on by general laws, which produce constancy and uniformity in the operations of nature. Among many reasons for this, we can clearly discover one, which is unfolded in a former Essay,* that were not nature uniform and constant, men and other sensible beings would be altogether at a loss how to conduct themselves. Our nature is adjusted to these general laws; and must therefore be subjected to all their varieties, whether beneficial or hurtful. We are made sensitive beings, and therefore equally capable of pleasure and pain. And it must follow from the very nature of the thing, that delicacy of perception, which is the source of much pleasure, may be equally the source of much pain. It is true, we cannot pronounce it to be a contradiction, that a being should be susceptible of pleasure only and not of pain. But no argument

---

* Knowledge of Future Events.

can be founded upon this supposition but what will conclude, that a creature such as man ought to have no place in the scale of beings; which surely will not be maintained: for it is still better, that man be as he is, than not to be at all. It is further to be observed in general, that aversion to pain is not so great, at least in mankind, as to counterbalance every other appetite. Most men would purchase an additional share of happiness, at the expence of some pain. And therefore it can afford no argument against the benevolence of the Deity, that created beings from their nature and condition are capable of pain, supposing upon the whole their life to be comfortable. Their state is still preferable to that of inanimate matter, capable neither of pleasure nor pain.

Thus it appears, even from a general view of our subject, that natural evil affords no argument against the benevolence of the Deity. And this will appear in a stronger light, when we go to particulars. It is laid open in the first Essay, that the social affections, even when most painful, are accompanied with no degree of aversion, either in the direct feeling or in subsequent reflection. We value ourselves the more for being so constituted; being conscious that such a constitution is *right* and *meet* for sociable creatures. Distresses therefore of this sort cannot be called evils, when we have no aversion to them, and do not repine at them. And if these be laid aside, what may be justly termed natural evils, are reduced within a small compass. They will be found to proceed necessarily, and by an established train of causes and effects, either from the imperfection of our nature, or from the operation of general laws. Pain is not distributed thro' the world blindly, or with any appearance of malice; but ends, proportions, and measures, are observed in the distribution. Sensible marks of good tendency are conspicuous, even in the harshest dispensations of Providence; and the good tendency of general laws, is a sure pledge of benevolence, even in those instances where we may be puzzled to explain their good effects. One thing is certain, that there is in man a natural principle to submit to these general laws, and their consequences. And were this principle cultivated as it ought to be, men would have the same consciousness of right conduct in submitting to the laws of the natural world, that they have in submitting to the laws of the moral world, and would as little repine at the distresses of the one kind, as at those of the other.

But justice is not done to the subject, unless we proceed to show, that pain and distress are productive of manifold good ends, and that they are in a measure necessary to the present system. In the first place, pain is necessary, as a monitor of what is hurtful and dangerous to life. Every man is trusted with the care of his own preservation; and he would be ill qualified for that trust, were he left entirely to the guidance of reason: he would die for want of food, were it not for the pain of hunger: and, but for the pain arising from fear, he would precipitate himself every moment into the most destructive enterprises. In the next place, pain is the great sanction of laws, both human and divine: there would be no order nor discipline in the world without it. In the third place, the distresses and disappointments that arise from the uncertainty of seasons, from the variable tempers of those we are connected with, and from other cross accidents, are wonderfully well adapted to our constitution, by keeping our hopes and fears in constant agitation. Man is an active being, and is not in his element but when in variety of occupation. A constant and uniform tenor of life without hopes or fears, would soon bring on satiety and disgust. Pain therefore is necessary, not only to enhance our pleasures, but to keep us in motion.* And it is needless to observe a second time, that to complain of man's constitution in this respect, is in other words to complain, that there is such a creature

---

* One argument used against Providence, I take to be a very strong one in its defence. It is objected,

> That storms and tempests, unfruitful seasons, serpents, spiders, flies, and other noxious or troublesome animals, with many more instances of the like kind, discover an imperfection in nature, because human life would be much easier without them.

But the design of Providence may clearly be perceived in this. The motions of the sun and moon, the whole system of the universe as far as Philosophers have been able to discover and observe, are in the utmost degree of regularity and perfection; but wherever God hath left to man the power of interposing a remedy by thought or labour, there he hath placed things in a state of imperfection, on purpose to stir up human industry, without which life would stagnate, or indeed rather could not subsist at all: *Curis acuunt mortalia corda.*

Swift's thoughts on various subjects ["Thoughts on Various Subjects" was published in Volume 1 of the four-volume *Miscellanies in Prose and Verse* (1727–32; 4th ed., 1742), by Alexander Pope, Jonathan Swift, and John Gay.]

as man in the scale of being. To mention but one other thing, pain and distress have a wonderful tendency to advance the interests of society. Grief, compassion, and sympathy, are strong connecting principles, by which every individual is made subservient to the general good of the whole species.

I shall close this branch of my subject with a general reflection, which is reserved to the last place, because in my apprehension it is a decisive argument for the benevolence of the Deity. When we run over what we know of the formation and government of this world, the instances are without number, of good intention and of consummate wisdom in adjusting things to good ends and purposes. And it is equally true, that as we advance in knowledge, scenes of this kind multiply upon us. This observation is enforced above. But I now observe, that there is not a single instance to be met with, which can be justly ascribed to malevolence or bad intention. Many evils may be pointed out; evils at least as to us. But when the most is made of such instances, they appear to be consequences only from general laws which regard the whole more than particulars; and therefore are not marks of malevolence in the Author and Governor of the world. Were there any doubt about the tendency of such instances, it would be more rational to ascribe them to want of power, than want of benevolence, which is so conspicuous in other instances. But we cannot rationally ascribe them to either, but to the pre-established order and constitution of things, and to the necessary imperfection of all created beings. And after all, laying the greatest weight upon these natural evils that can reasonably be demanded, the account stands thus. Instances without number of benevolence in the frame and government of this world, so direct and clear as not to admit of the slightest doubt. On the other side, natural evils are stated, which at best are very doubtful instances of malevolence, and may be ascribed, perhaps obscurely, to another cause. In balancing this account, where the evil appearances are so far outnumbered by the good, why should we hesitate to ascribe pure benevolence to the Deity, and to conclude these evils to be necessary defects in a good system; especially when it is so repugnant to our natural perceptions, to ascribe great benevolence and great malevolence to the same being?

It will be remarked, that in answering the foregoing objection to the benevolence of the Deity, I have avoided urging any argument from our future existence; though it affords a fruitful field of comfort, greatly over-balancing the transitory evils of this life. But I should scarce think it fair reasoning, to urge such topics upon this subject; which would be arguing in a circle; because the benevolence of the Deity is the only solid foundation upon which we can build a future existence.

Having discussed what occurred upon natural evil, we come now to con-sider moral evil as an objection against the benevolence of the Deity. And some writers carry this objection so far, as to conclude, that God is the cause of moral evil, since he hath given man a constitution, by which moral evil doth and must abound. It is certainly no satisfying answer to this objection, that moral evil is the necessary consequence of human liberty; when it is a very possible supposition, that man might have been endued with a moral sense, so lively and strong as to be absolutely authoritative over his actions. Waving therefore the argument from human liberty, we must look about for a more solid answer to the objection; which will not be difficult, when we consider this matter as laid down in a former essay.* It is there made out, it is hoped, to the satisfaction of the reader, that human actions are all of them directed by general laws, which have an operation no less infallible, than those laws have which govern mere matter. Thus, as all things in the moral as well as material world, proceed according to settled laws estab-lished by the Almighty, we have a just ground of conviction, that all matters are by Providence ordered in the best manner; and therefore that even hu-man vices and frailties are made to answer wise and benevolent purposes. Every thing possesses its proper place in the Divine plan. All our actions contribute equally to carry on the great and good designs of our Maker; and therefore there is nothing which in his sight is ill, at least nothing which is ill upon the whole.

Considering the objection in the forgoing light, which is the true one, it loses its force. For it certainly will not be maintained as an argument against the goodness of the Deity, that he endued man with a sense of moral evil; which in reality is one of the greatest blessings bestowed upon him, and which eminently distinguishes him from the brute creation.

* Essay upon Liberty and Necessity.

But if the objection be turned into another shape, and it be demanded, Why was not every man endued with so strong a sense of morality, as to be completely authoritative over all his principles of action, which would prevent much remorse to himself, and much mischief to others? it is answered, first, That this would not be sufficient for an exact regularity of conduct, unless man's judgment of right and wrong were also infallible. For, as long as we differ about what is *yours* and what is *mine,* injustice must be the consequence in many instances however innocent we be. But in the next place, to complain of a defect in the moral sense, is to complain that we are not perfect creatures. And if this complaint be well founded, we may with equal justice complain, that our understanding is but moderate, and that in general our powers and faculties are limited. Why should imperfection in the moral sense be urged as an objection, when all our senses, internal and external, are imperfect? In short, if this complaint be in any measure just, it must go the length, as above observed, to prove, that it is not consistent with the benevolence of the Deity to create such a being as man.

After putting the last hand to this book for a third edition, Dialogues by David Hume, Esq.; concerning Natural Religion were published.[6] Their purpose is to illustrate what the author had laid down on that subject in his former works, without adding any new matter. He has given a satisfactory reason for preferring the dialogue form; which is, that dialogue or conversation is the best suited to loose reasoning upon subjects obscure and uncertain. The execution justifies his choice; for the subject is treated in a more pleasing manner than strict and concise reasoning can admit. He has attained the true spirit of dialogue: the characters are finely supported, the stile animated, and the arguments properly enforced. One thing indeed surprised me, that there is not the slightest notice taken of the evidence of our senses for the existence of a Deity, one urged above, another in Sketches of the History of Man, vol. 4th.[7] These books are in the hands of every

6. Kames refers to Hume's posthumously published *Dialogues Concerning Natural Religion* (1779; reprint, ed. Richard H. Popkin, Indianapolis: Hackett Publishing, 1980).
7. A reference to the sketch on the "Principles and progress of theology," in Kames, *Sketches,* vol. 4, bk. 3, sketch 3.

one, and could not have been unknown to Mr. Hume. Did he think them so trifling as to merit nothing but contempt? I cannot believe it. May I not then suspect him of an artifice, not uncommon, That if an argument cannot be answered, to say nothing about it.

In another point Mr. Hume is equally liable to censure. An argument strenuously insisted on in the dialogues, is, that supposing a Deity unbounded in power and intelligence, the prevalence of evil both natural and moral is a clear proof that he must be deficient in benevolence.[8] These evils are displayed at great length and with persuasive eloquence; but not a word of what is above urged on the other side; and as little of what is urged in Sketches of the History of Man,* where it is made evident, that evil both natural and moral are so far beneficial to man, as that without them he would be a most abject creature. Doth not our author's silence in this instance as well as in the former, seem as if he had been more studious of victory than of truth?

As censure is to me not an agreeable amusement, I shall add but a single word. In explaining the system of nature, Mr. Hume, by an unaccountable bias, professes to have no reliance on the evidence of our senses. And by this strange opinion, he has been misled into many an inextricable labyrinth. Can it be thought wonderful, that an author who rejects the evidence of his senses for the existence of the objects around him, should think such evidence insufficient for the existence of a Deity?[i]

Recapitulation

We have thus gone through a variety of subjects, not without labour and expence of thought. And now, like a traveller, who, after examining the different parts of a country, ascends some eminence to review the whole; let us refresh ourselves, by looking back, and enjoying the discoveries we have made.

The subject of these Essays is man. We have formed no imaginary

8. Hume, *Dialogues Concerning Natural Religion,* Part XI, p. 67ff.
* Vol. 2d. p. 203. edit. 2d. ["Appetite for society—Origin of national societies," in Kames, *Sketches,* vol. 2, bk. 2, sketch 1.]

schemes, for exalting or for depressing his nature. The inquiry has been, Whether his capacities and powers suit his present circumstances, and fit him for acting a proper part in this life? We begin with examining some of the great springs of action. Upon accurate scrutiny, it is found, that self-love or desire of good, is not our sole principle of action; but that we are furnished beside with a variety of impelling powers. Mingled in society for the convenience of mutual help, it is necessary that we feel for each other. But as the feeling for the distress of others, cannot but be painful, here is traced an admirable contrivance to reconcile us to this virtuous pain, by removing that aversion to pain, which in all other cases is an overruling principle. This explains a seemingly strange phaenomenon, that we should seek entertainment from representations that immerse us in affliction. From man as a social, we proceed to him as a moral agent. We find him sensible of beauty, in different ranks and orders; and eminently sensible of it, in its highest order, that of sentiment, action, and character. But the sense of moral beauty is not alone sufficient. The importance of morality requires some stronger principle to guard it; some checks and restraints from vice, more severe than mere disapprobation. These are not wanting. To the sense of beauty, is superadded a sense of obligation, a perception of *right* and *wrong,* which constitutes a law within us.* This law injoins the primary virtues, those which are essential to society, under the strictest sanctions. Pain, the strongest monitor, is here employed to check transgression; whilst in the sublimer more heroic virtues, where strict obligation ends, pleasure is employed to reward the performance. No action is made a duty, to which we are not antecedently disposed by some principle. An exact proportion is maintained betwixt the strength of our internal principles, and their usefulness. From self, the object of our most vigorous principles, affection spreads through all our connections with others; till, by distance of con-

---

* Conscience! conscience! instinct divin; immortelle & celeste voix; guide assuré d'un être ignorant & borné, mais intelligent & libre; juge infaillible du bien & du mal, qui rends l'homme semblable à Dieu; c'est toi qui fais l'excellence de sa nature & la moralité de ses actions. ROUSSEAU ["Conscience, conscience! Divine instinct, immortal and celestial voice, certain guide of a being that is ignorant and limited but intelligent and free; infallible judge of good and bad which makes men like unto God; it is you who make the excellence of his nature and the morality of his actions." *Emile,* bk. IV, p. 290.]

nection, it ceases to be felt. After it is thus lost, by the distance of particular objects, nature revives its force, by directing it to the abstract idea of a public and a whole; which idea, though faint and obscure in the conception, is yet equal to any of our ideas in force and energy. Man, by this artful contrivance is fitted for acting a proper and useful part in the system to which he belongs. But this system could not be regulated upon any pre-adjusted plan, the actions of man could not proceed with any order nor be subject to any government, unless all men were determined by motives. At the same time, man could not answer the purposes of active life, without being a free agent. Having made out, that morals are established on an immoveable foundation, we proceed to show, by what inward powers we are led to the knowledge and belief of some of the most important truths; particularly, the existence of the Deity. To this we pave the way, by a full preparation of reasoning. We first consider the nature of that act of the mind which is termed *belief;* of which the immediate foundation is the testimony of our senses. If the testimony they give to the real existence of a material world, be a mere illusion, as some have held, all belief founded on our own perceptions is at an end. Hence appears the absurdity of denying the evidence of our senses. And here we find full satisfaction. In other cases, where there is any thing like artifice in the conduct of nature, means are afforded, both of discovering the truth, and of discovering the end for which truth is artfully concealed; for nature never deceives us but for our good. Dispersing, with no great labour, that philosophic dust which sceptics have raised about material substance, we find upon examination that we have a conception of it, no less clear than of qualities; both being equally displayed to us by the sense of sight. But belief is not more solidly founded upon our external senses, than upon our internal feelings. Not the greatest sceptic ever doubted of his own personal identity, continued through the successive periods of life; of his being the same man this year he was the last: which, however, is a discovery made by no reasoning; resting wholly upon an inward sense and consciousness of the fact. Upon a like foundation rests our belief of cause and effect. No relation is more familiar than this, nor sooner takes hold of the mind. Yet certain it is, that no reasoning, no experience, can discover the power or energy of what we term a *cause,* when we attempt to trace it to its source. It is necessary for the well-being of man, first, that he should perceive the objects which exist around him; and next, that he should perceive them in their true state, not detached and loose, but as causes and effects, as producing and produced. Nature hath furnished us with senses for the perception of objects, not only as simply existing, but as existing thus related to each other. Nor without such faculties could we ever have attained the idea of cause and effect. The same provision is made by nature, in another case, no less remarkable. Our senses can only inform us of objects as presently existing. Yet nothing is more common, than from our knowledge of the present, and our experience of the past, to reason about the future. Now, reasonings about futurity, which have extensive influence on our conduct, would be utterly destitute of a foundation, were we not endued with a sense of uniformity and constancy in the operations of nature: an innate sense dictates to us, that the future will be like the past. Thus there is established a marvellous harmony betwixt our perceptions and the course of events. In the above-mentioned instances, we attribute to our boasted reason, what in truth is performed by sense. We act upon its informations, with equal confidence as we do upon the clearest conclusions of reason. Nature is thus our preceptor in things the most necessary to be known. But this is not all. We pursue the argument into an intuitive perception of the Deity. He hath not left us to collect his existence from abstract or perplexed arguments, but makes us perceive intuitively that he exists. When external objects are presented to our view, some are immediately distinguished to be effects, not by any process or deduction of reasoning, but by an internal sense, which gives us the perception of cause and effect. In the same manner, this whole world is seen to be an effect produced by some invisible designing cause. The evidence of this perception cannot be rejected, without introducing universal scepticism; and without obliging us to doubt of things, of which no man ever doubted. For, as in viewing an external object, the sense of sight produces the idea of substance as well as of quality; as by an intuitive perception we discover some things to be effects requiring a cause; as from experience of the past, we judge of the future; in fine, as by the sense of identity the reader is conscious of being the same person he was when he began to read; as all these conclusions upon which mankind rest with the fullest assurance, are the dictates of senses external and internal; in the very same way, and upon the same evidence, we conclude the existence of a first Supreme Cause. Reason gives us all its aid, both to confirm the certainty of his being, and to discover his perfections. From effects great and good display'd through the universe, we necessarily infer the cause to be both great and good. Mixed or imperfect qualities cannot belong to that cause. The difficulties from apparent evil, are found capable of a satisfactory solution. All the general laws of the universe are confessedly wise and good. Pain is found not to be useful only, but necessary, in the present system. If this be an argument of an imperfect state, must it not however be admitted, that somewhere in the scale of existence, an imperfect order of beings must be found? And why not man such a being? unless we extravagantly demand, that, to prove the benevolence of the Deity, all the possible orders of being should be advanced to the top of the scale, and all be left void and waste below; no life, no existence, allowed, except what is perfect. The more we know of nature, the less of evil appears. New discoveries of wisdom, order, and good intention, are the never-failing effects of enlarged knowledge; an intimation, not obscure, of its being owing to our imperfect and bounded views that evil is supposed to take place at all. Now, when we consider all these things in one complex view, so many striking instances of final causes, such undeniable proofs both of wise design and skilful execution: banishing cold distrust of the great universal cause, are we not raised to the highest admiration! And doth it not encourage us to attempt a higher strain?

> For, do not all these wonders, *O Eternal Mind,* Sovereign Architect of all, form a hymn to thy praise![9] If in the dead inanimate works of nature, thou art seen; if in the verdure of the fields and the azure of the skies, the ignorant rustic admire thy creative power; how blind must that man be, who, contemplating his living structure, his moral frame, discerns not thy forming hand? What various and complicated machinery is here! and reg-

---

9. This deist prayer was composed for Kames by the liberal clergyman Hugh Blair (1718–1800), who defended Kames and Hume against the charges of heresy leveled by the "high-flyers" (i.e., strictly orthodox Calvinists). In addition to his *Critical Dissertation on the Poems of Ossian* (1763) and his influential *Lectures on Rhetoric and Belles Lettres* (1783), Blair was the author of an enormously popular collection of *Sermons* (5 vols., 1777–1801), a work so moderate and ecumenical in orientation that it earned the Presbyterian minister a pension from the Crown.

ulated with what exquisite art! While man pursues happiness as his chief aim, thou bendest self-love into the social direction. Thou infusest the generous principle, which makes him feel for sorrows not his own: nor feels he only, but, strange indeed! takes delight in rushing into foreign misery; and with pleasure goes to drop the painful tear over real or imaginary wo. Thy divine hand thus formed the connecting tye, and by sympathy linked man to man; that nothing might be solitary in thy world, but all tend toward mutual association. For that great end man is not left to a loose or arbitrary range of will. Thy wise decree hath erected within him a throne for virtue. There thou hast not decked her with beauty only to his admiring eye, but hast thrown around her the awful effulgence of authority divine. Her persuasions have the force of a precept; and her precepts are a law indispensable. Man feels himself bound by this law, strict and immutable. And yet the privilege of supererogating is left: a field opened for free and generous action; in which, performing a glorious course, he may attain the high reward by thee allotted of inward honour and self-estimation. Nothing is made superfluously severe, nothing left dangerously loose, in thy moral institution; but every active principle made to know its proper sphere. In just proportion, man's affections spread from himself to objects around him. Where the rays of affection, too widely scattered, begin to lose their warmth: collecting them again by the idea of a public, a country, or the universe, thou rekindlest the dying flame. Converging eagerly to this point, behold how intense they glow! and man, though indifferent to each remote particular, burns with zeal for the whole. All things are by thee pre-ordained, great Mover of all! Throughout the wide expanse, every living creature runs a destin'd course. While all under a law irresistible fulfil thy decrees, man alone seems to himself exempt; free to turn and bend his course at will. Yet is he not exempt; but ministers to thy decree omnipotent, as much as the rolling sun, or ebbing flood. What strange contradictions are in thy great scheme reconciled! what glaring opposites made to agree! Necessity and liberty meet in the same agent, yet interfere not. Man, though free from constraint, is under bonds. He is a necessary agent, and yet acts with perfect liberty. Within the heart of man thou hast placed thy lamp, to direct his otherways uncertain steps. By this light, he is not only assured of the existence and entertained with all the glories of the material world, but is enabled to penetrate into the recesses of nature. He perceives objects joined together by the mysterious link of cause and effect. The connecting principle, though he can never explain, he is made to perceive; and is thus instructed to refer even things unknown, to their proper origin. Endued with a prophetic spirit, he foretels things to come. Where reason is unavailing, sense comes in aid; and bestows a power of divination, which discovers the future by the past. Thus thou gradually liftest him up to the knowledge of thyself. The plain and simple sense, which in the most obvious effect reads and perceives a cause, brings him straight to thee, the first great Cause, the ancient of days, the eternal source of all. Thou presentest thyself to us, and we cannot avoid thee. We must doubt of our own existence, if we can doubt of thine. We see thee by thine own light. We see thee, not existing only, but in wisdom and in benevolence supreme, as in existence first. As spots in the sun's bright orb, so in the universal plan, scattered evils are lost in the blaze of superabundant goodness. Even by the research of human reason, weak as it is, those seeming evils diminish and fly away apace. Objects, supposed superfluous or noxious, have assumed a beneficial aspect. How much more, to thine all-penetrating eye must all appear excellent and fair! It must be so.—We cannot doubt. Neither imperfection nor malice dwell with thee. Thou appointest as salutary, what we lament as painful. Even the follies and vices of men minister to thy wise designs: and as at the beginning of days thou sawest, so thou seest and pronouncest still, that *every thing thou hast made is good.*

FINIS

APPENDIX

Significant Variant Readings

Kames published three editions of his *Essays* (1751, 1758, and 1779). The first two editions were published anonymously; in the third edition Kames signed his name to the Preface.

With each new edition, Kames made many changes, some of them stylistic, some of them concerning substantive issues. In revising his text for the second edition (of 1758), Kames focused on Part I, and especially on the "Liberty and Necessity" essay, which had involved him in a heated controversy with a group of Church of Scotland ministers headed by George Anderson. Many of the essays in Part II of the second edition were reprinted with only minor stylistic changes. For the third edition (of 1779), Kames made two kinds of significant revisions. First, in terms of altering and correcting previously published material, Kames again focused his energies on Part I, and especially on Essays II and III ("Foundation and Principles of Morality" and "Liberty and Necessity"). Once again, many of the essays in Part II appeared with only minor stylistic variations. Where Kames did make a significant revision to Part II was in the addition of two entirely new essays.

This appendix records some of the variations between the three editions. It does not offer a complete and exhaustive list of textual variants but rather provides a partial list based on two criteria. First, I have emphasized places in the text where Kames significantly qualifies or retracts an argument made in the previous editions. Second, I have briefly noted changes in the organization and presentation of the essays. Superscript roman numerals in the text indicate where the following variations occur.

Editions

A. *Essays on the Principles of Morality and Natural Religion.* In Two Parts. Edinburgh, 1751.

B. *Essays on the Principles of Morality and Natural Religion.* In Two Parts. The Second Edition. With Alterations and Additions. London, 1758.

C. *Essays on the Principles of Morality and Natural Religion.* Corrected and improved, in a third edition. Several Essays added concerning the Proof of a Deity. Edinburgh and London, 1779.

Variant Readings to Part I

II. FOUNDATION AND PRINCIPLES OF MORALITY

i. In A and B, this essay is entitled "Of the Foundations and Principles of the Law of Nature."[1]

ii. In A and B (with slight stylistic variations from A), this paragraph reads:

It is but a superficial account which is given of morality by most writers, that it depends upon Approbation and Disapprobation. For it is evident, that these terms are applicable to works of art, and to objects beneficial and hurtful, as well as to morality. It ought further to have been observed, that the approbation or disapprobation of actions, are feelings, very distinguishable from what relate to the objects now mentioned. Some actions are approved of as good and as fit, right and meet to be done; others are disapproved of as bad and unfit, unmeet and wrong to be done. In the one case, we approve of the actor as a good man; in the other, disapprove of him as a bad man. These feelings don't apply to objects as fitted to an end, nor even to the end itself, except as proceeding from deliberate intention. When a piece of work is well executed, we approve of the artificer for his skill, not for his goodness. Several things inanimate, as well as animate, serve to extreme good ends. We approve of these ends as useful in

---

1. But throughout the text, C continues to speak of the principles and foundations of the law of nature. For Kames, and for most Scottish moral philosophers of the period (with the important exception of Hume), the laws of morality are the laws of nature.

themselves, but not as morally fit and right, where they are not considered as the result of intention.[2]

iii. This paragraph was added to C.[3]
iv. In A, the next two paragraphs read:

Upon a small degree of reflection, it will appear, that the whole system of morals is founded upon the supposition of liberty of action.* If actions were understood to be necessary, and no way under our power or controul, we could never conceive them as fit or unfit to be done; as what we are indispensibly bound to do or not to do. To have such a feeling of human actions, upon the supposition of necessity, would be as inconsistent as to have such a feeling of the actions of matter. The celebrated dispute about liberty and necessity is reserved to be discussed in a following essay. But without entering upon the subject at present, one fact is certain, that in acting we have a feeling of liberty and independency. We never do a wrong, however strong the motive be, which is not attended with a severe reflection, that we *might* have done otherways, and *ought* to have done otherways. Nay, during the very action, in the very time of it, we have a sense of feeling of wrong, and that we *ought* to forbear. So that the moral sense, both in the direct feeling, and in the act of reflection, plainly supposes and implies liberty of action.

This, if we mistake not, will clear the difficulty above stated. If in the moral sense be involved liberty of action, there must of consequence be the highest sense or feeling of morality where liberty is greatest. Now, in judging of human actions, those actions, which are essential to the order and preservation of society, are considered to be in a good measure necessary. It is our strict duty to be just and honest. We are bound by a law in our nature, which we ought not to transgress. No such feeling of duty or obligation attends those actions which come under the denomination of *generosity, greatness of mind, heroism.* Justice, therefore, is considered as less free than generosity; and, upon that very account, we ascribe less merit

2. C reads "no clear account" rather than "superficial account," but makes the point about the application of approbation/disapprobation to morally irrelevant and possibly superficial categories through its examples (esp., "I approve an elegant dress on a fine woman").
3. Here Kames emphasizes the practical danger of failing to distinguish between duty and benevolence.

to the former, than to the latter. We ascribe no merit at all to an action which is altogether involuntary; and we ascribe more or less merit, in proportion as the action is more or less voluntary.

*Doctor Butler, preface to his sermons, page 11, says, "Our constitution is put into our own power: we are charged with it; and therefore are accountable for any disorder or violation of it."[4]

v. A does not list "love of justice," but includes "friendship" and "love to children," both of which are omitted from B and C.[5]

vi. In place of the above three paragraphs (beginning, "The surface of the globe"), A reads:

Man is by nature fitted for labour, and his enjoyment lyes in action. To this internal constitution his external circumstances are finely adapted. The surface of this globe does scarce yield spontaneously food for the greatest savages; but, by labour and industry, it is made to furnish not only the conveniencies, but even the luxuries of life. In this situation, it is wisely ordered, that man should labour for himself and his family, by providing a stock of necessaries for them, before he thinks of serving others. The great principle of self-preservation directs him to this course. Now this very disposition of providing against want, which is common to man with many other creatures, involves the idea of property. The ground I cultivate, and the house I build, must be considered as mine, otherways I labour to no purpose. There is a peculiar connection betwixt a man and the fruits of his industry felt by every one; which is the very thing we call property. Were all the conveniencies of life, like air and water, provided to our hand without labour, or were we disposed to labour for the publick, without any selfish affections, there would be no sense of property, at least such a sense would be superfluous and unnecessary. But when self-preservation, the most eminent of our principles of action, directs every individual to

4. Kames quotes from Butler, *Works,* 2:10. B and C make a similar distinction between justice (now called a primary virtue) as a matter of law, and generosity (now classed as a secondary virtue) as a matter of choice, but the reference to "the supposition of liberty of action" is omitted and the issue is no longer explicitly framed around the liberty and necessity debate.

5. An example of Kames's increased concern to demonstrate (contra Hume) that justice is a primary virtue, rooted in our very nature: while A does not even list justice, B and C give it pride of place.

labour for himself in the first place; man, without a sense or feeling of property, would be an absurd being. Every man therefore must have a notion of property, with regard to the things acquired by his own labour, for this is the very meaning of working for one's self: property, so far, is necessarily connected with self-preservation. But the idea of property is essentially the same, whether it relates to myself, or to another. There is no difference, but what is felt in surveying the goods of any two indifferent persons. And, were it consistent for a man to have the idea of his own property, without having a notion of property in another; such a man would be a very imperfect being, and altogether unqualified for society. If it could be made out, that such is the constitution of mankind in general, I should be much disposed to believe that we were made by a fortuitous concourse of atoms. But the constitution of man is more wisely framed, and more happily adjusted to his external circumstances. Not only man, but all provident creatures who have the hoarding quality, are endued with the sense or feeling of property; which effectually secures each individual, in the enjoyment of the fruits of its own labour. And accordingly we find, in perusing the history of mankind, as far back as we have any traces of it, that there never has been, among any people or tribe, such a thing as the possession of goods in common. For, even before agriculture was invented, when lived upon the natural plenty of the earth, tho' the plenty of pasture made separate possessions unnecessary, yet individuals had their own cattle, and enjoyed the produce of their cattle separately.[6]

6. B and C suggest the influence of a stadial model of historical development, according to which mankind progresses through four stages of material subsistence, from hunting to pasturage to agriculture to commerce. Thus, Kames acknowledges an original hunting stage ("men originally made shift to support themselves, partly by prey, partly by the natural fruits of the earth"), a pastoral stage ("man found it necessary, therefore, to abandon this manner of life, and to become shepherd"), and an agricultural stage ("a bit of land is divided from the common; it is cultivated with the spade or plough"). Given this stadial understanding of historical development, Kames can no longer assert that "there never has been, among any people or tribe, such a thing as the possession of goods in common." Moreover, rather than state at the outset that provision against want necessarily involves the idea of property, in B and C Kames is at pains to first establish the universality of the "hoarding principle," from which the sense of property can then be inferred. Thus, while Kames continues to argue that the sense of property is natural rather than artificial, he must now take stock of a theory of historical progress that tends to support Hume's position: that is, that the idea of property is not based on a natural sense or instinct but is rather the outcome of a complex process of material and social

vii. A adds:

Here then is property established by the constitution of our nature, antecedent to all human conventions. We are led by nature to consider goods acquired by our industry and labour as belonging to us, and as our own. We have the sense of feeling of property, and conceive these goods to be our own, just as much as we conceive our hands, our feet, and our other members to be our own; and we have a sense of feeling equally clear of the property of others. What is here asserted is a matter of fact, of which there can be no other decisive evidence, than to appeal to every man's own feelings. At the same time we need scarce any other proof of this fact, than that *yours* and *mine* are terms familiar with the greatest savages, and even with children. They must have feelings which correspond to these terms; otherways the terms would not be intelligible to them.[7]

viii. This paragraph added to B and C.[8]

ix. A and B end here; the remainder of this section added to C.

III. LIBERTY AND NECESSITY

i. A inserts:

An extreme beautiful scene opens to our view, when we consider with what propriety the ideas, feelings, and whole constitution of the mind of man, correspond to his present state. The impressions he receives, and the notions he forms, are accurately adapted to the useful purposes of life, tho' they do not correspond in every instance to the philosophic truth of things. It was not intended that man should make profound discoveries.

---

developments (though at the same time, natural in the sense that the establishment of property can be seen as the outcome of a natural process of historical development).

In his sketch on "The Progress of Property," Kames continued to assert that the "sense of property" was "inherent in man," while conceding that "the sense of property is slower in its growth toward maturity, than the external senses" (*Sketches,* vol. 1, bk. 1, sketch 2, p. 116).

7. B and C argue the same point but through an indirect approach: having established that the "hoarding appetite" is natural, Kames can then infer a sense of property from the instinct to hoard ("What sort of creature would man be, endued as he is with a hoarding appetite, but with no sense or notion of property?").

8. Another example of the stronger emphasis that Kames places on justice in his later revisions to the work.

He is framed to be more an active than a contemplative being; and his views both of the natural and moral world are so adjusted, as to be made subservient to correctness of action rather than of belief. Several instances there are of perceptions, which, for want of a more proper term, may be called deceitful; because they differ from the real truth. But man is not therefore misled in the least. On the contrary, the ends of life and action are better provided for by such artifice, than if these perceptions were more exact copies of their objects.

In the natural world, somewhat of this kind is generally admitted by modern philosophers. It is found, that the representations of external objects, and their qualities conveyed by the senses, sometimes differ from what philosophy discovers these objects, and their qualities to be. Thus a surface appears smooth and uniform, when its roughness is not such as to be hurtful. The same surface, examined with a microscope, is found to be full of ridges and hollows. Were man endowed with a microscopic eye, the bodies that surround him, would appear as different from what they do at present, as if he were transported into another world. His ideas, upon that supposition, would indeed be more agreeable to strict truth, but they would be far less serviceable in common life. Further, it is now universally admitted, that the qualities called secondary, which we by natural instinct attribute to matter, belong not properly to matter, nor exist really without us. Colour in particular is a sort of visionary beauty, which nature has spread over all her works. It is a wonderful artifice, to present objects to us thus differently distinguished: to mark them out to the eye in various attires, so as to be best known and remembered: and to paint on the fancy, gay and lively, grand and striking, or sober and melancholy scenes: whence many of our most pleasurable and most affecting sensations arise. Yet all this beauty of colours, with which heaven and earth appear clothed, is a sort of romance and illusion. For, among external objects, to which colours are attributed by sense, there is really no other distinction, than what arises from a difference in the size and arrangement of the contingent parts, whereby the rays of light, are reflected or refracted in such different ways, as to paint various colours on the retina of the eye. From this, and other instances of the same kind which be adduced, it appears, that our perceptions some times, are less accommodated to the truth of things, than to the end for which our senses are designed. Nature, at the same time, has provided a remedy; for she seldom or never leaves us without means of discovering the deception, and arriving at the truth. And it is wonderful, that, even when we act upon these deceitful impressions, we are not betrayed into any thing that is hurtful. On the contrary, life and action are better provided for, and the ends of our being fulfilled to more advantage, than if we conducted ourselves by the strictest truth of things.

Let us carry on this speculation from the natural to the moral world, and examine whether there are not here also, analogous instances of deceitful impressions. This will lead us into an unbeaten tract. We are to open a scene entirely new; which, like most other things that are new, may perhaps surprize the reader. But he will suspend his judgment, 'till he has leisurely reviewed the whole: and then let him pronounce, whether our hypothesis does not solve all the phaenomena: whether it does not tally with the nature of man, and illustrate the wisdom and goodness of the author of his nature.

B also inserts the above, but replaces "for want of a better term, may be called deceitful" with "for want of a better term, must be called deceitful or delusive,"* and then adds the following footnote:

*I am sensible that these terms are unhappy, because they are generally taken in a bad sense. Let it only be considered, that in Latin there is a *dolus bonus* [good or permissible deceit] as well as a *dolus malus* [bad deceit]. By the art of perspective painting, a plain surface appears raised, and an object near the eye appears at a great distance. We are deceived, it is true; but the deceit contributes to our entertainment.[9]

ii. In place of the remainder of this paragraph, A and B (with slight stylistic variations from A) read:

We agree with the doctor, that the immediate efficient cause of motion is not the motive, but the will to act. No person ever held, that the pleasure of a summer-evening, when a man goes abroad into the fields, is the immediate cause of the motion of his feet. But what does this observation avail, when the prevailing motive, the will to act, and the action itself, are three things inseparably linked together? The motive, according to his own concession, necessarily determines the will; and the will necessarily produces the action, unless it be obstructed by some foreign force. Is not the action, by consequence, as necessary, as the will to act; tho' the motive be

---

9. While B responds to criticisms of Kames's notion of deceit by qualifying the terms, C drops the language of deceit altogether.

the immediate cause of the will only, and not of the action or beginning of motion? What does this author gain, by showing, that we have a power of beginning motion, if that power never is, never can be, exerted, unless in consequence of some volition or choice, which is necessarily caused? But, says he, it is only a moral necessity which is produced by motives; and a moral necessity, he adds, is no necessity at all, but is consistent with the highest liberty. If these words have any meaning, the dispute is at an end. For moral necessity, being that sort of necessity which affects the mind, and the physical necessity that which affects matter, it is plain, that, in all reasonings concerning human liberty, moral necessity, and no other, is meant to be established. The laws of action, we say, which respect the human mind, are as fixed as those which respect matter. The different nature of these laws, occasions the fixed consequences of the one to be called moral, and of the other to be called physical necessity. But the idea of *necessary, certain, unavoidable,* equally agrees to both. And to say that moral necessity is no necessity at all, because it is not physical necessity, which is all that the doctor's argument amounts to, is no better, than to argue, that physical necessity is no necessity at all, because it is not moral necessity.

iii. A and B add another paragraph:

Thus far then we have advanced in our argument, that all human actions proceed in a fixed and necessary train. Man being what he is, a creature endowed with a certain degree of understanding, certain passions and principles, and placed in certain circumstances, it is impossible he should will or chuse otherways, than in fact he wills or chuses. His mind is passive in receiving impressions of things as good or ill: according to these impressions, the last judgment of the understanding is necessarily formed; which the will, if considered as different from the last judgment of the understanding, necessarily obeys, as is fully shown; and the external action is necessarily connected with the will, or the mind's final determination to act.

iv. The next two paragraphs are new to C.
v. The paragraph is new to C.
vi. In place of this paragraph and the preceding paragraph, A reads:

What then shall be done in this case, where truth contradicts the common feeling and natural notions of mankind; where it presents to us, with irresistible evidence, a system of universal necessity upon which we never act; but are so formed, as to conduct ourselves by a system of notions quite opposite? Shall we sacrifice abstract truth to feeling? Or shall we stand by truth, and force our feelings into compliance? Neither of these will do. Truth is too rigid to bend to mere feeling; and our feelings are incapable of being forced by speculation. The attempt is vain, *pugnantia secum, frontibus adversis, componere.* [10] Let us be honest then. Let us fairly own, that the truth of things is on the side of necessity; but that it was necessary for man to be formed, with such feelings and notions of contingency, as would fit him for the part he has to act. This thought requires illustration.

vii. From this point on, A and B each offer a different version. A reads:

And, what is wonderful, tho' in this he acts upon a false supposition, yet he is not thereby misled from the ends of action, but, on the contrary, fulfills them, to the best advantage. Long experience has made him sensible, that some things, such as the sun's rising and setting, depend upon immutable laws. This is contradicted by no feeling, as it is no way for his benefit, that he should act upon any other supposition, Such things he reckons upon as necessary. But there are other things, which depend upon the spontaneous choices of men, or upon a concurrence of natural and moral causes. As to these, he has not knowledge enough, to foresee and determine by what law they will happen: and his ignorance of the event, is made to have the same effect upon his mind, as if the event were what we vulgarly call contingent. Its *uncertainty as to him* produces the same feeling, and stirs him up to the same activity, as if it were *uncertain in itself,* and had no determined cause of its futurition. This feeling then of contingency, and all the ideas connected with it, may be treated as secondary qualities, which have no real existence in things; but, like other secondary qualities, are made to appear as existing in events, or belonging to them, in order to serve the necessary purposes of human life.

Some objections shall be considered, after discussing the other branch of the disquisition concerning liberty of action. These subjects are so closely connected, that they cannot fail to throw light upon each other.

10. "You are going to make things tally, that are contradictory in their natures." Horace, *Satires,* 1.1, 102–3.

Contingency in events is analogous to liberty in actions. The one is a supposed quality of the thing; the other of the actor.

The extent of human liberty is above ascertained. It consists in spontaneity, or acting according to our inclination and choice. It may be therefore distinguished from *constraint,* but must not be opposed to necessity. For, as has been fully shown, the mind, in the most calm choice, the most deliberate action, is necessarily, *i. e.* unavoidably and certainly, determined by the prepollent motive. When we examine accurately, how far our feelings correspond to this system; we find, as was hinted before, first, that, antecedent to any particular action, we generally think and reason upon the scheme of necessity. In considering or guessing at future events, we always conclude, that a man will act consistently with his character; we infer what his actions will be, from the knowledge we have of his temper, and the motives that are fitted to influence it; and never dream of any man's having a power of acting against motives. Here we have a very weak feeling, if any at all, of liberty, as distinguished from necessity: and wisely so ordered, that a clue, as it were, might be afforded, to guide us in the labyrinth of future actions, which, were it not for the connection betwixt an action and its motive, would appear like a rope of sand, loose and unconnected; and no means left of reasoning upon, or foreseeing future actions. It is to be observed in the next place, that, during the action, the feeling begins to vary; and, unless in cases where the motive is so strong and overbearing, as to approach to the nature of constraint; unless, in these, a man has a feeling of liberty, or of a power of acting otherways than he is doing. But, in the third place, it is principally in reflecting and passing judgment upon a past action, that the feeling of liberty is sensible and strong. Then it is, that our actions are not considered as proceeding in a necessary unavoidable train: but we accuse and blame others, for not having acted the part they *might* and *ought* to have acted, and condemn ourselves, and feel remorse, for having been guilty of a wrong we *might have* refrained from. The operations of moral conscience plainly proceed upon this supposition, that there is such a power in man of directing his actions, as rendered it possible for the person accused, to have acted a better part. This affords an argument, which the advocates for liberty have urged in its full force, against the doctrine of necessity. They reason thus: If actions be necessary, and not in our own power, and if we know it to be so, what ground can there be for reprehension and blame, for self-condemnation and remorse? If a clock had understanding to be sensible of its own motions, knowing, at the same time, that they proceed according to necessary laws, could it find fault with itself for striking wrong? Would it not blame the artist, who had ill adjusted the wheels on which its movements depended? So that, upon this scheme, say they, all the moral constitution of our nature is overturned. There is an end to all the operations of conscience about right and wrong. Man is no longer a moral agent, nor the subject of praise or blame for what he does.

This difficulty is great, and never has been surmounted by the advocates for necessity. They endeavour to surmount it, by reconciling feeling to philosophic truth, in the following manner. We are so constituted, they say, that certain affections, and the actions which proceed from them, appear odious and base; and others agreeable and lovely; that, wherever they are beheld, either in ourselves or others, the moral sense necessarily approves of the one, and condemns the other; that this approbation is immediate and instinctive, without any reflection on the liberty or necessity of actions; that, on the contrary, the more any person is under the power of his affections and passions, and, by consequence, the greater necessity he is under, the more virtuous or vicious he is esteemed.

But this account of the matter is not satisfactory. All that is here said, is in the main true, but is not the whole truth. I appeal to any man who has been guilty of a bad action, which gives him uneasiness, whether there is not somewhat more in the inward feeling, than merely a dislike or disapprobation of the affection, from which his action proceeded? whether the pain, the *cruciatus* of remorse, is not founded on the notion of a power he has over his will and actions, that he might have forborn to do the ill thing? and whether it is not upon this account, that he is galled within, angry at himself, and confesses himself to be justly blameable? An uneasiness somewhat of the same kind, is felt upon the reflection of any foolish or rash action, committed against the rules of wisdom. The sting is indeed much sharper, and for very wise reasons, when a man has trespassed against the rules of strict morality. But, in both cases, the uneasiness proceeds upon the supposition, that he was free, and had it in his power to have acted a better part. This indeed is true, that to be so entirely under the power of any bad passion, (lust, for instance, or cruelty) as to be incapable of acting otherways than they direct, constitutes a very hateful character. I admit, that all such ill affections are naturally, and in themselves, the objects of dislike and hatred, where-ever they are beheld. But I insist upon it, that mere dislike and hatred, are not the whole, but only a part of the moral feeling. The person, thus under the dominion of bad passions, is accused, is condemned, singly upon this ground, that it was *thro' his own fault* he became so subject to them; in other words, that it was in his power, to have kept his mind free from the enslaving influence of corrupt affections. Were not this the case, brute animals might be the objects of moral blame, as well as man. Some beasts are reckoned savage and cruel, others treacherous and false: we dislike, we hate creatures so ill constituted: but we do not blame nor condemn them, as we do rational agents; because they are not supposed to have a sense of right and wrong, nor freedom and power of directing their actions according to that inward rule. We must therefore admit, that the idea of freedom, of a power of regulating our will and actions according to certain rules, is essential to the moral feeling. On the system of universal necessity, abstracted from this feeling, tho' certain affections and actions might excite our approbation, and others our dislike, there could be no place for blame or remorse. All the ideas would entirely vanish, which at present are suggested by the words *ought* and *should,* when applied to moral conduct.

Here then is another instance of a natural feeling, opposed to philosophic truth, analogous to what is before considered. It is the more remarkable, that it has given rise to those disputes about liberty and necessity, which have subsisted thro' all ages in the inquiring world; which, since the earliest accounts of philosophy, have run thro' all different sects of philosophers, and have been ingrafted into most of the religious systems. We are now able, I imagine, to give a clear and satisfactory account why the different parties never could agree; because, in truth, the feeling of liberty, which we have, does not agree with the real fact. Those who were boldest in their inquiries, traced out the philosophic truth: they saw that all things proceeded in a necessary train of causes and effects, which rendered it impossible for them, to act otherways than they did; and to this system they adhered, without yielding to natural feelings. Those again, who had not courage to oppose the first and most obvious feelings of their heart, stopped short, and adhered to liberty. It is observable, that the side of liberty has always been the most popular, and most generally embraced: and, upon this system, all popular discourses and exhortations must needs proceed. Even those persons, whose philosophical tenets are built upon the system of necessity, find themselves obliged to desert that system, in popular argument, and to adopt the stile and language of those who espouse liberty. Among the antients, the great assertors of necessity were the

Stoicks; a severe and rigid sect, whose professed doctrine it was, to subdue all our feelings to philosophy. The Platonics, Academics and Epicureans, who embraced a softer scheme of philosophy, and were more men of the world than the Stoics, leaned to the side of liberty. Both parties have their own advantages in reasoning; and both, when pushed, run into difficulties, from which they can never extricate themselves. The advocates for liberty talk with great advantage upon the moral powers of man, and his character as an accountable being: but are at a loss, how to give any view of the universe, as a regular pre-adjusted plan; and when urged with the connection betwixt the motive and the action, and the necessary train of causes and effects, which results from admitting it to be a fixed connection, they find themselves greatly embarrassed. Here the patrons of necessity triumph. They have manifestly all the advantages of speculative argument; whilst they fail in accounting for man's moral powers, and struggle in vain to reconcile to their system, the testimony which conscience clearly gives to freedom.

Let us then fairly acknowledge, concerning both these classes of philosophers, that they were partly in the right, and partly in the wrong. They divided, as it were, the truth betwixt them. The one had abstract reason on their side: the other had natural feeling. In endeavouring to reconcile these opposites, both parties failed; and the vain attempt has rendered the controversy difficult and perplexed. After having ascertained the foundation, upon which the doctrine of necessity is built, and which seems incapable of being shaken, let us fairly and candidly take our nature as we find it, which will lead us to this conclusion, that tho' man, in truth, is a necessary agent, having all his actions determined by fixed and immutable laws; yet that, this being concealed from him, he acts with the conviction of being a free agent. It is concealed from him, I say, as to the purposes of action: for whatever discoveries he makes as a philosopher, these affect not his conduct as a man. In principle and speculation, let him be a most rigid fatalist; he has nevertheless all the feelings which would arise from power over his own actions. He is angry at himself when he has done wrong. He praises and blames just like other men: nor can all his principles set him above the reach of self-condemnation and remorse, when conscience at any time smites him. It is true, that a man of this belief, when he is seeking to make his mind easy, after some bad action, may reason upon the principles of necessity, that, according to the constitution of his nature, it was impossible for him to have acted any other part. But this will give him little relief. In spite of all reasonings, his remorse will subsist. Nature never intended us to act upon this plan; and our natural principles are too deeply rooted, to give way to philosophy. This case is precisely similar to that of contingency. A feeling of liberty, which I now scruple not to call deceitful, is so interwoven with our nature, that it has an equal effect in action, as if we were really endued with such a power.

Having explained, at full length, this remarkable feeling of liberty, and examined, as we went along, some arguments against necessity that are founded upon it; we now proceed to handle this feeling, as we have done that of contingency, with regard to its final cause. And in this branch of our nature are displayed the greatest wisdom, and the greatest goodness. Man must be so constituted, in order to attain the proper improvement of his nature, in virtue and happiness. Put the case, he were entirely divested of his present ideas of liberty: suppose him to see and conceive his own nature, and the constitution of things, in the light of strict philosophic truth; in the same light they are beheld by the deity: to conceive himself, and all his actions, necessarily linked into the great chain of causes and effects, which renders the whole order both of the natural and moral world unalterably determined in every article: suppose, I say, our natural feelings, our practical ideas to suit and tally with this, which is the real plan; and what would follow? Why, an entire derangement of our present system of action, especially with regard to the motives which now lead us to virtue. There would still indeed be ground for the love of virtue, as the best constitution of nature, and the only sure foundation of happiness; and, in this view, we might be grieved when we found ourselves deficient in good principles. But this would be all. We could feel no inward self-approbation on doing well, no remorse on doing ill; because both the good and the ill were necessary and unavoidable. There would be no more place for applause or blame among mankind: none of that generous indignation we now feel at the bad, as persons who have abused and perverted their rational powers: no more notion of accountableness for the use of those powers: no sense of ill desert, or just punishment annexed to crimes as their due; nor of any reward merited by worthy and generous actions. All these ideas, and feelings, so useful to men in their moral conduct, vanish at once with the feeling of liberty. There would be field for no other passions but love and hatred, sorrow and pity: and the sense of *duty*, of being *obliged* to certain things which we *ought* to perform, must be quite extinguished; for we can have no conception of moral *obligation,* without supposing a power in the agent over his own actions.

It appears then most fit and wise, that we should be endued with a sense of liberty; without which, man must have been ill qualified for acting his present part. That artificial light, in which the feeling of liberty presents the moral world to our view, answers all the good purposes of making the actions of man entirely dependent upon himself. His happiness and misery appear to be in his own power. He appears praiseworthy or culpable, according as he improves or neglects his rational faculties. The idea of his being an accountable creature arises. Reward seems due to merit; punishment to crimes. He feels the force of moral obligation. In short, new passions arise, and a variety of new springs are set in motion, to make way for new exertions of reason and activity. In all which, tho' man is really actuated by laws of necessary influence, yet he seems to move himself: and whilst the universal system is gradually carried on to perfection by the first mover, that powerful hand, which winds up and directs the great machine, is never brought into sight.

It will now be proper to answer some objections, which may be urged against the doctrine we have advanced. One, which at first, may seem of considerable weight, is, that we found virtue altogether upon a deceitful feeling of liberty, which, it may be alledged, is neither a secure nor an honourable foundation. But, in the first place, I deny that we have founded it altogether upon a deceitful feeling. For, independent of the deceitful feeling of liberty, there is in the nature of man a firm foundation for virtue. He must be sensible that virtue is essentially preferable to vice; that it is the just order, the perfection and happiness of his nature. For, supposing him only endued with the principle of self-love; this principle will lead him to distinguish moral good from evil, so far as to give ground for loving the one, and hating the other: as he must needs see that benevolence, justice, temperance, and the other virtues, are the necessary means of his happiness, and that all vice and wickedness introduce disorder and misery. But man is endued with a social as well as a selfish principle, and has an immediate satisfaction and pleasure in the happiness of others, which is a further ground for distinguishing and loving virtue. All this, I say, takes place, laying aside the deceitful feeling of liberty, and supposing all our notions to be adjusted to the system of necessity. I add, that there is nothing in the above doctrine, to exclude the perception, of a certain beauty and excellency in virtue, according to lord *Shaftesbury* and the antient

Philosophers; which may, for ought we know, render it lovely and admirable to all rational beings. It appears to us, unquestionably, under the form of intrinsick excellency, even when we think not of its tendency to our happiness. Ideas of moral obligation, of remorse, of merit, and all that is connected with this way of thinking, arise from, what may be called, a wise delusion in our nature concerning liberty: but, as this affects only a certain modification of our ideas of virtue and vice, there is nothing in it, to render the foundation of virtue, either unsecure or dishonourable. Unsecure it does not render it, because, as now observed, virtue partly stands firm upon a separate foundation, independent of these feelings; and even where built upon these feelings, it is still built upon human nature. For though these feelings of liberty vary from the truth of things, they are, nevertheless, essential to the nature of man. We act upon them, and cannot act otherways. And therefore, tho' the distinction betwixt virtue and vice, had no other foundation but these feelings, (which is not the case) it would still have an immoveable and secure foundation in human nature. As for the supposed dishonour done to virtue, by resting its authority, in any degree, on a deceitful feeling, there is so little ground for this part of the objection, that, on the contrary, our doctrine most highly exalts virtue. For the above described artificial sense of liberty, is wholly contrived to support virtue, and to give its dictates the force of a law. Hereby it is discovered to be, in a singular manner, the care of the Deity; and a peculiar sort of glory is thrown around it. The Author of nature, has not rested it, upon the ordinary feelings and principles of human nature, as he has rested our other affections and appetites, even those which are most necessary to our existence. But a sort of extraordinary machinery is introduced for its sake. Human nature is forced, as it were, out of its course, and made to receive a nice and artificial set of feelings; merely that conscience may have a commanding power, and virtue be set as on a throne. This could not otherways be brought about, but by means of the deceitful feeling of liberty, which therefore is a greater honour to virtue, a higher recommendation of it, than if our conceptions were, in every particular, correspondent to the truth of things.

A second objection which may be urged against our system, is, that it seems to represent the Deity, as acting deceitfully by his creatures. He has given them certain ideas of contingency in events, and of liberty in their own actions, by which he has, in a manner, forced them to act upon a false hypothesis; as if he were unable, to carry on the government of this world,

did his creatures conceive things, according to the real truth. This objection is, in a great measure, obviated, by what we observed in the introduction to this essay, concerning our sensible ideas. It is universally allowed
by modern philosophers, that the perceptions of our external senses, are
not always agreeable to strict truth, but so contrived, as rather to answer
the purposes of use. Now, if it be called a deceit in our senses, not to give
us just representations of the material world, the Deity must be the author
of this deceit, as much as he is, of that which prevails in our moral ideas.
But no just objection can ly against the conduct of the Deity, in either
case. Our senses, both internal and external, are given us for different ends
and purposes; some to discover truth, others to make us happy and virtuous. The senses which are appropriated to the discovery of truth, unerringly answer their end. So do the senses, which are appropriated to virtue and happiness. And, in this view, it is no material objection, that the
same sense does not answer both ends. As to the other part of the objection, that it must imply imperfection in the Deity, if he cannot establish
virtue but upon a delusive foundation; we may be satisfied how fallacious
this reasoning is, by reflecting upon the numberless appearances, of moral
evil and disorder in this world. From these appearances, much more
strongly, were there any force in this reasoning, might we infer imperfection in the Deity; seeing the state of this world, in many particulars, does
not answer the notions we are apt to form, of supreme power conducted
by perfect wisdom and goodness. But, in truth, there is nothing in our
doctrine, which can justly argue imperfection in the Deity. For it is abundantly plain, first, that it is a more perfect state of things, and more worthy
of the Deity, to have all events going on with unbroken order, in a fixed
train of causes and effects; than to have every thing desultory and contingent. And, if such a being as man, was to be placed in this world, to act
his present part; it was necessary, that he should have a notion of contingency in events, and of liberty in his own actions. The objection therefore,
on the whole, amounts to no more, than that the Deity cannot work contradictions. For, if it was fit and wise, that man should think and act, as a
free agent, it was impossible this could be otherways accomplished, than
by endowing him with a sense of liberty: and if it was also fit and wise,
that universal necessity should be the real plan of the universe, this sense
of liberty could be no other than a deceitful one.

Another objection may perhaps be raised against us in this form. If it
was necessary for man to be constituted, with such an artificial feeling,

why was he endowed with so much knowledge, as to unravel the mystery? What purpose does it serve, to let in just so much light, as to discover the disguised appearance of the moral world, when it was intended, that his conduct should be adjusted to this disguised appearance? To this, I answer, first, that the discovery, when made, cannot possibly be of any bad consequence; and next, that a good consequence, of very great importance, results from it. No bad consequence, I say, ensues from the discovery, that liberty and contingency are deceitful feelings; for the case is confessedly parallel in the natural world, where no harm has ensued. After we have discovered, by philosophy, that several of the appearances of nature, are only useful illusions, that secondary qualities exist not in matter, and that our sensible ideas, in various instances, do not correspond to philosophic truth; after these discoveries are made, do they, in the least, affect even the philosopher himself in ordinary action? Does not he, in common with the rest of mankind, proceed, as it is fit he should, upon the common system of appearances and natural feelings? As little, in the present case, do our speculations about liberty and necessity, counteract the plan of nature. Upon the system of liberty we do, and must act: and no discoveries, made concerning the illusive nature of that feeling, are capable of disappointing, in any degree, the intention of the Deity.

But this is not all. These discoveries are also of excellent use, as they furnish us with one of the strongest arguments, for the existence of the Deity, and as they set the wisdom and goodness of his providence, in the most striking light. Nothing carries in it more express characters of design; nothing can be conceived more opposite to chance, than a plan so artfully contrived, for adjusting our impressions and feelings to the purposes of life. For here things are carried off, as it were, from the straight line; taken out of the course, in which they would of themselves proceed; and so moulded, as forcibly, and against their nature, to be subservient to man. His mind does not receive the impression of the moral world, in the same manner, as wax receives the impression of a seal. It does not reflect the image of it, in the same manner, as a mirror reflects its images: it has a peculiar cast and turn given to its conceptions, admirably ordered to exalt virtue, to the highest pitch. These conceptions are indeed illusive, yet, which is wonderful, it is by this very circumstance, that, in man, two of the most opposite things in nature, are happily reconciled, liberty and necessity; having this illustrious effect, that in him are accumulated, all the prerogatives both of a necessary and free agent. The discovery of such a marvelous adjustment, which is more directly opposed to chance, than any other thing conceiveable, must necessarily give us the strongest impression of a wise designing cause. And now a sufficient reason appears, for suffering man to make this surprising discovery. The Almighty has let us so far into his councils, as to afford the justest foundation, for admiring and adoring his wisdom. It is a remark worthy to be made, that the capacities of man seem, in general, to have a tendency beyond the wants and occasions of his present state. This has been often observed with respect to his wishes and desires. The same holds as to his intellectual faculties, which, sometimes, as in the instance before us, run beyond the limits of what is strictly necessary for him to know, in his present circumstances, and let in upon him some glimmerings of higher and nobler discoveries. A veil is thrown over nature, where it is not useful for him to behold it. And yet, sometimes, by turning aside that veil a very little, he is admitted to a fuller view; that his admiration of nature, and the God of nature, may be increased; that his curiosity and love of truth may be fed; and, perhaps, that some *augurium,* some intimation, may be given, of his being designed for a future, more exalted period of being; when attaining the full maturity of his nature, he shall no longer stand in need of artificial impressions, but shall feel and act according to the strictest truth of things.

B reads:

It will now be proper to answer some objections which may be urged against the doctrine we have advanced.* One, which at first may seem of considerable weight, is, That it seems to represent the Deity as acting deceitfully by his creatures.[11] He hath given them certain notions of contingency in events, by which he hath, in a manner, forced them to act upon a false hypothesis; as if he were unable to carry on the government of the world, did his creatures conceive things according to the real truth. This objection is, in a great measure, obviated, by what is observed in the introduction to this essay. It is universally allowed by modern philosophers, that the perceptions of our external senses do not always correspond in

---

11. In A, Kames had anticipated this objection: "A second objection which may be urged against our system, is, that it seems to represent the Deity as acting deceitfully toward his creatures." What he had not anticipated was the degree of opposition that he would encounter upon publication of this doctrine.

strict truth, but are so contrived, as rather to answer useful purposes. Now, if it be called a deceit in our senses, not to give us just representations of the material world, the Deity must be the author of this deceit, as much as he is of that which prevails in the moral world. But no just objection can lie against the conduct of the Deity, in either case. Our senses, both internal and external, are given to us for different ends and purposes; some to discover truth, others to make us happy and virtuous. The senses which are appropriated to the discovery of truth, unerringly answer their end. So do the senses which are appropriated to virtue and happiness. And, in this view, the objection vanisheth, because it amounts but to this, that the same sense does not answer both ends. As to the other branch of the objection, That it must imply imperfection in the Deity, if he cannot govern this world without deluding his creatures; I answer, That there is nothing in the foregoing doctrine which can justly argue imperfection in the Deity. For it is abundantly plain, first, that it is a more perfect state of things, and more worthy of the Deity, to have all events going on with unbroken order, in a fixed train of causes and effects, than to have every thing desultory and contingent. And if such a being as man was to be placed in this world, to act his present part, it was necessary, that he should have a notion of contingency in events, and of power to direct and controul them. The objection therefore, on the whole, amounts to no more, than that the Deity cannot work contradictions. For if it was fit and wise, that man should think and act as an independent being, having power to regulate his own actions, and, by means of these, to regulate also future events; it was impossible this could be otherways accomplished, than by enduing him with a sense of this power: and if it was also fit and wise, that universal necessity should be the real plan of the universe, this sense must be delusive. And, after all, seeing our happiness, in many instances, is placed upon delusive perceptions, why should it puzzle us, that our activity is promoted by the same means? No one considers it as an imputation on the Deity, that we are so framed as to perceive what is not, *viz.* beauty, grandeur, colour, heat or cold, as existing in objects, when such perceptions, though delusive, contribute to our happiness: and yet our happiness depends greatly more on action than on any of these perceptions.

The foregoing objection may perhaps be turned into a different shape. If it was necessary for man to be constituted with such an artificial sense, why was he endued with so much knowledge as to unravel the mystery? What purpose does it serve, to let in just so much light, as to discover the disguised appearance of the moral world, when it was intended that his conduct should be adjusted to this disguised appearance? To this I answer, first, That the discovery, when made, is not attended with any bad consequence; and next, that a good consequence, of very great importance, results from it. No bad consequence, I say, ensues from the discovery, that contingency, and power to regulate our own conduct, are delusive perceptions: for the case is confessedly parallel in the material world, where no harm hath ensued. After we have discovered, by philosophy, that several of the appearances of nature are only useful illusions; that secondary qualities exist not in matter; and that the perceptions of our external senses, in various instances, do not correspond to philosophic truth; after these discoveries are made, do they in the least affect even the philosopher himself, in ordinary action? Doth not he, in common with the rest of mankind, proceed, as it is fit he should, upon the common system of appearances and natural perceptions? As little, in the present case, do our speculations about liberty and necessity unhinge the plan of nature. Upon the common system we do and must act; and no discoveries made concerning the illusive nature of our perceptions, can disappoint in any degree the intention of the Deity.

But this is not all. These discoveries are also of excellent use; as they furnish us with one of the strongest arguments for the existence of the Deity, and as they set the wisdom and goodness of his providence in the most striking light. Nothing carries more express characters of design, nothing can be conceived more opposite to chance, than a plan so artfully contrived, for adjusting our impressions and feelings to the purposes of life. For here things are carried off, as it were, from the straight line; taken out of the course in which they would of themselves proceed; and so moulded, as forcibly, and against their nature, to be subservient to man. He doth not receive the impression of the moral world in the same manner as wax receives the impression of a seal; he doth not reflect the image of it in the same manner as a mirror reflects its images. He hath a peculiar cast and turn given to his conceptions, admirably adjusted to the part allotted him to act. These conceptions are indeed illusive; yet, which is wonderful, it is by this very circumstance, that, in man, two of the most opposite things in nature are happily reconciled, liberty and necessity; having this illustrious effect, that in him are accumulated all the prerogatives both of a necessary and a free agent. The discovery of such a marvellous adjustment, which is more directly opposed to chance than any other thing conceivable, must necessarily give us the strongest impression of a wise designing cause. And now a sufficient reason appears, for suffering man to make this surprising discovery. The Almighty hath admitted us so far into his counsels, as to afford the justest foundation for admiring and adoring his wisdom. It is a remark worthy to be made, that the capacities of man seem in general to have a tendency beyond the wants and occasions of his present state. This hath often been observed with respect to his wishes and desires. The same holds as to his intellectual faculties, which sometimes, as in the instance before us, run beyond the limits of what at present is necessary for him to know, and let in upon him some glimmerings of higher and nobler discoveries. A veil is thrown over nature, where it is not useful for him to behold it: and yet sometimes, by turning aside that veil a very little, he is admitted to a fuller view; that his admiration of nature, may be increased; that his curiosity and love of truth may be fed; and perhaps that some *augurium,* some intimation may be given, of his being designed for a future, more exalted state of being; when attaining the full maturity of his nature, he shall no longer stand in need of artificial impressions, but shall perceive and act according to the strictest truth of things.

* I acknowledge it to have been once my opinion, that we have a delusive sense of power to act against motives, or to act against our own inclination and choice, commonly termed *liberty of indifference.* I was carried along by the current of popular opinion; and I could not dream this sense to be a pure imagination, when I found it vouched by so many grave writers. I had at the same time a thorough conviction, from the clearest evidence, that man is a necessary agent; and therefore I justly concluded, that the sense of liberty of indifference, like that of contingency, must be delusive. I yielded to another popular opinion, That the perceptions of the moral sense, praise and blame, merit and demerit, guilt and remorse, are inconsistent with necessity, and must be founded upon the delusive sense of liberty of indifference. From these premises, I was obliged, though reluctantly, to admit, that some of the most noted perceptions and emotions of the moral sense are entirely built upon this delusive sense of liberty. The subject being handled after that manner in the first edition of this book, I was sensible of the odium of a doctrine that rests virtue in any measure upon a delusion; and I stated this as the first objection, in order to remove it the best way I could. Candor I shall always esteem essential in speaking to the public, not less than in private dealings; and my opinion of the wisdom of providence in the government of this world, is so firmly established, that I never can be apprehensive of harm in adhering to truth, however singular it may appear upon some occasions. I now chearfully acknowledge my errors; and am happy in thinking, that I have at last got into the right track. It appears to me at present a harsh doctrine, that virtue in any part should be founded on a delusion, though formerly the supposed truth of the doctrine reconciled me to it. It gives me solid satisfaction, to find the moral sense entirely consistent with voluntary necessity, which I must pronounce to be the system of nature. The moral sense makes a chief branch of the original constitution of man; and it can never lose its authority, while we have any feeling of pleasure and pain. According to this plan of morality, the objection, That it is partly founded on a delusion, vanisheth; and the objection, for that reason, is dropt in the present edition.

IV. PERSONAL IDENTITY

i. In A, this essay reads:[12]

Had we no original impressions but those of the external senses, according to the author of the treatise of human nature, we never could have any consciousness of *self*; because such consciousness cannot arise from any external sense. Mankind would be in a perpetual reverie; ideas would be constantly floating in the mind; and no man would be able to connect his ideas with *himself.* Neither could there be any idea of *personal identity.* For a man, cannot consider himself to be the same person, in different circumstances, when he has no idea or consciousness of *himself* at all.

Beings there may be, who are thus constituted: but man is none of these beings. It is an undoubted truth, that he has an original feeling, or consciousness of himself, and of his existence; which, for the most part, accompanies every one of his impressions and ideas, and every action of his mind and body. I say, for the most part; for the faculty or internal sense, which is the cause of this peculiar perception, is not always in action. In a dead sleep, we have no consciousness of self. We dream sometimes without this consciousness: and even some of our waking hours pass without it. A reverie is nothing else, but a wandering of the mind through its ideas, without carrying along the perception of self.

12. In A and B, this much briefer essay is found in Part II. As Kames explains in the Preface to C, "In correcting the Essay on Personal Identity, having discovered its intimate connection with the moral system, I transferred it from the second Part to the first." Thus, in C Kames argues that moral agency requires a sense of continuous selfhood: "The knowledge I have of my personal identity is what constitutes me a moral agent, accountable to God and to man for every action of my life. Were I kept ignorant of my personal identity, it would not be in my power to connect any of my past actions with myself. . . . It would answer no good purpose, to reward me for a benevolent act, or to punish me for a crime."

This consciousness or perception of self, is, at the same time, of the liveliest kind. Self-preservation is every one's peculiar duty; and the vivacity of this perception, is necessary to make us attentive to our own interest, and, particularly, to shun every appearance of danger. When a man is in a reverie, he has no circumspection, nor any manner of attention to his own interest.

'Tis remarkable, that one has scarce any chance to fall asleep, 'till this perception vanish. Its vivacity keeps the mind in a certain degree of agitation, which bars sleep. A fall of water disposes to sleep. It fixes the attention, both by sound and sight, and, without creating much agitation, occupies the mind, so as to make it forget itself. Reading of some books has the same effect.

It is this perception, or consciousness of self, carried through all the different stages of life, and all the variety of action, which is the foundation of *personal identity*. It is, by means of this perception, that I consider myself to be the same person, in all varieties of fortune, and every change of circumstance.

The main purpose of this short essay, is to introduce an observation, that it is not by any argument or reasoning, I conclude myself to be the same person, I was ten years ago. This conclusion rests entirely upon the feeling of identity, which accompanies me through all my changes, and which is the only connecting principle, that binds together, all the various thoughts and actions of my life. Far less is it by any argument, or chain of reasoning, that I discover my own existence. It would be strange indeed, if every man's existence was kept a secret from him, 'till the celebrated argument was invented, that cogito ergo sum. And if a fact, that to common understanding, appears self-evident, is not to be relied on without an argument; why should I take for granted, without an argument, that I think, more than that I exist? For surely I am not more conscious of thinking, than of existing.

Upon this subject, I shall just suggest a thought, which will be more fully insisted on afterwards; that any doctrine, which leads to a distrust of our senses, must land in universal scepticism. If natural feelings, whether from internal or external senses, are not admitted as evidence of truth, I cannot see, that we can be certain of any fact whatever. It is clear, from what is now observed, that, upon this sceptical system, we cannot be certain even of our own existence.*

*The deceitful feeling of liberty, unfolded in the essay upon liberty and ne-
cessity, may perhaps embarrass some readers, as in some measure contradictory to
the position here laid down. But the matter is easily cleared. Natural feelings are
satisfying evidence of truth; and, in fact, have full authority over us, unless in some
singular cases, where we are admonished by counter-feelings, or by reasoning, not
to give implicit trust. This is a sufficient foundation for all the arguments, that
are built upon the authority of our senses, in point of evidence. The feeling of
liberty is a very singular case. The reasons are clearly traced for the necessity of
this delusive feeling, which distinguishes it in a very particular manner, and leaves
no room, to draw any consequence from it, to our other feelings. But there is,
besides, a circumstance yet more distinguishing, in this delusive feeling of liberty,
which entirely exempts it, from being an exception to the general rule above laid
down. It is this; that the feeling is by no means entire on the side of liberty. It is
counter-balanced by other feelings, which, in many instances, afford such a conviction of the necessary influence of motives, that physical and moral necessity
can scarce be distinguished. The sense of liberty operates chiefly in the after reflection. But, previous to the action, there is no distinct or clear feeling, that it can
happen otherways, than in connection with its proper motive. Here the feelings
being, on the whole, opposite to each other, nothing can be inferred from this
case, to derogate from the evidence of feelings that are clear, cogent and authoritative; and to which, nothing can be opposed, from the side of reason or counter-
feeling. So that our principle remains safe and unshaken, that a general distrust
of our senses, internal or external, must land us in universal scepticism.

B reads as above, but removes the footnote.

APPENDIX

i. Added to B, and reprinted without revision in C.

Variant Readings to Part II

II. EXTERNAL SENSES

i. In place of the two brief introductory paragraphs, A opens:

In a former essay are pointed out some instances, in which our senses
may be called deceitful.* They are of two sorts. One is, when the deception
is occasioned by indisposition of the organ, remoteness of place, grossness
of the medium, or the like; which distort the appearances of objects, and
make them be seen double, or greater or less, than they really are. In such
instances, the perception is always faint, obscure or confused: and they
noway invalidate the authority of the senses, in general, when, abstracting

from such accidental obstructions, the perception is lively, strong and distinct. In the other sort, there is a deception established by the laws of nature; as in the case of secondary qualities, taken notice of in that essay; whence it was inferred, that nature does not always give us such correct perceptions, as correspond to the philosophic truth of things. Notwithstanding of which, the testimony of our senses still remains, as a sufficient ground of confidence and trust. For, in all these cases, where there is this sort of established deception, nature furnishes means for coming at the truth. As in this very instance of secondary qualities, philosophy easily corrects the false appearances, and teaches us, that they are rather to be considered, as impressions made upon the mind, than as qualities of the object. A remedy being thus provided to the deception, our belief, so far as it can be influenced by reason, is the more confirmed, with regard to our other sensations, where there is no appearance of illusion. But this is not the whole of the matter. When any sense presents to our view, an appearance that may be called deceitful, we plainly discover some useful purpose intended. The deceit is not the effect of an imperfect or arbitrary constitution; but wisely contrived, to give us such notice of things, as may best suit the purposes of life. From this very consideration, we are the more confirmed in the veracity of nature. Particular instances, in which, our senses are accommodated to the uses of life, rather than to the strictness of truth, are rational exceptions, which serve, the more firmly, to establish the general rule. And, indeed, when we have nothing but our senses to direct our conduct, with regard to external objects, it would be strange, if there should be any just ground, for a general distrust of them. But there is no such thing. There is nothing to which all mankind are more necessarily determined, than to put confidence in their senses. We entertain no doubt of their authority, because we are so constituted, that it is not in our power to doubt.

    *Essay upon liberty and necessity.

B opens with the same paragraph, but revises the first sentence to: "In several instances things appear to us different from what they truly are; and so far our senses may be termed delusive."[13]

13. B qualifies the description ("and so far may be termed deceitful"), while C drops the term from the text.

ii. The section on "Perceptions of External Sense" was added to C.[14]

III. DIFFERENT THEORIES OF VISION

i. This essay in its entirety was added to C.[15]

IV. MATTER AND SPIRIT

i. This essay in its entirety was added to C.

VIII. KNOWLEDGE OF THE DEITY

i. The last three paragraphs on Hume's posthumously published *Dialogues Concerning Natural Religion* (1779) added to C.[16]

14. A and B are not divided into separate sections and present the material in a different order than is found in C. But apart from the introductory material, there are no substantial differences between the three editions.

15. Kames briefly considers the sense of vision in A and B, as part of his essay on "External Senses." In C, since sight is "one of the most simple and distinct" of the senses, vision represents a test case for the veracity of the human senses.

16. Kames's censure of this posthumously published work represents his harshest treatment of Hume. Though Hume's *Treatise* was one of the main targets of the *Essays,* shortly after the publication of A, Hume described Kames's work as "well wrote" and "an unusual instance of an obliging method of answering a Book" (Hume to Michael ⌐msay, 22 June 1751, in *The Letters of David Hume,* 2 vols., ed. J. Y. T. Greig [Oxford: ⌐n Press, 1932], I:162).

BIBLIOGRAPHY

Works Cited or Alluded to by Kames

Aesop. *Fables*. Retold by Joseph Jacobs. Vol. 17, *The Harvard Classics*. New York: Collier & Son, 1909–14.

Aristotle. *On the Soul*. Translated by J. A. Smith. Vol. I, *The Complete Works of Aristotle*. Edited by Jonathan Barnes. Princeton: Princeton University Press, 1984.

Berkeley, George. *A Treatise Concerning the Principles of Human Knowledge*. 1710. Edited by Jonathan Dancy. New York: Oxford University Press, 1998.

Bolingbroke, Henry St. John, Viscount. *Reflections Concerning Innate Moral Principles*. 1752.

Buffon, Georges Louis Leclerc, Comte de. *De L'Homme*. Vols. 2 and 3, *Histoire naturelle, générale et particulière*. 15 vols. Paris, 1749.

Butler, Joseph. *Fifteen Sermons Preached at the Rolls Chapel*. 1726. In *The Works of Joseph Butler*, 3 vols. Oxford: Clarendon Press, 1896. Reprint, Bristol, England: Thoemmes Press, 1995.

Calvin, Jean. *Tractatus Theologici Omnes*. Geneva, 1576.

Chesterfield, Philip Dormer Stanhope, 4th Earl of. *Letters written by the late Right Honourable Philip Dormer Stanhope, Earl of Chesterfield, to his son, Philip Stanhope, Esq.*, 2 vols. London, 1774.

Cicero. *On Fate (De Fato)*. Edited and translated by R. W. Sharples. Warminster, England: Aris & Phillips, 1991.

———. *On the Nature of the Gods (De Natura Deorum)*. Translated by P. G. Walsh. Oxford: Clarendon Press, 1997.

Clarke, Samuel. *A Discourse concerning the Being and Attributes of God, the Obligations of Natural Religion, and the Truth and Certainty of Christian Revelation*. 9th ed., London, 1738.

Descartes, René. *Discourse on Method*. 1637. Translated by Donald A. Cress. Indianapolis: Hackett Publishing, 1998.

Dubos, Jean-Baptiste. *Réflexions critiques sur la poésie et sur la peinture.* Paris, 1719.

Edwards, Jonathan. *A Careful and Strict Inquiry into the Modern Prevailing Notions of That Freedom of Will, Which Is Supposed to Be Essential to Moral Agency, Virtue and Vice, Reward and Punishment, Praise and Blame.* Boston, 1754; London, 1762.

Euclid. *The Thirteen Books of Euclid's Elements.* Edited and translated by Thomas L. Heath. Cambridge: Cambridge University Press, 1925.

Helvétius, Claude-Adrien. *De l'esprit.* Paris, 1758.

Hobbes, Thomas. *Leviathan or the Matter, Forme and Power of a Commonwealth Ecclesiastical and Civill.* 1651. Edited by Richard Tuck. Cambridge: Cambridge University Press, 1996.

Horace. *Epistles. Satires. Arts Poetica.* Translated by H. Rushton Fairclough. Loeb Classical Library, No. 194. Harvard: Harvard University Press, 1926.

Hume, David. *Dialogues Concerning Natural Religion.* 1779. Edited by Richard H. Popkin. Indianapolis: Hackett Publishing, 1980.

———. *An Enquiry Concerning Human Understanding.* First published as *Philosophical Essays concerning Human Understanding.* 1748. Edited by Tom L. Beauchamp. Oxford: Oxford University Press, 1999.

———. *An Enquiry Concerning the Principles of Morals.* 1751. Edited by Tom L. Beauchamp. Oxford: Oxford University Press, 1998.

———. *A Treatise of Human Nature.* 1739. Edited by David Fate Norton and Mary J. Norton. Oxford: Oxford University Press, 2000.

Hutcheson, Francis. *An Inquiry concerning the Original of Our Ideas of Virtue or Moral Good.* Inquiry II of *An Inquiry into the Original of Our Ideas of Beauty and Virtue.* London, 1725.

Livy. *History of Rome.* Translated by Rev. Canon Roberts. New York: E. P. Dutton, 1912.

Locke, John. *An Essay Concerning Human Understanding.* 1690. Edited by Peter H. Nidditch. Oxford: Clarendon Press, 1975.

———. *Locke's Reply to the Right Revered the Lord Bishop of Worcester's Answer to his Letter.* 1697.

———. *Some Familiar Letters between Locke and several of his Friends.* In Vol. 8 of *The Works of John Locke,* 10 vols. 12th ed. London, 1823.

Milton, John. *Paradise Lost.* 1674. Edited by Scott Elledge. New York: W. W. Norton, 1993.

Newton, Isaac, Sir. *Opticks: or, A treatise of the reflexions, refractions, inflexions and colours of light.* London, 1704.

Pictet, Benedict. *Theologia Christiana.* 2 vols. Geneva, 1696.

Porterfield, William. "An essay concerning the motions of our eyes. Part I. Of their external motions" (1737). In *Medical Essays and Observations, Published by a Society in Edinburgh,* 5 vols. 5th ed. London and Edinburgh, 1771.

———. *A Treatise on the Eye, the Manner and Phaenomena of Vision,* 2 vols. London: A. Miller, and Edinburgh: G. Hamilton and J. Balfour, 1759.

Reid, Thomas. *Correspondence of Thomas Reid.* Edited by Paul Wood. University Park, Pa.: Pennsylvania State University Press, 2002.

Rousseau, Jean-Jacques. *Emile, or, On Education.* 1762. Edited and translated by Allan Bloom. New York: Basic Books, 1979.

Shaftesbury, Anthony Ashley Cooper, Third Earl of. *Inquiry Concerning Virtue or Merit.* In *Characteristics of Men, Manners, Opinions, Times.* 1711. Edited by Lawrence E. Klein. Cambridge: Cambridge University Press, 1999.

Smith, Adam. *The Theory of Moral Sentiments.* 1759. Edited by D. D. Raphael and A. L. Macfie. Indianapolis: Liberty Classics, 1982.

Swift, Jonathan. "Thoughts on Various Subjects." In Vol. I of Alexander Pope, Jonathan Swift and John Gay, *Miscellanies in Prose and Verse.* 1727–32.

Terence. *Heautontimorumenos: The Self-Tormentor.* In *The Comedies of Terence.* Edited by Henry Thomas Riley. New York: Harper & Brothers, 1874.

Turrettini, François. *Institutio theologiae elencticae,* 3 vols. Geneva, 1679–85.

Virgil. *The Aeneid.* Translated by Robert Fitzgerald. New York: Vintage Books, 1990.

Voltaire, François Marie Arouet de. *La Henriade.* Rouen, 1723. English translation 1728.

Wollaston, William. *The Religion of Nature Delineated.* London, 1724.

Secondary Literature

Emerson, Roger L. "Henry Home, Lord Kames." In *British Prose Writers, 1660–1800,* 2nd series, *Dictionary of Literary Biography,* vol. 104. Edited by Donald T. Siebert. Detroit: Gale Research Company, 1991, pp. 224–25.

Haakonssen, Knud. *Natural Law and Moral Philosophy: From Grotius to the Scottish Enlightenment.* Cambridge: Cambridge University Press, 1996.

Helo, Ario. "The historicity of morality: Necessity and necessary agents in the ethics of Lord Kames." *History of European Ideas,* 27 (2001): 239–55.

Lehmann, William C. *Henry Home and the Scottish Enlightenment: A Study in National Character and in the History of Ideas.* The Hague: Martinus Nijhoff, 1971.

McGuiness, Arthur E. *Henry Home, Lord Kames.* New York: Twayne Publishers, 1970.

Moore, James, and Michael Silverthorne. "Gershom Carmichael and the natural jurisprudence tradition in eighteenth-century Scotland." In *Virtue and Commerce: The Shaping of Political Economy in the Scottish Enlightenment.* Edited by Istvan Hont and Michael Ignatieff. Cambridge: Cambridge University Press, 1983, pp. 73–87.

Ross, Ian Simpson. *Lord Kames and the Scotland of His Day.* Oxford: Oxford University Press, 1972.

Ross, Trevor. "Copyright and the invention of tradition." *Eighteenth-Century Studies,* 26 (Autumn 1992): 1–27.

Smellie, William. "The Life of Henry Home, Lord Kames." In *Literary and Characteristical Lives.* 1800. Reprint, edited by Stephen Brown, Bristol: Thoemmes Press, 1997.

Stewart, M. A. "Religion and rational theology." In *The Cambridge Companion to the Scottish Enlightenment.* Edited by Alexander Broadie. Cambridge: Cambridge University Press, 2003.

Stocking, George W. "Scotland as the model of mankind: Lord Kames's philosophical view of civilization." In *Toward a Science of Man: Essays in the History of Anthropology.* Edited by Timothy H. H. Thorensen. The Hague: Mouton, 1975, pp. 65–89.

Tytler, Alexander Fraser, Lord Wordhouselee. *Memoirs of the Life and Writing of the Honourable Henry Home of Kames.* 1814. Reprint, Bristol: Thoemmes Press, 1996.

INDEX

ness of God; Proofs for existence of God

Good and evil: human knowledge of, 197–98; Hume on, 229; moral evil, problem of, 227–28; natural evil, problems raised by, 222–27; proofs of existence of God and, 204–5, 233; right and wrong, human sense of, 230. *See also* Benevolence as principle of moral action

Goodness of God, 218–29; causation, argument from, 206, 220–21; created world, lack of perfection in, 223–26; future existence and, 227; Hume on, 229; increase in knowledge leading to further instances of, 221–22, 226, 233; independence and self-sufficiency of Deity, 221; mixed nature, difficulties raised by, 222; moral evil, problem of, 227–28; natural evil, problems raised by, 222–27; pain and distress reconciled with, 223–26; reason *vs.* intuitive knowledge, 219–21

Gratitude as principle of moral action, 45, 56, 58–59, 79

Gravity, 154, 179

Greenlander's argument for existence of God, 206 n.

Grief, human attraction to, 14–15, 16

Grotius, Hugo, ix

Hearing, 149–50; double organs producing single perception, 173, 174; primary and secondary qualities, 154–55; reality of perception of external objects, 155–56; substance and quality, 151

Heat, 154

Helvetius, 74, 77 n.

La Henriade (Voltaire), 110

Henry of Navarre, 110 n. 3

Heretical doctrines: goodness of God (Manichaeanism), 222; liberty and necessity (Pelagianism and Arminianism), 133, 135, 138, 139

Heroes, deification of, 216–17

Historical Law-Tracts (Kames), xii

Historicism in *Essays* and *Sketches,* xviii–xix

History *vs.* fiction and nature of belief, 145–46

Hobbes, Thomas, xiii, 33 n., 49, 86

Home, Henry. *See* Kames, Henry Home, Lord

Hope, 147

Horace, 189

Human nature: *Essays,* as theme of, xii–xiii, xviii–xix, 229–30; evidence of existence of God from principles wrought into, 206–8; moral foundations derived from, 24–26, 40–41; origins, development from (*See* Origins of human nature, development from); pain, role of, 230, 233; primary laws of nature deduced from, 55–61; right and wrong, sense of, 230; thinking, human action of, 181–84

Human will: liberty or free will (*See* Liberty and necessity); physical motions directed by, 180

Hume, David: Anderson, George, opprobrium of, xvi; belief, 143 n. 1; causation, argument against, xviii; goodness of God and existence of evil, 218–19, 229; justice and morality, x, xiv, 46–47, 51–54, 82–88, 94; Kames's appreciation of, 94–95; Kames praised by, 264 n. 16; personal identity, xvii; power and causation, 186–88; proofs of existence of God, 228–29, 264; skepticism, Humean, x, xiii, xiv; sympathy,

This book is set in Adobe Garamond, a modern adaptation by Robert Slimbach of the typeface originally cut around 1540 by the French typographer and printer Claude Garamond. The Garamond face, with its small lowercase height and restrained contrast between thick and thin strokes, is a classic "old-style" face and has long been one of the most influential and widely used typefaces.

Printed on paper that is acid-free and meets the requirements of the American National Standard for Permanence of Paper for Printed Library Materials, z39.48-1992 ⊗

Book design by Louise OFarrell
Gainesville, Florida
Typography by Apex Publishing, LLC
Madison, Wisconsin
Printed and bound by Edwards Brothers, Inc.
Ann Arbor, Michigan